THESE HUNDRED YEARS

A CHRONICLE OF THE TWENTIETH CENTURY

As recorded in the pages of the

Youngstown Vindicator

THE VINDICATOR PRINTING COMPANY / YOUNGSTOWN, OHIO

THESE HUNDRED YEARS
A Chronicle Of The Twentieth Century
As Recorded in the Pages of The Youngstown Vindicator

© The Vindicator Printing Company

FIRST EDITION 2000

Published by
The Vindicator Printing Company
107 Vindicator Square
Youngstown, Ohio 44503

ISBN 0-9675834-0-3

Printed in the United States of America

Library of Congress Cataloging in Publication Data

Cart, Sarah
Jagnow, Paul
McFerren, Robert

Library of Congress Catalog Card Number: 99-67573

TABLE OF CONTENTS

ACKNOWLEDGMENTS

THESE HUNDRED YEARS is a deluxe issue of THE YOUNGSTOWN VIN-DICATOR, which each day delivers a lasting record of the lives and times of the people of the Mahoning and Shenango valleys. This chronicle of the twentieth century is made possible by the efforts of many people, not the least of whom are the past and present employees of THE VINDICATOR and the carriers who deliver the paper to our faithful readers, without whom there would be no VINDICATOR.

Special thanks for help in the making of this book also goes to:

▶ George H. Kelley (1904–1985), VINDICATOR editorial writer and assistant managing editor, who knew Youngstown, its history, and its people as few of us ever will and blazed the trail for us.

▶ The Mahoning Valley Historical Society, Youngstown, Ohio.

▶ The Arms Family Museum of Local History and the MVHS Library.

▶ H. William Lawson and Pamela Pletcher.

▶ William F. Maag, Sr. (1850–1924), a courageous publisher whose optimism and abiding faith in Youngstown should inspire us all.

———————

Dates in chronological lists are the days news events appeared in the paper and may or may not be the days on which the events occurred.

———————

THE INTRODUCTORY PARAGRAPHS for chapters two through ten and a quotation on Page 137 derive from the following sources and are gratefully acknowledged.

Chapter Two, Page 14
THE OHIO ALMANAC, 1992–1993, Damaine Vonada, editor. ©1992. Published by Orange Frazer Press Wilmington, Ohio. Used with permission.

Chapter Three, Page 24
THE 20S: FORDS, FLAPPERS & FANATICS. From the introduction by George E. Mowry, editor. ©1963. Published by Prentice Hall, Englewood Cliffs, New Jersey.

Chapter Four, Page 34
MAHONING MEMORIES by Frederick J. Blue, William D. Jenkins, H. William Lawson, Joan M. Reedy. ©1995, Mahoning Valley Historical Society. Donning Company Publishers, Virginia Beach, Virginia. Used with permission.

Chapter Five, Page 46
THE 1940S: DECADE OF TRIUMPH AND TROUBLE by Cabell Phillips. ©1975 by THE NEW YORK TIMES. Macmillan Publishing Company, Inc., New York, N.Y.

Chapter Six, Page 60
THE DECLINE OF AMERICAN STEEL: HOW MANAGEMENT, LABOR AND GOVERNMENT WENT WRONG by Paul A. Tiffany. ©1988. Published by Oxford University Press, New York, N.Y. Used with permission.

Chapters Seven and Eight, Pages 70 and 80
THE BUCKEYE EMPIRE: AN ILLUSTRATED HISTORY OF OHIO ENTERPRISE by Eugene C. Murdock. ©1988. Published by Windsor Publications, Inc., Northridge, California.

Chapters Nine and Ten, Pages 90 and 106
GOING, GOING, GONE: VANISHING AMERICANA by Susan Jonas and Marilyn Nissenson. ©1994. Published by Chronicle Books, San Francisco, California. Used with permission.

Chapter Eleven, Page 137
THE REBEL ANGELS by Robertson Davies. ©1981. Published by Viking Press, New York, N.Y.

*"**History is the witness** that testifies to the passing of time; it illumines reality, vitalizes memory, provides guidance in daily life, and brings us tidings of antiquity."*

CICERO
106–32 B.C.

Introduction & Dedication

THIS CELEBRATION of Youngstown and the Mahoning Valley owes a debt of gratitude to the hundreds of men and women who have worked tirelessly to witness and report the times and the challenges, the joys and the sorrows, the victories and the defeats of the past hundred years in the pages of THE VINDICATOR, the people's paper.

Not intended to be an exhaustive history of the twentieth century in the valley, it is rather a mosaic crafted from pieces of the day-to-day lives of the local citizenry, each fragment reflecting but one small piece of a larger whole.

Taken together, those fragments—a person here, an advertisement there, a few headlines, an occasional front page, a multitude of triumphs and tragedies, many photos, and much, much more—provide a densely detailed picture of a proud community. The rise and fall of the American steel industry and its impact on the hearts and souls of the people of the Mahoning Valley cement this mosaic of the twentieth century together.

Many of the stories told and some of the people introduced will be familiar. Others will be strangers. A few will shock and surprise us. Many will amuse us. At their best,

may they entertain and educate us, throwing light on our lives and guiding us into the next millennium.

And so this work is dedicated not only to those who have peopled THE VINDICATOR's newsroom, pressroom, darkroom, advertising department, art department, circulation department, administrative offices, library, and delivery vans through the decades, but also to the people of Youngstown and the Mahoning Valley who came from countries and communities all over the world to build one proud citizenry—a citizenry that as it grew repeatedly shared its resources, strengths, and honor with the rest of the United States.

Over the past ten decades, this area and its people have witnessed the establishment and destruction of the American steel industry, weathered economic highs and lows, faced social challenges, endured political struggles, and sacrificed through World War I, the Depression, World War II, Korea, Vietnam, and the Gulf War.

May this book deepen our appreciation of and respect for the efforts of all of those who have led the way.

Betty H. Brown Jagnow
President and Publisher
THE VINDICATOR

News from the Mahoning and Shenango Valleys

1900

FEB. 9: At the Erie's Hazel Street crossing, workers accidentally push rail cars into a mail wagon, smashing it and fatally injuring the horse.

FEB. 9: Pennsylvania's Penrose sponsors a U.S. Senate bill for incorporation of the Lake Erie & Ohio River Canal Company.

APRIL 8: Motion pictures debut at The Opera House–"the strongest attraction of the theatrical season." Featured: "the Boston horseless fire department" in action.

JULY 12: Rampaging Mill Creek destroys three Youngstown Ice Company houses on Price Road, "hurling great cakes of ice in every direction."

JULY 29: Due to changing fashions, "the horse is rapidly coming into use again, and...the bicycle will have to take second place," a dealer in horses and bicycles says.

OCT. 28: Beyond being a pleasure vehicle, the "horseless carriage" is useful to business, sports and warfare, THE VINDICATOR reports.

1901

FEB. 7: A dozen or so Poland subscribers await service from the Central Union Telephone Company. "It is only a question of time until every township in Mahoning county will be connected up."

MAY 10: Mike Gulach, Struthers, pleads guilty to bewitching Annie Lukac, causing her to "suffer greatly by the false and malicious stories."

MAY 13: The Iron & Steel Institute of London says Youngstown has the world's finest mill machinery.

SEPT. 14: President McKinley, Niles native and former Poland resident, dies of assassin's bullet at 2:15 a.m. THE VINDICATOR updates the death watch in bulletins posted at Federal and Phelps streets.

OCT. 28: Idora Park to build a 240-foot roller coaster using sixty-five thousand feet of Georgia yellow pine. "Trips will cost a nickel and the fun will be worth the price," THE VINDICATOR reports.

1902

MARCH 24: Two freight trains collide on the Pennsylvania line near Upper Union Mill, killing four and injuring several others. Mistaken orders and dense fog are blamed

for the crash, Youngstown's worst.

JULY 5: The New Castle Limited and a regular train, carrying two hundred passengers between them, collide west of Edinburg, Pennsylvania, killing two and injuring more than a dozen others. Their crews misconstrued signals.

AUG. 23: The Youngstown-made Fredonia auto is "a marvel...the highest-powered, simplest and strongest machine in its class," THE VINDICATOR reports.

NOV. 11: Oil fever hits Mahoning and Columbiana counties. A well in the headwaters of the Mahoning discharges two million gallons of water a day, drying up springs and water wells and angering farmers.

1903

FEB. 3: Quarrymen, on strike for more money, clash with deputy sheriffs at the Hillsville, Pennsylvania, quarries of the Lake Erie Limestone Company.

MARCH 22: Two clerics deliver simultaneous Lenten sermons in St. John's Episcopal Church. On one side of the pulpit, the Rev. Mr. Mann, a deaf clergyman from Cleveland, delivers his message in sign language to twenty deaf churchgoers. Rector Abner L. Frazer, meanwhile, speaks to the rest of the congregation.

MAY 3: The solicitor and Youngstown Council meet privately and suppress details to prevent The Sunday VINDICATOR from scooping the Republican papers, which don't publish on Sunday. Reporters on hand from New York City, Chicago and Washington papers report the gag order.

DEC. 10: The need for more pesthouse facilities is felt as Youngstown Township Hospital fills "to the doors" with victims of the latest smallpox epidemic.

1904

JAN. 2: Pittsburgh headquarters shuts Carnegie Steel's Warren mill, laying off all but "the man who takes care of the horses." The mill isn't covered by Amalgamated Association concessions that allow independent mills to cut wages and operate at a profit.

JAN. 16: President Theodore Roosevelt congratulates a Girard couple on the birth of triplets. The couple has sixteen children.

SEPT. 15: In Trumbull County Com-

mon Pleas Court, Carnegie Steel seeks to enjoin strikers at the steel-hoop mills in Girard. It marks the first time a Mahoning Valley company has sought injunctive relief in a labor dispute.

SEPT. 29: THE VINDICATOR prints the Democratic ticket directly under its masthead as a show of support for the party's candidates for president, vice president, state, district, county, township and city offices, as well as the Citizens' Ticket for the seven-member Youngstown School Board.

1905

MAY 16: Grease smeared on the Youngstown & Southern tracks stalls trains climbing the hill between Eureka and Lima. Suspicion settles on farmers who favor electric over steam power.

JULY 14: Simms & Company of Pittsburgh wins a contract to divert the Mahoning River in East Youngstown (later Campbell). The project is expected to employ five hundred.

OCT. 25: A ladle of molten metal explodes at Struthers Furnace, killing one and injuring two others seriously. A fourth man is missing.

1906

APRIL 5: The Youngstown Board of Service will replace the broken town pump on Central Square with one that will "day and night spout forth good clear .999 percent pure filtered Mahoning river water."

MAY 23: Worms threaten to defoliate trees in Mill Creek Park. THE VINDICATOR hopes for federal or state help, lest the park "have to be abandoned as a pleasure resort during the summer."

AUG. 4: On Phelps Street, the three-story Erie Hotel is "out of plumb and leaning over the Erie tracks at a perceptible angle." Worries arise that the fifteen-year-old structure might fall. "[A]side from the probable loss of life, such an accident would necessarily block the railroad tracks."

AUG. 14: In a large advertisement, Harry B. Burt invites VINDICATOR readers to visit his "New Story & Arbor Room" and candy and ice cream factory at 25 North Phelps Street. Burt's confections would gain national fame later under the "Good Humor" product label.

1907

MAY 16: THE VINDICATOR exposes a trumped up investigation at the Canfield Infirmary for "county charges." Director Weir used a phony "investigation of unsanitary conditions...as he groomed himself for a future race for county commissioner." The exposé helps clear infirmary Superintendent Taylor and his wife of false accusations.

OCT. 1: George Tod bequeaths his six-hundred-acre Brier Hill Farm to Youngstown for a cemetery. The farm was home to David Tod, Ohio's Civil War governor.

OCT. 21: Mayor Frank Baldwin protects vice, THE VINDICATOR charges, noting that police face dismissal or transfer if they "arrest dive keepers without orders from the mayor." The paper reprints a March 15, 1906, Youngstown Telegram editorial calling the Republican regime a "wretched failure."

1908

FEB. 25: Youngstown Council pays $11,299 for 204 acres in Berlin Township for construction of a reservoir.

FEB. 28: One hundred foreigners get their signals crossed and jam the post office for a bread giveaway, snarling mail service. They should have assembled behind Westminster Presbyterian Church.

JUNE 10: Carnival Night of the Old Home Week Pioneer Reunion provides entertainment for "happy joyous throngs." THE VINDICATOR calls it "the greatest event of its kind ever seen in Youngstown."

OCT. 27: A local-option election in Warren pits "drys" against "wets." The drys, led by women at every voting booth, banish alcohol from Trumbull County.

1909

JAN. 16: Area puddlers look longingly at the new wrought-iron mill at the A.M. Byers Company, Girard.

AUG. 10: Ernest Hensch, Seventh Ward councilman, finds that Carnegie Steel has dammed the Mahoning at the Ohio Works. Carnegie dumped cinder to get water during a dry spell.

AUG. 24: By fall, not an idle blast furnace in the valley. Carnegie's Bessemer stacks now total seven. Niles Ohio Works, Lowellville's Mary furnace and the rebuilt Struthers furnace to restart.

1900 **1** 1909

THE CENTURY DAWNS

WEST FEDERAL STREET, 1900: At the turn of the century, electric trolleys were a convenient, and important, mode of transportation. The automobile was a crude thing then—a sputtering, backfiring novelty that frightened horses and excited dreamers. When it ran.

The coming of the twentieth century brought major changes to the everyday lives of all citizens—in Youngstown and across the nation.

Modern Youngstown may be said to have had its beginning in 1900.

THE VINDICATOR, MARCH 27, 1938

SEPTEMBER 1900: Though remembered more for foreign-policy achievements, Niles-born William McKinley guided the U.S. through a period of prosperity. The Republican president's "full dinner pail" platform capitalized on good times as he ran for a second term.

VINDICATORS FROM THE turn of the century reflect a community and way of life on the brink of phenomenal change. The country was only thirty-five years past the Civil War (today we're forty-six years past the Korean conflict) and the Union boasted forty-five states.

In Youngstown, with not quite forty-five thousand people, electric lights were just coming into use. The city was home to only one automobile and was adjusting to its first electric streetcars.

The novelty of telephones was only beginning to penetrate the Mahoning Valley. People retrieved mail from the post office, which regularly advertised unclaimed letters in the paper, and the tallest buildings were four stories. Cattle grazed the land south of the Mahoning.

The Market Street viaduct, which reached to the top of the bluff on the river's south side, had just opened in 1899, replacing a smaller bridge that had spanned the river but had not scaled the heights above its bank. Almost simultaneously, a new streetcar line had been built from downtown Youngstown to Mill Creek Park and the area of Lanterman's Falls.

The City of Youngstown encompassed 6,150 acres, or 9.5 square miles, and seventy acres of water, exclusive of the Mahoning River. Within its limits ran ninety-six miles of streets and thirty-one miles of sewers.

Calculations were that one horse a day died in the city, a trend that gave way gradually with the rise of electric streetcars,

CRUCIAL LINK: The Market Street viaduct, opened in 1899, scaled the south heights for the first time and cleared the way for expansion south of the Mahoning River.

trucks, and automobiles. In the early days of Mill Creek Park, signs along its dirt roads required automobiles to take the outside of the drive, regardless of left or right, so frightened horses would not bolt down the slopes.

Until the twentieth century, a majority of Youngstown's families had been here for generations. After 1900, however, with the rise of the steel industry and the immigration of workers drawn to the mills, the population began to change rapidly. By decade's end, the population within the city limits had multiplied seventy-six percent, notwithstanding epidemics of typhoid, smallpox, infantile paralysis (what we know as polio), and diphtheria.

Downtown, bootblacks buffed gentlemen's shoes, farriers shoed horses, and newsies hawked THE VINDICATOR and its competitors in the streets. Regular and extra editions reported everything from illicit cockfighting and illegal boxing matches to the national pastime, baseball, and Youngstown's standing in its interstate league. Interspersed with notices of daily travels undertaken by horse

1904: Federal Street looking east from Central Square on a bleak winter day.

and buggy or bicycle were reports of traffic accidents typically caused by runaway hacks and bolting horses. Advertisements peddled a wealth of goods, from rustproof corsets to front-page pitches for hardware. The pal-

lid, the powerless, and the perturbed could avail themselves of such nostrums as "Dr. Williams' Pink Pills for Pale People," "Dr. Coderre's Red Pills for Pale & Weak Women," and "Paine's Celery Compound to strengthen the nerves."

Cobblestones paved Federal Street, a watering trough stood at Spring Common, and the old bridge that crossed the river there landed level with the Pennsylvania Railroad tracks. The McGuffey Road Bridge didn't come about until 1902, and the Mahoning Avenue Bridge until a year later.

The Commerce Street blacksmith shop stood opposite the yard in which brawny teamsters loaded McKelvey's delivery wagons. When fire struck, proud horses pulled a steam pumper out of the Hazel Street firehouse, smoke billowing behind.

Grocery stores stood on nearly every corner, smelling of chocolate candy, vegetables, and home-baked ice-cream cones. As the decade progressed, livery stables frequently advertised horses that didn't fear automobiles, and for an evening out, dandies hired buggies to

FOR WHAT AILS YOU: Patent tonics offer a one-size-fits-all regimen of self-medication.

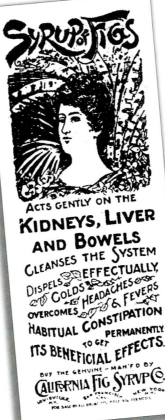

▲

1905: The Wick Building towers over its West Federal Street neighbors in this northwest view from Central Square. The Greek Revival building is First National Bank. Bank One occupies that location today. The Chelekis Building, in the foreground, was later torn down.

PARADING PACHYDERMS: The Barnum & Bailey Circus marched its elephants up West Federal Street flanked by large crowds and electric trolleys. Every year, big-name circuses came to Youngstown and worked their magic under the big top at Wright Field. ▼

1901: Minstrels, variety shows rich in song and humor, were popular with Youngstown audiences. The "end men," made up in blackface, provided the comedy skits.

take their girls for long drives to Hubbard or New Bedford and a romantic dinner.

The papers tracked the continuity of the coal and water supplies, which were often in question and of serious concern to all in that day and age. And while the newspapers brought news of the outside world to the Mahoning Valley, in 1900 trains provided the most immediate physical connection; man's first flight at Kitty Hawk, North Carolina, was still three years away.

Trains were everywhere, their uneven crossings dashing whatever hopes one might have held for a smooth ride along the area's dirt streets. (Only eight miles of the city's ninety-six were paved.) Soot from the trains, dust from the streets, and smoke from burning coal, the fuel of necessity for industry, commerce, and homeowner alike, were unavoidable nuisances.

Minstrels and Theater —A Dash of Soap Opera

While providing news about the world beyond and the community up close, THE VINDICATOR also offered such diversions as sheet music of popular songs, historical notes, geography, comics, fashion, and fiction— even serialized stories not unlike the radio and television soap operas that would develop three and four decades later.

For live entertainment, Mr. and Mrs. Youngstown went to minstrel shows, the theater or opera, or watched and listened as celebrities performed or spoke here on their circuits of the country. Once or twice a year, a big-name circus came to town—Ringling Brothers or Barnum & Bailey or Wallace or Forepaugh-Sells—setting up near Wright Field, having paraded up West Federal Street (when the Erie Railroad's trains weren't blocking Westlake's Crossing).

Many of the greatest performers of the day came to Youngstown, returning time and again to regale local audiences. Stars appeared at the Park Theater and the old Opera House (managed one summer a couple of decades later by Youngstown's

VALLEY SPORTS

I N 1938, THE VINDICATOR, in a special seventieth anniversary issue, reported:

"Those who have lived in maturity, or near maturity, since 1900 may well claim to have witnessed the development of [a] unique era with regard to the recreational side of life. Organized play came into being with the 'turn of the century.' Playgrounds, too, came into being, and such games as baseball, football, boxing and later basketball did not receive the real impetus that has lifted them and set them apart as necessary to national life, until after 1900."

BASEBALL fever ran high (Wright Field was built for professional ball), but Ohio law forbade Sunday play until 1911. That didn't stop local players or fans.

"It was May of 1907 that the first game of baseball was played at Willis Park, at Glenwood and Sherwood Aves. Mr. Willis Park was president of the ball club. A number of times the Youngstown team played on Sunday, then on Monday appeared in Squire Miskell's court, in Phelps St., pleaded guilty and paid a fine of $1 each. Large crowds turned out for the Sunday games."

AS PART of the Interstate League, which included Toledo, New Castle, Fort Wayne, Springfield, Dayton, Mansfield, and Wheeling, Youngstown won the championship in 1907.

Jimmy McAleer was perhaps the area's premier big-leaguer. After a career as an outfielder, McAleer held several major-league posts, including manager of the Saint Louis Browns from 1902-1909. Fame as a big-league pitcher came to Lou Schettler, who played with the Philadelphia Phillies until 1910.

Warner brothers, who later gained Hollywood fame), which subsequently became the site of First Baptist Temple.

George M. Cohan first appeared here as "Little Georgie" in the melodrama "On the Frontier," traveling with his father and mother. Cohan was one of the original stockholders of the Park Theater Company. As a child, the comedian Buster Keaton often played Youngstown with his father, who would carry him on stage in a suitcase. When the Marx family played for Jack Elliott at the Hippodrome, the brothers were children with careers managed by their mother. Buffalo Bill's Wild West Show, featuring an Indian attack on a covered wagon, generated unbridled excitement.

As the decade advanced, THE VINDICATOR tracked the birth of the local steel industry: from the report November 23, 1900, of the incorporation of the Youngstown Iron Sheet & Tube Company by several area men and their purchase of a swampy field for one hundred dollars an acre five miles east of Central Square; to the headline of September 4, 1901,

HEADQUARTERS: From 1893 to 1937, THE VINDICATOR published from this building at Boardman and Phelps streets. The WFMJ-TV Building occupies that location today.

Youngstown Vindicator

HALF A MILLION GOES UP IN SMOKE.

The Most Disastrous Fire Ever Chronicled in the City Calls the Entire Fire Department Out at Midnight to Fight the Flames.

INFERNO: In 1906 fire destroyed the Stambaugh-Thompson Company. In 1900 and again in 1907 the H.L. McElroy Company furniture store and J.N. Euwer's Sons department store incurred devastating losses. A man's death in the 1907 fire was attributed to fright.

FINEST SHEET MILL OPENED; to subsequent plans to change the course of the Mahoning River; to the struggles that befell those who labored in the mills; to the horrendous accidents; to the (sometimes violent) labor strikes; to the unpredictable fluctuations in employment.

The Hot News: Horseshoes, Smoke Abatement, Mail

So what were the day-to-day topics reported in THE VINDICATOR, a charter member of the Associated Press, as the new century arrived?

In March 1900 the Master Horseshoers convened in Youngstown and "painted the town red." In July, clerics and dignitaries laid the cornerstone of Saint Columba Roman Catholic Church. In October, the new Republic Bessemer on East Front Street produced two hundred tons of steel a day. Other notices told of committee meetings to discuss smoke-abatement,

HOME AWAY FROM HOME: Hotels were being built throughout Greater Youngstown in the early 1900s. As the population increased, so did the need for temporary housing. Braun's Hotel was on Wilson Avenue, near Center Street, in the Haselton district.

MILL CREEK PARK

Volney Rogers founded Mill Creek Park, the second largest urban park in the United States (Central Park in New York City is the largest). Preserving the park's natural state proved to be a challenge.

the success of rural mail delivery, and the Opera House production of Uncle Tom's Cabin (admission ten, twenty, and thirty cents).

THE VINDICATOR devoted its front page to national and international news. Items of local interest ran inside, except in such extreme situations as the story February 2, 1900, headlined HALF A MILLION GOES UP IN SMOKE—THE EUWER-McELROY-McKELVEY FIRE. A review of Sunday's news ran Monday on page two for those who hadn't seen the Sunday issue.

The paper printed the news in tiny type flowed into eight columns a page on weekdays and seven columns on Sundays; daily issues contained eight pages.

Social notices appeared by neighborhood under the banner "Subrosa": Haselton, Pine Hill, West End, East End, Woodworth, Brushville, Milton, Fairwatch, Calla, Rosemont, Scienceville, Knowledge Hill, New Albany, Milville, Four-Mile-Run....

The Sunday paper, usually thirty-two pages, contained three sections. The first covered news, including commentary on local politics in a column titled "Over the Telephone," and such milestones as births, engagements, weddings, and deaths. The second section related the latest sports information, under such headings as "Ring News," "The Races," "Horse Talk," and "Golf Gossip." The third section offered a collection of history, fiction, geography, fashion, housekeeping notes, and comics (the first color version of which

ONE OF THE COMMUNITY'S brightest jewels, Mill Creek Park owes its existence and early preservation to the visionary Volney Rogers, who with his brother, Bruce, invested time and energy to ensure the preservation of its seven-mile-long gorge from six hundred feet to a mile wide.

Two serious threats he worked tirelessly to avert during the century's first decade were waterworks and district sewer proposals.

THE OLDEST LAKE in the park, Cohasset, was built in the eighteen-nineties. Construction of Lake Glacier took place in 1904 and 1905. With beach areas on either shore, Lake Glacier quickly became a favorite spot for swimming.

Lanterman's Mill and waterfall.

appeared in May 1907).

Throughout the decade, the daily paper cost two cents; Sunday issues were a nickel. Every headline appeared in the same typeface, and advertisements, along with letters to the editor, were mixed among, and barely distinguishable from, the news, even on the front page. Many advertisements were testimonials, as in the thank you that sang the praises of "Mrs. Pinkham's Vegetable Compound": "I have gained in weight from ninety-five to 140; everyone asks what makes me so stout."

A New Social Consciousness Spreads Through the Valley

Flowery language adorned everything from hard news (from January 17, 1900: "THE VINDICATOR this morning came into possession of information, which is regarded as perfectly reliable since it comes from an official source....") to obituaries that spoke of "The Sleep," "The Death Angel's Call," "The Tolling of the Bell," and being "At Rest until the Resurrection Morn."

In a crusade that would come to infuse many aspects of daily life, local churches, like their counterparts round the world, discovered at the turn of the century a new "social Gospel," particularly people's relationships in economic, political, and interracial affairs.

People worked for women's suffrage and temperance, causes that would find their way into the U.S. Constitution in the next decade. (In a prophetic editorial, THE VINDICATOR clearly stated its opinion of prohibition in April 1909). The crash of the U.S. stock market and the Panic of 1907 prompted concern for feeding the local poor.

In 1900 a mayor and a board of four commissioners ran the city. An Ohio Supreme Court decision in 1902 ended that form of government, and the legislature created statutory government comprising a mayor, a council, a three-member elected board of public

LAW, ORDER, AND THE GALLOWS: The first courthouse in Youngstown opened in 1876 at Wick and Wood streets. The courthouse yard was the setting for Youngstown's only legal execution, in which the county strung up Charles Theodore Sterling in 1877 for killing a fourteen-year-old girl.

service, and a two-member appointed board of public safety.

While the population within the city limits of Youngstown grew seventy-six percent in the first ten years of the twentieth

City Hospital opened in 1883 in a house on Oak Hill Avenue. When it expanded in 1902, it looked much like it does in this 1906 photo. When North Side Hospital was built in the late twenties, this complex became South Side Hospital.

MODERN MEDICINE: THE FIRST STEPS

MEDICINE, too, progressed. Although a hospital had been organized in Youngstown in 1882, not until 1902 was the first facility of the modern era built on Oak Hill Avenue. In 1909 efforts began for the development of Saint Elizabeth Hospital (which officially opened in 1911).

No discussion of medicine in the city at that time would be complete without mention of W.L. and W.H. Buechner, father and son, who contributed immeasurably to the community's medical and civic development for seventy years that bridged the turn of the century.

The senior Buechner, a medical practitioner more than fifty years and one of the leaders in the movement to form a city hospital, died tragically when a runaway horse dragged his carriage through a fence and plunged down a twenty-foot ravine at Bear's Den in 1904.

The younger Dr. Buechner studied in Europe and specialized in surgery; in many instances he was the first to perform particular surgical procedures locally, operations that later became commonplace. The first president of the Youngstown Automobile Club (organized in 1916), he died of pneumonia in 1920.

century, expenditures about tripled during that period. With a tax duplicate of $10,282,440 in 1899, the city's general fund expenditures totaled $215,996. By 1908, the city's tax duplicate totaled $32,485,980 (the county's was $32,521,780). The budget request for city expenditures in 1909 totaled $638,451, with the police department costing the city $102,000 and the fire department just over $110,000.

The criminal court, solicitor, and mayor's office requested $3,040, $4,350, and just over $4,500 for their operations.

Youngstown Telephone First Tenant of Dollar Bank Bldg.

In 1902 the Dollar Savings & Trust Company moved into a new six-story building. Although the building was known as the Dollar Savings & Trust Building, the bank was not the first tenant; when the building was under construction its third floor was devoted to the new offices of the Youngstown Telephone Company.

To enable the new telephone exchange to open on schedule, the

STAMBAUGH-THOMPSON'S 1900: The company sold anything and everything at its West Federal Street store—from shotguns to house plants. And hardware, of course.

third story was completed before the first two, and the telephone operator climbed a ladder to get to and from work. In 1902 a residential phone cost two dollars a month. Business lines were three dollars apiece. About the same time, telephone extensions came into use, but they cost seven dollars more a month residential and ten dollars a month commercial. Two-party lines offered a less expensive option: two dollars a

month for offices, a dollar fifty for homes.

When Dollar Bank added two stories to become eight in 1907, it became the city's first skyscraper. Thereafter, as reporter Clingan Jackson wrote January 29, 1950, "The skyscrapers of downtown Youngstown grew like mushrooms for more than a decade."

Water resources were a grave concern as the century dawned. For a long time, domestic supplies

TRANSPORTATION: THE CRAZY QUILT RAILROADS

TRAINS provided the only practical means of mass transportation at the turn of the century, but maneuvering around them and on them provided a daily challenge. Trains and switching operations often blocked traffic at the Erie crossings from Watt Street to Westlake's Crossing.

THE PENNSYLVANIA Railroad came to Youngstown late in the nineteenth century through consolidation of small railroads, including the Ashtabula, Youngstown & Pittsburgh, Alliance, Niles & Ashtabula, Erie & Pittsburgh, Liberty & Vienna, and Lawrence Line.

With construction of the Mahoning Valley & Western between Niles and Ravenna, the

Pennsylvania established a new route between Pittsburgh and Cleveland by way of Youngstown in 1905. Just after the turn of the century, a Youngstown-Ravenna line was set up for the Pennsylvania by a company that bought right-of-way and unfinished grading from the Cleveland & New Castle Railway Company.

THE BALTIMORE & OHIO began serving Youngstown about 1875, but its city line didn't become an integral part of the great B&O system until 1891, when the B&O set a shorter route between Pittsburgh and Chicago by purchasing the Pittsburgh & Western Railroad and its subsidiary companies. Acquisition of the P&W and construction of a line from Ak-

ron to Chicago Junction (now Willard, southwest of Cleveland) gave the B&O a better run from the East to Chicago through Pittsburgh, Youngstown and Akron. By the 1950s that would become known as the Akron division of the B&O.

LOCALLY, PEOPLE could ride the Youngstown & Southern. Originated in 1903 as a steam railroad, the line went broke and was reorganized as an electric line in 1907, becoming known as the Youngstown & Suburban. It became important to Youngstown's transportation picture because of links with the Youngstown & Ohio River Railroad for East Liverpool and the Stark Electric Railway for Alliance and Canton.

were pumped from the Mahoning River, but by 1895 the city had incurred an abnormal number of typhoid cases. Mill Creek was proposed as the most logical source for a new water supply, but Lake Erie also had its supporters. By fall 1905 the city was being supplied with Mahoning River water filtered by the latest methods.

Purer Water, but Not Enough To Meet Consumer Demand

Although filtration solved the problem of purity, consumption rapidly proved the river to be an inadequate source. While consideration was given to Mill Creek, Yankee Run, Meander Valley, Lake Erie, Liberty Lake, and Lake Hamilton, it was eventually determined that damming the Berlin watershed would be the ideal, and it might have been but for realty interests that drove up the cost beyond reason. As the decade ended, city council pursued damming the Milton Township basin.

Water as a means of transportation was also a topic of frequent discussion as the idea formed of a Lake Erie and Ohio River canal, similar to those that operated at the time of the Civil War.

In March 1902, Joseph G. Butler incorporated a canal company. By December, Congress was asked to approve the Ship Canal Company. In 1905 a Columbiana County company also proposed a Lake Erie to Ohio River canal, and that fall the paper reported that a construction survey was nearly complete. The idea faded from view until the next decade, however, despite a VINDICATOR feature in March 1906 laying out the benefits of a canal.

The William B. Pollock Company was probably Youngstown's oldest active industry to thrive well into the twentieth century. Originally founded in 1863 by William B. Pollock, a blast furnace operator, it was first located on

1910: The old Mahoning National Bank Building was dismantled to make way for the bank's thirteen-story structure on the southwest corner of Central Square.

Basin Street, then Market, where it was destroyed by fire.

A new plant was built in 1901 to make blast furnaces, steel plant equipment, hot metal ladles, hot metal cars of various kinds and other heavy steel fabrications. For generations, it built blast furnaces all over the world and its equipment was found in virtually every steel plant in the United States.

The Steel Trust, Forerunner Of U.S. Steel, Takes Shape

But the steel plants themselves held the key to Youngstown's twentieth-century industrial fate.

As the century began, the area's first steel concern, the Ohio Steel Company, was eight years old. Its plant, completed in 1895 on the riverbank beyond Youngstown's west edge, helped make the city the nation's second-largest steel center for a time, and Thomas McDonald, an old steel man for whom the village of McDonald would later be named, was hired to run it. The first Youngstown steel was blown in the new Bessemer converters Feb. 4, 1895, a day old timers would later recall as having been four below zero.

In February 1899 the National Steel Company was formed as the

first step in organizing the so-called "steel trust" that would later become U.S. Steel Corporation. National purchased Ohio Steel and with it local plants of Union Iron & Steel Company, which had been organized by merging a number of nineteenth-century rolling mills in the area.

Big Steel Acquires Most Independent Producers

The Ohio Steel plant became known as the "Ohio Works," and the Union plants became known as "Upper Union Mill" (abandoned around 1949) and "Lower Union Mill" (dismantled around 1930).

In 1900 the Ohio Works comprised just a couple of blast furnaces and two small Bessemer converters. But they grew so quickly that when Carnegie Steel, the biggest steel-making subsidiary of U.S. Steel, was organized in 1903, it took over the Ohio Works as one of its main plants. By 1909 the Ohio Works included six blast furnaces; that year, too, twelve open hearths were built and the plant produced Youngstown's first open hearth steel. Three more open hearths would be added later.

Other district iron and steel plants eventually drawn into the U.S. Steel fold included Shenango Valley Steel Company at New Castle, Buhl Steel at Sharon, and Thomas Furnace at Niles. The New Castle property would be dismantled during the Depression, the Thomas Furnace was razed even before that, and the Sharon property went to Sharon Steel just after World War II.

Also of vital significance at the end of the nineteenth century was the merger that formed Republic Iron & Steel Company, forerunner of what became Republic Steel.

While the "steel trust" had engulfed virtually all the steel plants, the new Republic round-ed up many of the iron plants, some of them unprofitable little producers known as "cats and dogs."

Among Republic's acquisitions were Brown-Bonnell & Company, which at that time had the country's largest rolling mills (part of Republic's local plant would long be known as the Brown-Bonnell Works), Andrews Brothers & Company, Mahoning Valley Iron Company, and the Sharon Iron Works. With construction of its Bessemer in 1900, Republic Iron & Steel became Youngstown's second official steel concern.

Sharon Interests Set Their Sights on Barrel-Hoop Trade

As U.S. Steel and Republic gobbled up the small plants of the Shenango Valley, some Sharon industrialists, eager to put to work the money they had received, decided they, too, would organize a new steel concern in 1900.

Because the new outfit aimed to grab a big share of an important business of that era—the barrel hoop trade—it was named Sharon Steel Hoop Company and eventually included a substantial rolling mill and a small steel plant with seven open-hearth furnaces. The sale of Ohio Steel to the steel trust had furnished Youngstown's industrialists and financiers the cash that would bring about some

of the city's most important enterprises through the coming decades. The first of these was Youngstown Iron Sheet & Tube ("Iron" was later dropped from the name); others included Republic Rubber, Ohio Leather, General Fireproofing, and Standard Textile Products.

Youngstown Sheet & Tube was incorporated November 23, 1900, and sold $600 thousand worth of stock. Among those who bought heavily were families that profited heavily in the Ohio Steel and Union sales—the Wicks, Tods, Stambaughs, and others. James A. Campbell, a dominant figure in steel then and for many years afterward, lost his executive job with the old Union Iron & Steel Company in the National Steel sale. Although Republic quickly hired him as district manager, Campbell was unhappy there and decided to make a switch to the struggling new Sheet & Tube, working under Col. George Wick, its capable president.

The new company bought a swamp and

JAMES CAMPBELL

COL. GEORGE WICK

wheat field for one hundred dollars an acre five miles east of Central Square as the site for its plant and originally intended to build four sheet mills, fourteen double puddling furnaces, some muck bar mills, a skelp mill, and three tube mills.

The first contract called for $450 thousand, but after facing a shortage of cash, battling floods that held up construction, and confronting many other problems, the capital was increased to $2 million in June 1901. By February 1902 the puddling furnaces were operational; the sheet mills began rolling the next month. In the meantime, to help with cash flow, the company bought the Alice furnace from the Mathers of Cleveland for $300 thousand and found itself in the iron business. Although the new company's mills rolled both iron and steel, it didn't get around to producing its own steel until 1906, when it built Bessemer converters of its own. Until then, it bought steel by furnishing Republic with pig

KIDNAPPED!

IN MARCH 1909 the kidnapping of Billy Whitla created a sensation in Ohio and Pennsylvania.

The boy, son of a prominent Sharon lawyer and nephew of a Sharon industrialist and philanthropist, was found in Cleveland within a week and his kidnappers were caught.

So intense was interest in the case, that this photo was sold at the time as a postcard. That's Billy in the window.

1909: Downtown Youngstown and the steel mills as they appeared from the south bank of the Mahoning River. The next decade would bring phenomenal growth in the industry. By the end of that decade, the district's steel industry would be almost fully organized.

iron and paying a fee for the conversion to steel. Wick retired in May 1902, leaving his vice president and general manager, Jim Campbell, as top officer for two years until he assumed the presidency July 26, 1904, a role he would fill for more than twenty-five years.

For Youngstown Sheet & Tube, A Succession of Developments

Youngstown Sheet & Tube grew quickly and steadily. In 1908 the company built two five hundred-ton blast furnaces to augment the Alice furnace and more puddle furnaces, giving it twenty-four double units. More pipe mills were built as well. In 1909, Sheet & Tube bought the Struthers sheet mill and Morgan Spring Works in Struthers. In 1911, it would buy Western Conduit & Manufacturing's Harvey, Ill., plant, and, in 1912, move it to join the others in Struthers.

Other industrial concerns that flourished in the valley as the century got under way included Ohio Leather, formed in 1901; Republic Rubber Company, also organized in 1901, which for years made outstanding rubber products, including fire hose, garden hose, solid truck tires, and mechanical rubber goods; and General Fireproofing Company, which originally specialized in fireproof office furniture, metal lath, and steel joists.

Truscon Steel (originally Trussed Concrete) came to the area in 1906

from Detroit. A supplier of steel products for the construction business, Truscon came to Youngstown to better meet its need for large quantities of bars, wire, and flat-rolled steel. The executive offices followed in 1914, and in 1935 the company was acquired by Republic Steel Corporation as a subsidiary and as an outlet for its steel.

In 1906, the A.M. Byers Company, which owned a blast furnace at Girard, built a puddling furnace that grew to be the largest of its kind and was chiefly responsible for Girard's widespread reputation as a source of wrought iron.

In 1907, Falcon Bronze was organized to produce brass and bronze castings, mainly for iron and steel plants. Youngstown Sheet & Tube and its successors gave the Mahoning Valley a reputation as the "American Ruhr," named for the German river valley that was the world's most famous steel-producing region.

Though Greater Youngstown had been one of Ohio's major industrial centers for a hundred years, the first half of the twentieth century would see its greatest growth. Its industrial expansion would furnish jobs for a thriving population and stand as a tribute to the initiative, courage, energy, enterprise, and abilities of the pioneer industrialists and financiers—the Fords, Tods, Wicks, Armses, and others—as well as the industry and know-how of Youngstown's workers.

News from the Mahoning and Shenango Valleys

1910

MARCH 19: Youngstown's water-filtration plant must be improved and enlarged by 1912, the Ohio Board of Health says. Filth entering the Mahoning upstream will require moving the intake beyond Brier Hill.

APRIL 5: A cyclone rips through Lansingville and Haselton, toppling houses and barns and crippling factories. Seventeen are injured.

JUNE 20: In Lordstown, the Pennsylvania Flyer strikes a horse-drawn rig at seventy miles an hour, killing a couple on their way to church and badly injuring their daughter.

JULY 6: The Barnum & Bailey circus arrives with its own "city"–stores, hospital, shops, hotel, laundry, and light plants. The circus has 1,280 people, seven hundred horses, forty elephants, and twelve hundred other animals.

DEC. 18: With Christmas nearing, passenger and freight traffic swamp the Youngstown & Southern, requiring the addition of another trailer to the regular Leetonia car.

1911

MARCH 11: Lowellville residents vote 139-107 to allow the Lowellville Water Company to install a water system fed by artesian wells.

MAY 1: In Struthers, C.A. Windle, editor of Chicago's ICONOCLAST MAGAZINE, represents wets as he and Youngstown lawyer D.F. Anderson, debate the topic "Is Prohibition Right?"

AUG. 19: A "week-old American baby boy" is available for adoption. Childless couples on the Humane Society list didn't "care for a baby so young" so any interested party should contact the society agent.

SEPT. 12: A six-foot black snake bites a Sharon lad's left hand at the tile works. A doctor cauterizes the wound to ward off blood poisoning.

OCT. 17: "Humming, Singing or Whistling of 'Alexander's Ragtime Band' is prohibited," reads a sign in Squire Welsh's office. Clerks said the noise made it hard to work.

1912

JAN. 11: At Brady Lake near Ravenna, German Buehrle and his company are cutting ice "twelve inches thick and of the finest quality." Patrons may buy it next summer for twenty-seven cents a block.

APRIL 4: A blast rocks the Quaker Falls plant of the Burton Powder

Company, killing two workmen and shattering lights in Lowellville and windows in New Castle.

MAY 8: First National Bank directors honor Titanic victim George D. Wick, fellow director and vice president, for his many important contributions to the bank.

DEC. 8: Panama Canal locks use gate-moving machines made by Youngstown's William Tod Company. The work took more than a year and filled 275 rail cars.

1913

JAN. 22: Pennsylvania's health commissioner bans milk-bottle returns by Sharon and Farrell families afflicted with typhoid fever.

FEB. 18: Council allows THE VINDICATOR to erect a lighted bulletin rack at Phelps and Federal streets.

MARCH 25: Elkton, Columbiana County, awash in eight feet of water as record floods swamp Ohio. Many residents are living in upper stories without food, potable water or fuel.

SEPT. 16: Fire levels Ferrin & Waller, a livery stable at South Walnut and Boardman streets, killing twenty-nine horses and causing a loss of nineteen thousand dollars.

DEC. 13: THE VINDICATOR receives Youngstown's first wireless message; THE CLEVELAND PLAIN DEALER congratulates the city on its first wireless telegraph office. "Neither fire, flood, nor tornado can now cut off these cities from each other or from the world," the paper said.

1914

JAN. 5: The Youngstown Board of Education welcomes its first woman member, Mrs. R.S. Baker.

FEB. 4: A cholera-like ailment hits Grove City, Pennsylvania. Many of the thousand cases are collegians.

AUG. 1: Dynamite causes damage of two hundred dollars at the home of Samuel McClure, editor and publisher of THE YOUNGSTOWN TELEGRAM. McClure considers it an attempt to intimidate him and his newspaper.

OCT. 27: Newly poured floors of the Hippodrome Arcade collapse, killing three laborers.

NOV. 12: The board of health quarantines the Canfield farm of John Neff to contain an outbreak of hoof and mouth disease.

1915

FEB. 11: A bobsled coasting down

Shady Run Road into Campbell Street strikes a Poland Avenue streetcar, injuring seven people. About fifteen riders were aboard when the sled started its run at the top of Flint Hill, more than a mile above Poland Avenue.

MARCH 24: A census of Youngstown religion by the Mahoning County Sunday School Association provides "considerable food for both faith and fancy," THE VINDICATOR reports. The top ten faiths: Catholic (3,972); Methodist (2,905); Presbyterian (1,332); Christian (1,272); Baptist (1,198); Lutheran (1,089); Episcopal (549); United Presbyterian (537); Reformed (404); and Jewish (266).

JULY 22: The Petersburg Fair is discontinued because the 25-cent admission doesn't cover the cost of renting grounds and organizing a picnic, horse race and ball games.

AUG. 9: The Grocers Association will prosecute corner stores if they open on Sundays.

NOV. 4: The Eastern Ohio Fish & Game Preservation Society will restock Lake Cohasset and several ponds and streams with fish obtained from the state.

1916

MAY 6: A flatcar carrying a cage of leopards derails at the New York Central depot as the Hagenback-Wallace Circus leaves for Sharon, Pennsylvania. No animals escaped.

JULY 6: Spontaneous combustion ignites a $25,000 fire at the Youngstown Carriage Company, Walnut and Boardman streets. Autos on the first and second floors are saved, but the fire destroys many on the third floor.

JULY 15: THE VINDICATOR commends President Wilson's appointment of John H. Clarke to a seat on the Supreme Court of the United States. Clarke is a VINDICATOR investor.

DEC. 7: The Mahoning County Horticultural Society opens its first annual meeting at the Public Library. A five- by ten-foot map made from twelve bushels of apples shows each township in a different color.

1917

JAN. 18: The state's master bakers meet in Cleveland and predict the five-cent loaf of bread will soon go up to seven cents. One option: drop the small loaf and make only the standard twelve-cent size.

FEB. 6: Foreign-born Youngstowners need not "fear any invasion of ...personal or property rights" if the U.S. goes to war in Europe, Mayor Carroll Thornton says.

MAY 3: "Mahoning County's donation to patriotism," a lighted flag, is placed atop the courthouse.

MAY 17: Police Chief H. H. Hartenstein and Municipal Judge George Gessner declare war on speeders, promising arrests and jail sentences regardless of social position.

OCT. 5: Former President William Howard Taft (later chief justice of the United States) dedicates the McKinley Memorial. Niles businesses and schools close for the event.

1918

FEB. 21: Carnegie Steel will build more housing for McDonald Works employees at the new town of McDonald. With more mills, the company will need more men by summer.

MAY 20: Mahoning County patriots pledge $129,033 to the million-dollar war drive on its first day.

JULY 5: Youngstown has its first lady mail carrier, Ellen Vallery. Postmaster George B. Snyder and Herbert C. Williams, superintendent of South Side station, praise her work.

AUG. 1: The state Food Board, meeting at the Youngstown YMCA, raises the price of milk a penny to thirteen cents a quart.

DEC. 6: Eyes turn upward as a Martin bomber flies at 150 miles an hour above Youngstown's skyscrapers in the first nonstop flight from Cleveland to Washington, D.C.

1919

FEB. 19: World War I's toll in Mahoning County: one hundred-sixty dead, 221 wounded, 21 missing.

MAY 19: Three nationalities, Italian, Serbian and Hungarian, hold celebrations in East Youngstown (later Campbell), proving "that the melting pot is working in the right direction," THE VINDICATOR says.

JUNE 14: Boy Scouts observe Recognition Week and Flag Day with a parade downtown, then leave for Stambaugh Reservation, the late Henry Stambaugh's gift to Scouting.

JULY 7: Youngstown reports its first bootlegging arrest since Ohio went dry. A policeman grabs Pete Dangler and a grip filled with liquor.

1910 **2** 1919

BATTLES NATURAL & MAN-MADE

MARCH 26, 1913: The century's worst flood swamped Youngstown's Baltimore & Ohio station, filling its main floor halfway to the ceiling. The gondolas in the foreground probably floated off the railroad tracks. The Mahoning River would be a problem into the sixties.

Youngstown flourished in the second decade of the twentieth century. Housing, population, and industry boomed, but battles at home and abroad, from women's rights to World War I, occupied the minds of its people.

EVENTS BEYOND THE VALLEY

1910: Boy Scouts of America founded.

1911: Norwegian Roald Amundsen reaches South Pole.

EXTRA
COL. GEORGE D. WICK LOST

Cleveland, O., April 17. Another version of the message received by H. W. Bonnell at New York, from his sister Miss Caroline Bonnell, a Titanic survivor, was received here. It read:
"All women saved on board Carpathia. George lost."

1912: R.M.S. Titanic sinks ▲ on maiden voyage. Col. George Wick of Youngstown among the victims.

1913: Federal income tax begins in United States.

1914: Archduke Franz Ferdinand assassinated in Sarajevo.

• U.S. maintains neutrality amid world's growing hostilities.

• Panama Canal finally reaches completion.

1915: German submarine sinks R.M.S. Lusitania.

• German zeppelins bomb Great Britain.

1916: Trans-Siberian Railway completed.

• First tanks used in warfare as British troops assault German line at the River Somme.

1917: U.S. declares war on Germany.

• Russia's Tsar Nicholas II abdicates.

1918: Leon Trotsky organizes the Red Army.

• Civil war breaks out in Russia.

1919: U.S. Senate won't ratify Treaty of Versailles.

• League of Nations formed.

Heavy-metal manufacturing not only defined Youngstown's economy but also its culture. Immigrants by the thousands came from southern and eastern Europe to work in the steel mills, and generation by generation, ethnic neighborhoods and union halls displaced the city's Yankee roots.

DAMAINE VONADA, EDITOR
THE OHIO ALMANAC, 1992-1993

1918: World War I inspired unparalleled industrial growth for Youngstown and parades of soldiers down West Federal Street after the United States entered the war in 1917.

A S THE DECADE BEGAN, Youngstown had a population of nearly eighty thousand, and before the decade ended, the population would increase almost sixty-five percent. The Mahoning Valley experienced a housing boom of which construction of three hundred homes on Mahoning Avenue in a three-year period was but one example. Such dramatic increases led to civic improvements—paving of streets, laying of water and sewer mains, elimination of railroad grades, erection of bridges, construction of dams, and expansion of educational opportunities. However, battles at home and abroad, in social, financial, and military arenas, commanded the

AND THEY THOUGHT WE COULDN'T FIGHT

VICTORY LIBERTY LOAN

1918: American doughboys as they fought their way through the shell-shattered Argonne Forest during World War I.

1911: The Sisters of the Humility of Mary established Saint Elizabeth Hospital in three frame houses on Youngstown's Belmont Avenue. By 1915, the hospital had outgrown the structures and built what is now known as the north wing.

Mahoning Valley's attention as well. Between 1914 and 1920 the U.S. faced one hundred percent inflation. In Mexico, political unrest ran rampant, leading President Woodrow Wilson to send American troops to enforce democratic ideals there.

Destruction of Luxury Liner Nudges U.S. Closer to War

Battles also raged across the Atlantic. Not until 1915, however, with the sinking of the R.M.S. Lusitania by a German U-boat, did Wilson begin to consider that the U.S. had a role to play in war-torn Europe. At home, battles over women's rights, temperance, and labor unions were fought on editorial pages, from the pulpits, and in mass gatherings. Workers struck, revolted, rioted, and confronted

1917: Suffragettes, determined to gain the right to vote, marched on the White House from Women's Party headquarters.

the National Guard.

Natural disasters plagued the community as well. And Youngstown argued over what form of government—home-rule charter or executive management—would better serve the community.

Through the decade, people also debated transportation needs as jitneys, the forerunners of buses, raised doubts about the efficiency and fiscal practicality of the city's streetcars.

Time and time again, industrial growth and improved communications, along with ever-improving transportation, made the world seem smaller, but even an issue as basic as adopting a uniform time zone provoked argument. Not until the Erie Railroad adopted eastern time in April 1914 did Youngstown as well.

And although the hospitals were growing (Saint Elizabeth opened in 1911) and medicine made strides, the city still faced more than four hundred cases of diphtheria a year at the start of the decade, and struggled with outbreaks of hoof-and-mouth disease, typhoid, smallpox, and influenza that closed schools, banned theater-going, and shut down public places. During that time, THE VINDICATOR

enlivened downtown sidewalks with bulletin boards on which it hastily penciled summaries of the latest news flashes, and offered election night crowds the opportunity to track returns, projecting results on a screen from handwritten or typed slides.

The paper also reported everything from the holiday rush in 1911 that necessitated mail delivery on Sunday, December 24, to local history features, as in an eyewitness's reminiscence fifty years later of the firing on Fort Sumter April 12, 1861.

Bright Spots in the News, And an Armistice that Wasn't

Nor did the newspaper overlook stories of philanthropy, such as a fifty-thousand-dollar gift to the library from Pittsburgh's Andrew Carnegie in April 1910, and refreshing reports of natural events, such as an article in the July 15, 1916, issue about an eclipse of the moon. When the paper supported something, it "boomed" the issue.

As an Associated Press member, THE VINDICATOR was not deceived when United Press prematurely announced the signing of the Armistice on November 7, 1918. THE VINDICATOR accurately held off until the signing really came to pass November 11.

In that day and age, bobsledders could tear down Belmont Avenue from Broadway to Wood Street, and photographers plied their craft in studios with skylights and backdrops portraying Lanterman's Falls and Umbrella Rocks.

On Thanksgiving, the whole community mustered for the Rayen-South football game, South High School having opened in 1911 to meet the needs of a growing population. And by July 1910 Youngstown had more than six hundred autos.

Yet, while progress continued on some fronts, on others progress could be frustrated by the natural cycles of the Earth, as in 1913 when the mild winter prevented the annual ice harvest.

Downtown, Tall Buildings Rise Against the Skyline

Youngstown's skyline underwent dramatic change as skyscrapers multiplied: the Mahoning National Bank Building, thirteen floors, 1910; four more stories to the Stambaugh Building, 1915; Home Savings & Loan, 1919. And although two tries were needed, Joseph Butler succeeded in establishing an art museum, incorporating in November 1914, opening in 1915, suffering a fire in December 1917, then presenting a new gallery to the city in a service of rededication in September 1920.

The Black Hand and its members—"black hands"—inspired fear among many residents. Rumor associated the terrorist group, which had flourished in Sicily in the late nineteenth century, with the Mafia and the Camorra.

It was once estimated that ninety percent of the Italian population in New York City had received letters threatening death and bearing imprints of black hands. The Black Hand had been active in the Mahoning Valley as early as 1905. After 1910, however, bombings, arrests, trials, and raids on hidden headquarters became more and more common.

The population also faced many challenges from na-

1910: The first airplane in Youngstown drew a large crowd to see its initial flight. The plane flew from an airfield on Glenwood Avenue.

AS AUTOMOBILES became more and more popular, getting around became more of an adventure. The community experimented with a variety of paving materials, including slag generated in the mill furnaces. In 1912, the newspaper heralded the opening of the Austintown Road, with new brick pavement, and plans were unveiled in 1913 for a state highway connecting Youngstown to Cleveland.

AS POPULAR as cars were becoming, however, most people continued to rely on railroads and streetcars to get around, and the area's rail lines continued to expand. In 1913, the first passenger streetcar used the tracks from Youngstown to Poland. Such progress frustrated the city as it and the railroads continued year after year to negotiate whether and how to eliminate the bothersome railroad grades that disrupted other modes of transportation. The three choices were to do nothing, "depress the tracks," or "go into the hill." Traffic snarls became such a concern that the Supreme Court in 1911 forbade trains to bar any crossing for more than five minutes. On the other hand, construction of

bridges increasingly simplified getting from one part of the city to another. The first Spring Common Bridge went up in 1911, as did bridges at Dewey Avenue, Center Street and McKelvey Lake. In 1914, Lincoln Park got a bridge; in 1917, Oak Street Extension did. Throughout the 1910s, the old Elephant Bridge, with its plank surface, clattered under the wheels of wagons and buggies; its nickname reflected on the prohibitive cost of maintaining the city's "white elephant."

MEANWHILE, in the years leading up to World War I, the truly adventurous were taking to the skies, and observers would spread the news by shouting "Airplane!" whenever one heard a flying machine. One of the most noteworthy occasions came one day in 1910 when Eugene E. Ely flew his frail pusher plane before a huge crowd at Willis Park, the old ballfield near Fosterville, as part of a benefit exhibition for the planned construction of Saint Elizabeth Hospital. Just as aviation would make tremendous strides during the war, the war also ushered in the need for more varieties of efficient transportation and the birth of the trucking industry.

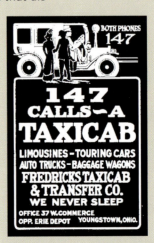

ARMISTICE: The end of World War I calls for a downtown celebration. Home Savings & Loan was under construction at the time.

ture during the decade. The quality of local water commanded the attention of the State Board of Health, and fear of water famines was discussed almost every other year.

In 1910 a tornado caused damage of fifty thousand dollars in the city's East End. In 1915 heavy frosts were reported May 27, and July was the coldest in thirty-three years, but the most devastating natural disaster of the decade had come two years earlier, in March 1913 when the Mahoning River rose twenty-two feet above low-water stage. Raging currents flooded the city, washing out three bridges, choking off water and

electricity, and causing a loss of more than $1 million (in 1913 dollars). Temporary pontoon bridges were later erected, one of which collapsed under the weight of a parade that August. To make matters worse, the heaviest snow since 1886 hit the region early that November, cutting Youngstown off from the outside world until communications were restored three days later.

Baseball, meanwhile, continued to occupy the hearts, bodies, and minds of area residents. The Central League took over the Ohio & Pennsylvania League in 1912.

That same year, inspired by the growing popularity of golf and cramped by the expanding population of Youngstown, the Youngstown Country Club moved from its nine-hole golf course on the North Side to Liberty Township and an eighteen-hole course.

YMCA Gets New Quarters; Night School a Necessity

Additional expansion of recreational facilities during the decade came with the construction of a new home for the YWCA, the opening of rooms by the Young Men's Hebrew Association, and the opening of a new YMCA.

MARCH 28, 1913: Once again, the Mahoning River torments Youngstown, rising twenty-two feet above low-water stage. This is Mahoning Avenue west of Spring Common.

ECONOMICS, POLITICS, AND CANAL TALK

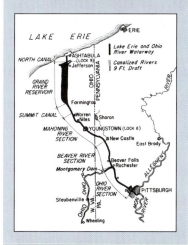

THE AREA'S financial worth was increasing along with population. Personal property in Mahoning County in 1910 totaled $14,734,352, and Youngstown real estate that year was valued at $97,354,666. In 1911, the county tax duplicate totaled $175 million, and, investments in the Mahoning Valley reached $50 million by 1915. Much to the consternation of wholesalers and retailers, the city adopted an ordinance in 1910 requiring weights to be marked on all goods sold in packages or cases.

THE MAKEUP of local government also changed when, in 1910, an act of the Ohio General Assembly abolished Youngstown's boards of Public Service and Public Safety and established the offices of service director and safety director. That form of government continued until the adoption of the City Charter in 1923.

OF INTEREST since before the turn of the century, the subject of a Lake Erie-to-Ohio River Canal again found its way into the headlines when Mayor Craver proposed it to council in 1910. At Christmas that year, a committee was formed to investigate the possibility and in April 1912 a recommendation for the canal was made to Congress.

Large numbers of immigrants and the round-the-clock nature of the steel industry necessitated the opening of night schools to teach English, and as the communities near the mills became more densely populated, THE VINDICATOR actively supported the Fresh Air Association, a program that provided time in the country for city children each summer.

Whether Alcohol Is to Be, Or Not to Be, Stirs Debate

Protestants, long the majority, tended to legislate morality by forbidding work or recreation on Sundays and preached against the evils of alcohol. The immigrant steelworkers, who endured long hours at physically demanding assignments in the heat of the mills, which ran round the clock, seven days a week, wanted to be able to relax when they had time off, no matter what day it was. The change of scene provided by the saloons proved especially popular.

The issue of alcohol consumption therefore provided material for energetic debate. Among others, Clarence Darrow, a Kinsman native and a lawyer of no little acclaim, spoke several times on behalf of the "wets." The "dry" position's most popular and vocal advocate was the former baseball player turned evangelist Billy Sunday, who preached often in Youngstown in many locations, including a basket picnic in 1910 at Southern Park.

FOR THE WETS: Kinsman lawyer Clarence Darrow, who later gained national fame in the Scopes "Monkey Trial," spoke against Prohibition.

Sunday, who was born in Ames, Iowa, had played professional ball in the 1880s, then worked at the Chicago YMCA, hooking up with an itinerant Presbyterian evangelist. After leading a successful revival in Garner, Iowa, in 1896, he decided to become a full-time evangelist himself.

Sunday's flamboyance made him popular in the Mahoning Valley and helped raise popular support for Prohibition. Although the pros and cons of prohibiting the manufacture, transportation, or sale of alcoholic beverages would be argued about and voted on repeatedly during the decade, Mahoning County did not go dry until 1917, and Prohibition did not enter the U.S. Constitution until 1919. Likewise, the issue of women's suffrage went to the male electorate only to be defeated time and again. The privilege of women to vote would have to wait until 1920 before gaining legal status.

As timing would have it, Prohibition also got a boost from the country's going to war. In May 1917, as a means of conserving the nation's food supply, the government forbade the use of grain in all liquor. The onset of Prohibition dictated that one of Youngstown's four oldest concerns, established as the George J. Renner Brewing Company, a partnership, in 1885 and incorporated in 1914 as the Renner Brewing Company, would

A FIRE DEPARTMENT AHEAD OF THE REST

The Youngstown Fire Department was just beginning to motorize when this picture was taken. By 1911, the city was in the vanguard of fire protection, with the first fully motorized department in the U.S. Even then, arsonists imperiled firefighters. The blaze at right was set by rioting steel strikers and destroyed businesses in East Youngstown in 1916.

change its name to the Renner Company in 1919.

Not surprisingly, the Great War brought with it increased demand for iron and steel, which exerted an astonishing impact on Youngstown's economy and its future as an industrial center.

A critical precursor of the wartime growth of the industries of the Mahoning Valley was the pursuit of an adequate and steady water supply. In 1910 the Milton site was chosen for a reservoir. Two years later, a dirt dam was built in Dry Run valley to supply water for industry, but the 1913 flood swept it away. In 1916, just in time for the war, Milton Reservoir was completed to provide the industrial water the Mahoning Valley needed to meet the increased demand produced by the conflict. Construction of the reservoir cost $1.1 million.

Carnegie Opens McDonald To Use Ohio Works Output

The Ohio Works had made the first open-hearth rails in industry history in 1910, and well before the war, in 1911, Carnegie Steel built its McDonald Mills to use the Ohio Works' heightened steel output. The Youngstown & Northern Railroad, another U.S. Steel property, connected the plants. In 1910 Republic Steel built an open-hearth plant in Lansingville to complement blast furnaces it had built at Haselton a few years earlier. Republic grew so much in Youngstown that it moved its general offices to the city in 1911, which led to even further expansion. In 1913 Republic built the valley's first byproducts coke plant, and in 1919 it bought DeForest Sheet & Tin Plate Company's plant at Niles, which would one day house its important electrolytic tinning lines.

In the meantime, another Youngstown steel concern evolved. Brier Hill Steel was founded in 1912, a descendent of the Brier Hill Iron & Coal Company, which had operated coal mines and blast furnaces in Brier Hill since the middle 1800s.

Sheet & Tube Predecessor Outstrips All Sheet Rollers

The company was capitalized with $15 million, mostly subscribed by the Stambaugh, Tod, Thomas, and Butler families and others that had fared well in the National Steel and Republic deals more than a decade earlier. Brier Hill Steel took in ore and coal properties of its predecessor, along with the Youngstown Steel, Thomas Steel, and Empire Steel companies, the latter being a Niles concern. Brier Hill's plant was built in 1913 with seven sev- enty-five-ton open hearths. It built new rolling mills and in 1916 acquired the Western Reserve Steel Company's Warren sheet plant. By then, owning twenty-eight sheet mills, Brier Hill became the largest sheet-rolling entity in the Steel Valley.

Sheet & Tube Acquisition Solidifies Specialty Line

Youngstown Sheet & Tube, which bought Western Conduit's plant in 1911 and moved it to Struthers in 1912, employed seventy-five hundred men with a payroll of $5 million, putting it solidly in the rod, wire, and conduit business. In 1912 and 1913 Sheet & Tube built two more blast furnaces and six open hearths at what was to become its Campbell Works, even though what came to be known as "Campbell" in honor of Jim Campbell himself continued to be called "East Youngstown" until 1926.

Another important steel plant that would later make its mark was organized in 1912 by Jonathan Warner.

Warner had been general manager of American Sheet & Tin Plate Company, a U.S. Steel subsidiary that bought the historic Empire Mill at Niles. However, Brier Hill's acquisition of Empire in 1912 left Warner without a job.

1913: The Brier Hill Iron & Coal Company decided that the future lay in steel, changed its corporate name to Brier Hill Steel Company, and added a steel mill near Youngstown's Division Street.

Warner had been prominent in the sheet and tin-plate business, a branch of the steel industry in which this district had excelled for years.

Not about to give up his career, Warner envisioned a bigger sheet and tin-plate plant than any already here. He hit on Warren as the place to build it and organized Trumbull Steel Company. His plant was soon the largest under one roof in the area, with thirty-four mills (nineteen tin, thirteen sheet, two jobbing). In 1916, he built the first strip mills.

THE STEEL VALLEY: Republic Steel and most other mills ran continuously. Output surged with the demand for iron and steel for munitions and materials to fight the war in Europe.

Sheet Mills Provide a Quick Return on Investment Dollar

Mills that rolled steel into sheets were profitable undertakings, and the Mahoning Valley had many. They did not require a big investment, and they paid a good return. Some owners found their investments paid off in as little as six months to a year.

Sheet-mill workers were the big shots among the steelworkers, too; rollers in sheet mills frequently earned twenty-five to fifty dollars a day when twenty-five dollars was considered an excellent week's pay.

Elsewhere, the William Tod Company's Youngstown machine shops were purchased in 1916 by Pittsburgh's United Engineering & Foundry Company, which at its organization in 1901 had taken in the Lloyd Booth Company of Youngstown, one of the country's principal makers of steel-machinery.

Industrial development did not come about easily. Concern for worker safety led U.S. Steel to set policies in 1910 for compensating injured employees and inspired Sheet &

Tube to adopt Jim Campbell's plan to care for the injured. In 1912, Carnegie, Sheet & Tube, and Republic changed from paying employees once every three weeks to twice a month, improving the employees' circumstances by increasing paychecks from seventeen to twenty-four a year.

Those measures were too small, however, to ward off labor discord that thrust Youngstown into the national headlines. Formation of the Youngstown Steel District occurred in 1915, a fitting result, given that all sorts of tonnage records had been broken that year, and that the valley's byproduct coke ovens had increased to 347, due mainly to the higher demand for iron and steel for the war in Europe. But as 1916 began, all hell broke loose in East Youngstown. While demand for iron and steel had increased, and therefore work, the employees had not received any corresponding increase in wages. Sixteen thousand employees struck Sheet & Tube

and Republic, attacking nonstriking workers and company guards.

Violence and mob rule overflowed into the center of East Youngstown. Strikers rioted, set fires, and looted, causing the governor to dispatch two thousand National Guard troops to restore order. More violence occurred in January as police battled a mob of four hundred at Carnegie Steel. That March, management faced more problems when a federal grand jury handed up indictments against Sheet & Tube, Republic, and Carnegie alleging a trust to fix wages.

War's End and Lower Steel Demand Renews Labor Strife

After the war ended, things grew ugly again as demand for iron and steel fell and the population continued to grow.

In August 1919, THE VINDICATOR reported that there were twelve families for every vacant house, and those on strike included brewery workers, sheet-metal laborers, phone girls, plumbers, and yard crews. In East Youngstown, police raided a meeting and arrested 118 Bolsheviks.

Through the rest of the year, strikers picketed, protesters were beaten, and many rioters, men and women, were jailed. On December 30, 1919, the newspaper

1913: The Republic Iron & Steel Company built a coke plant off Poland Avenue in Youngstown. In steelmaking, the ovens are filled with coal, which is then cooked. The coke residue, pure carbon, is then burned at high temperature in blast furnaces to smelt iron ore.

reported that Youngstown Mayor Alvin W. Craver had rescinded a ban on strike meetings.

The same war-inspired surge in demand for iron and steel that ignited the 1916 riots laid the foundation for Youngstown's future importance to the steel industry.

At that point, Sheet & Tube built its byproducts coke plant; use of the coke-oven gases and byproducts would play an important part in building the industry.

Sheet & Tube Beefs Up Open Hearths, Buys Blast Furnaces

At the same time, Sheet & Tube built six more open hearths, bought two blast furnaces at Hubbard (one of which was dismantled in the thirties) and built its Struthers merchant mills.

Meanwhile, Brier Hill's phenomenal growth during the war resulted in the construction of an eight-hundred-ton blast furnace and enlargement of the steel plant to twelve furnaces with ninety tons of steel-making capacity.

Brier Hill Steel also built a by-products coke plant and two mills to furnish armor plate for the U.S. government. With abundant steel capacity Brier Hill also sold large quantities of sheet bar to the many hand-sheet mills of the day.

The war also witnessed a push by Sharon Steel Hoop into the Mahoning Valley. It bought two small

concerns, Youngstown Iron & Steel and Ohio Iron & Steel, in 1917. Youngstown owned a good sheet-mill at Wilson Avenue and a three-furnace open-hearth plant at Lowellville. The other company owned a small, old-fashioned blast furnace named "Mary" at Lowellville. Sharon Steel Hoop set out to integrate the whole property. Using iron from Mary, it enlarged the Lowellville plant to six furnaces, abandoned the little Sharon steel plant, and instead shipped steel from Lowellville to Sharon for rolling.

Trumbull Steel, on the other hand, which depended on large quantities of semifinished steel it bought from other companies as slabs, billets, and sheet bars, had a rough time getting all it needed during the war.

Jonathan Warner, deciding to build his own steel plant so he could be independent of the basic steelmakers, erected a seven-furnace open hearth plant that was later enlarged to eight furnaces.

Trumbull Cliffs Furnace Company was organized and a blast furnace was built nearby to supply iron for Trumbull Steel. Originally the world's biggest blast furnace, it made one thousand tons of iron daily. Rebuilt and enlarged several times, it would become the world's biggest producer by 1950, casting more than fourteen hundred tons daily.

News from the Mahoning and Shenango Valleys

1920

MARCH 5: The election board will revise precincts "as the result of women of Ohio being able to exercise the franchise" for the first time in the fall election.

MARCH 24: Youngstowner Edmund H. Moore, a Democratic Party national committeeman, will head the presidential campaign of Ohio Gov. James M. Cox.

MAY 17: In Berlin Center, authorities catch two U.S. marshals from Pittsburgh in "a handsome Daniels touring car" escorting two truckloads of illegal whiskey to Cleveland.

OCT. 8: John Philip Sousa and his famous band pack the Park Theater. "Mr. Sousa knows what his audience wants and lets them have it," a VINDICATOR reviewer says.

OCT. 12: Youngstown schools close to honor Christopher Columbus and Volney Rogers. A bronze statue of Rogers, founder of Mill Creek Park, is unveiled in a ceremony.

1921

FEB. 12: In Leetonia, two of his intended victims shoot Dominic Gennario, a Black Hand leader, fifteen times as he tries to collect a fifteen-hundred-dollar shakedown.

FEB. 13: Ex-soldiers who became coffee lovers during the Great War might account for Youngstown's buying more coffee in 1920 than any other U.S. city of equal size.

APRIL 26: Fifteen hundred pounds of rat poison arrive from Chicago, the largest shipment ever to one city. Boy Scouts spread the word and turned in poison orders from residents for Youngstown's city-wide rat drive, the first in Ohio.

JULY 1: To prevent spread of skin diseases, the board of health requires rented bathing suits to be boiled before passing to the next users at Mill Creek Park beaches, city pools, the YMCA, and the YWCA.

1922

FEB. 8: Youngstown flappers like knickers. A front-page photo shows a flapper in "knicker costume" who chose "to leave the skirt behind."

FEB. 26: "Poor White," Sherwood Anderson's book about Mahoning County industrial growth, tells "of the power that dotted the Mahoning Valley with cities and towns and built the network of industry, making quick men rich and fearful

men poor," a VINDICATOR review says.

APRIL 19: Nine hooded Ku Klux Klansmen give twenty-five dollars to the New Castle YMCA at a fundraiser. Catholics, Jews and Negroes denounce the Klan as "sinister."

NOV. 17: Merchants planning the first "Buy on Market Street" promotion realize the benefits of forming a permanent organization.

DEC. 16: Justice John H. Clarke of the U.S. Supreme Court, a Youngstown native, will head a nonpartisan organization urging U.S. membership in the League of Nations.

1923

JAN. 22: Black damp, "the terror of miners," suffocates two men at abandoned Republic Rubber mine. Republic uses the Thorn Hill Road mine as a water source, and the men were there to repair a pump.

FEB. 2: High-tension lines from Warren and Beaver on the Ohio River join west of Sebring. A large transformer station will be built.

JUNE 10: Using the sky as a giant billboard, a pilot writes "Lucky Strike" in smoke, a new advertising twist that fascinates onlookers.

AUG. 7: Throngs form an "aisle of mourning" along the flower-strewn B&O tracks to await the train bearing the body of President Warren Harding. It passes through eight and one-half hours late.

SEPT. 16: Five hundred attend opening of Stambaugh Field, a nine-hole municipal golf course. After a ceremony, Louise Fordyce and Norman Hall play Clara Louise Krauter and Emmet French in a match.

1924

JAN. 11: Mill Creek Park receives two hundred-seventy acres bordering Mill Creek from Lanterman Falls to Shields Road. The main feature will be Lake Newport, predicted to be twice the size of Lake Glacier.

MARCH 13: Ohio Bell opens a campaign to teach residents how to use the dial telephone. "It is to the interest of every telephone user as well as to the county that all subscribers understand how to dial correctly," the utility says.

MARCH 25: William Jones, the last Civil War veteran in Mineral Ridge, is laid to rest with military honors in Riverside Cemetery.

MARCH 31: A hawker sells the roster of local Ku Klux Klan members

for a dollar. The price reflects the hazard of gathering the names.

NOV. 16: At Forest Glen, Boardman, fifty-nine elm trees are dedicated to the local men and women who gave their lives in the World War.

1925

FEB. 14: J.J. Brownlie offers the county commissioners land to eliminate Dead Man's Curve on Youngstown-Boardman Road. The property extends from Market and Midlothian southwest to Boardman Road.

JUNE 6: Two deaths attributed to the six-day heat wave. The mercury soars from 85 at 8 a.m. to 104 at 11.

JULY 5: Stunt pilots in seventeen planes thrill crowds at Watson Field as Youngstown holds the biggest July 4th air show in the U.S.

AUG. 16: Sam Swank, Akron, driving a Hal Special, wins the 150-lap Southern Park Speed Classic. The seventy-five-mile race took one hour thirty-one minutes.

NOV. 18: The Mahoning County Tuberculosis Institution on Kirk Road holds an open house. The building is said to be one of the finest of its kind in the state.

1926

APRIL 8: Rain has kept farmers from sowing twelve thousand acres of oats in Mahoning County.

AUG. 31: Three men set up illegal gambling using private phone lines at their Renner Building offices, the prosecutor's office says.

SEPT. 30: Some thirty booths display the latest radios at Youngstown's first radio show. WKBN airs the Sunnybrook Orchestra.

OCT. 13: Unannounced and unexpected, the first plane lands at Youngstown's yet-to-be-finished municipal airport. The pilot, Lt. A. G. Person of Chicago, launches several thousand balloons containing coupons for candy bars as he waits for the Lansdowne Field dedication.

NOV. 11: The New York Central's passenger station opens at Himrod and Wilson avenues. It will also be the line's division headquarters.

1927

APRIL 21: Airmail service opens with connections to the transcontinental line at Cleveland and rail deliveries out of Pittsburgh. A shipment of hats bought that morning in Cleveland arrives for Strouss-Hirshberg, the first local

company to use air transportation.

JULY 5: Inboard runabouts race ten miles, finishing five laps at speeds well over thirty miles an hour, in the Lake Milton Regatta Association's first annual race.

AUG. 16: Stunt aviatrix Gladys Roy, 25, steps into a spinning propeller while posing for publicity pictures at Watson Field. She was to be the opening draw at the Canfield Fair.

NOV. 22: In a letter on the front page of THE VINDICATOR'S second section, Santa promises to attend tomorrow's Christmas pageant.

1928

JAN. 9: Eulogy to Joseph G. Butler Jr.: "[A] supreme artist in friendship whose will proved his faith in his city by a princely gift which reveals that city as his only luxury."

JAN. 26: A Pitcairn Whirlwind airmail plane crashes at Lansdowne Field. The pilot escapes injury, but the plane incurs damage of two thousand dollars.

FEB. 12: Youngstown's tennis wonder, Carl Dennison, is fifteenth on the list of junior singles players of the U. S .Lawn Tennis Association.

OCT. 14: The Youngstown Real Estate Board, having studied the ad campaigns of eighteen cities, plans a strategy to market Youngstown to diversified industries.

1929

JAN. 25: Three hundred cars, streetcars and buses form a solid mass on the Market Street Bridge for more than ninety minutes in the worst ice storm ever to hit the Mahoning and Shenango valleys.

JUNE 1: The Men's Club of Rodef Sholom Temple holds a service with eight Protestant ministers and a rabbi to bring people of different faiths to a better understanding of one another. A large crowd hears four clergymen of different faiths extol good will and fellowship.

SEPT. 25: The U-Pilot-It Company has planes gassed, oiled and ready to fly at any hour of the day or night. The company also offers lessons in "the art of parachute jumping, which is being recognized by flyers as a precaution in flying."

DEC. 9: A new towboat for shallow waterways is important to the "effort for canalization of the Mahoning, Beaver and Shenango rivers," THE VINDICATOR editorializes.

CRIME, COMMUNISM, & COMMON CAUSES

WEST FEDERAL STREET: Youngstown changed rapidly as the century gained momentum. Vaudeville houses brought the stars of their circuits to town—big-name entertainers like Jack Benny and the Marx Brothers. Another form of entertainment made its appearance, too—motion pictures. Before long, films would be the entertainment of choice and vaudeville would be a memory.

The twenties produced major changes in the valley, including prohibition, motion pictures, and a radio station.

EVENTS BEYOND THE VALLEY

1920: ACLU founded.

• National Socialist German Workers Party (Nazis) founded.

1921: U.S. and Germany sign peace treaty.

1922: Permanent Court of International Justice opens in the Hague.

• U.S.S.R. formed.

• Mahatma Gandhi imprisoned in India for civil disobedience.

1923: Time Magazine founded.

1924: Adolf Hitler publishes Mein Kampf. ▶

• Josef Stalin comes to power with death of Vladimir Ilyich Lenin.

1925: Edwin Hubble develops classification scheme for galaxies.

• Clarence Birdseye markets quick-frozen foods.

• John T. Scopes tried in Tennessee for teaching theory of evolution.

1926: Robert Goddard launches first liquid propellant rocket. ▶

1927: Charles Lindbergh flies man's first solo flight across the Atlantic.

1928: British bacteriologist Alexander Fleming discovers penicillin.

1929: Lateran Treaty creates independent state of Vatican City.

• Saint Valentine's Day Massacre in Chicago.

Until the 20th century, despite the more or less democratic political apparatus, the country's social goals and aspirations had been traditionally set by small groups of preachers, politicians, lawyers, editors, and teachers, and later as well by the economic elite spawned by post-Civil War industrialism. But from 1920 on, the tastes of the crowd became an increasingly important determinant, first in popular culture and later in political and economic institutions. And this new mass culture differed vastly from the traditional culture that had been inspired from above.

THE 20S: FORDS, FLAPPERS & FANATICS,
GEORGE E. MOWRY, EDITOR

1920s: It would be a while before there were two cars in every garage, but the automobile was already proving itself to be an indispensable workhorse (no pun intended).

THE 1920S FOUND THE MAhoning Valley and the country facing the challenge of Prohibition, the reality of women's suffrage, and the rights of workers around the globe, as well as a world trying to make sense of such evolving forms of government as communism, fascism, and national socialism.

As recovery from the Great War began in earnest, Youngstown boasted 132,358 residents and was growing so fast that schools were asked to take over the Americanization of immigrants. Three hundred marriage licenses—a record—were issued in June 1920, and by 1922 the city was reported to have the third-highest birth rate in the country. At one point, the district ranked second in the number of residents who did not speak English.

Concurrent with such social changes, technological progress came on several fronts. The radio grew from infancy to adolescence in the 1920s. That inspired enthusiasts to organize a radio club in December 1920. The first commercial station would take to the airwaves here in 1926.

In 1923 the Mahoning Valley ranked second in Ohio in consumption of electricity, and Miss Youngstown opened the city's first all-electric home in 1924.

Even though farriers predicted in 1922 that horses would prevail over motors for short hauls, autos

APRIL 1923: Mayor William G. Reese and Police Officer James J. McNicholas look over the smashed bar of a speakeasy at South Avenue and Front Street. Speakeasies and illegal trafficking in liquor made a mockery of an unpopular law—Prohibition. Police once caught two federal marshals escorting an illegal shipment of bonded whiskey through Mahoning County to Cleveland.

continued to put horses out to pasture at a fast pace. By 1924 even auto theft was on the increase. By decade's end city residents owned 35,603 cars. In the county, cars totaled 49,550. Gasoline cost seventeen cents a gallon, and electric streetcars were gradually giving way to the gasoline engine and trolley buses.

The twenties brought medical advances, including immunization against the dreaded diphtheria. Once or twice a month, VINDICATOR obituaries recorded the death of a Civil War veteran.

The newspaper also revealed details about day-to-day life in the Mahoning Valley, reporting at one point that Youngstowners bought more coffee per capita than residents of any other city of similar size in the country; that the price of a shoeshine went up to fifteen cents in 1924; and that Youngstown voters turned down a proposal in 1928 to raise council salaries to three thousand dollars from six hundred dollars a year.

The newspaper also provided a community service that would fade with the growth of radio but was still going strong in the fall of 1924, when, as the paper itself recounted, people rallied round THE VINDICATOR's scoreboard during the World Series.

Many developments altered the face of the city during the twenties. Among the milestones were the New York Central's razing of its first station and dedication

of a new one in 1926, and only weeks later, the dedication of Stambaugh Auditorium, witnessed by five thousand people.

Changing daily life just a little in 1928 was the government's introduction of smaller greenbacks.

With the Eighteenth Amendment, local governments found themselves overwhelmed in their efforts to wage war against

CLEARING THE WAY: In the 1920s, electric streetcars gradually yielded to the more-convenient trolley buses in Youngstown.

Stambaugh Auditorium, destined to become a Fifth Avenue landmark, opened in 1926. Harvey Wiley Corbett designed it and Gaetana Ceceri sculptured the figures on the pediment.

▲ 1924: Building was booming in downtown Youngstown. The Realty Building, above, was going up, with the new First National Bank Building (now Bank One) to follow. Mahoning National Bank was preparing to double the size of its office building.

PRESIDENTIAL PASSAGE: Thousands of Youngstowners formed an "aisle of mourning" along the Baltimore & Ohio Railroad tracks to see the train bearing the body of President Warren G. Harding from Washington, D.C., to its final destination, Harding's hometown of Marion, Ohio. Harding died of a heart attack on Aug. 2, 1923, while returning from Alaska.
▼

bootlegging and vice. In November 1920, a typical report told of the discovery of a thousand cases of bonded whiskey in the B&O yards, underscoring the challenge communities faced trying to enforce the Volstead Act. The first local arrest for selling stills had come a month earlier. Safecrackings were frequent, and by January 1921, a grand jury had recommended acquisition of a submachine gun for the sheriff's office.

Arrests more than doubled those of the year before, perhaps the most notable being that of the Youngstown safety director, David J. Scott, in July. Indicted on twenty counts of illegal liquor activity, a jury found Scott guilty of accepting bribes and sentenced him to two to ten years in prison.

One of the stranger happenings occasioned by Prohibition took place in February 1923 when the federal government ordered $500 thousand worth of liquor stored at the Youngstown Post Office dumped into the city sewers or sold. In 1924, the newspaper began to run stories about banks stocking up on armored cars.

Coal shortages led to frequent conflicts between industry and government as residents were driven to steal and nearly riot to meet household heating needs. Often, large industrial companies were forced to suspend operations or consider burning oil as an alternative. In September 1920, the mills received eight thousand carloads of coal, versus sixty carloads for domestic consumption.

At the beginning of the decade, THE VINDICATOR reported that ice was in short supply, noting that 1920 produced the first successful harvest in three years. By summer 1921, demand exceeded three hundred tons a day. In an interesting twist on one decade's progress, ice was making news by 1930 as a driving hazard in the Mahoning and Shenango valleys.

Hospital Care: Beds Number 450; YHA adds its North Unit

Besides the infirmaries and hospitals the steel companies built near the mills to ease labor concerns and to address jobtime medical emergencies, Youngstown had about four hundred-fifty beds between South Side and Saint Elizabeth hospitals by 1920. In 1929 the Youngstown Hospital Association would include not only South Side but a new North Side unit.

As for the day-to-day health concerns of area residents, a local doctor termed the goiter situation "alarming" in 1921, and in March 1926 THE VINDICATOR reported thousands ill with grippe, the term back then for influenza. By 1926, Youngstown was still dealing with about one hundred-fifty diphtheria cases yearly, but that changed dramatically by 1929, when the city Board of Education and Health Department arranged to give the Schick test to schoolchildren and urged those found susceptible to diphtheria to undergo immunization.

Lucy Buechner, daughter of W.L. and sister of W.H. Buechner, upon her death in 1926 left half a million dollars to the Youngstown Hospital Association for orthopedic surgery and one million dollars for development of a home

1929: Saint Elizabeth Hospital expanded to care for Youngstown's exploding population, adding its north wing in 1915 and a south wing in 1929.

for working girls. Miss Buechner's death brought about the demolition, in 1927, of the family homestead, described as sitting "amid skyscrapers" at Federal and Champion streets.

Other changes to the city's skyline had come in 1924 with construction of the Realty Building; in 1925 with enlargement of the Mahoning National Bank Building; and in 1926 with construction of the First National Bank Building. The most dramatic change to Youngstown's skyline occurred in 1929 with construction of the tallest building of all, Central Tower, an Art Deco classic comprising seventeen floors.

Tragedies and scandals made headlines, too, including reports of rats gnawing children in East and West End tenements; a freak accident in which one of the cars of the Firefly ride at Idora Park broke loose and killed the ride's manager; the murder of a bellgirl by a porter at the Hotel Salow; and frequent court cases wherein a man or woman would be sued for "alienating the affections" of another's spouse. In September 1924 a man shot his wife and then himself in a senseless act of desperation because his sixth child was another girl.

In what perhaps was the trial of the decade, Alta Koehler found herself under suspicion after the death of her sons, ages three and five, in a fire in December 1920. According to the earliest reports, on December 5, Mrs. Koehler suffered a bullet wound to her left arm when sons William and Warren burned to death in the family home at Kansas Corners, Hubbard.

The next day, a bullet was found in the shoulder of one of the boys, and three days after that, THE VINDICATOR reported that Thomas Koehler had been refused permission to remove his wife from a Youngstown hospital. Two days before Christmas, authorities filed a charge of second-degree murder against Alta Koehler. On Christmas Eve, she pleaded not guilty, with the paper reporting her bond fixed at ten thousand dollars and noting that she could not post the money. In 1921 Trumbull County Common Pleas Court had to call seventy-one men before a complete jury could be seated. Four days after the trial began, the young mother was convicted. That May, Alta Koehler was sentenced to life imprisonment in Saint Mary's Reformatory.

The 1920s headlines made by Mother Nature were not nearly as

ROUNDING UP REDS

BOLSHEVISM and its alter ego, communism, appeared on the scene early in the century. Government agents arrested twenty local communists the day after New Year's 1920, and less than a week later, a hearing for seventy-seven reds made headlines. Before the end of the month, fresh headlines announced the discovery of a communist Sunday School in Youngstown.

THE VINDICATOR carried headlines January 3, 1920, announcing the overthrow of the government of South Russia, and in the days that followed, spoke of a local campaign against "active members of radical parties."

Warrants for the arrest of officers and leaders of local branches of the Communist Party of America were issued out of Washington, D.C., and the newspaper referred to the party as "the most radical and dangerous organization which aims at the violent overthrow of the government" using "coal and steel strikes as basis." "Arrests were made in the homes of the suspects or at the mills, where many are found at work," the newspaper reported, and thousands were arrested across the country.

ANOTHER ISSUE was the constitutionality of an ordinance in East Youngstown (now Campbell) against "the holding of public meetings," elsewhere referred to as "strike meetings." That law, passed the previous year, had recently been struck down.

Of those arrested, the newspaper referred to their "right to representation by counsel." The hearings were conducted by immigration inspectors, who were also termed "special agents."

dramatic, but some unusual conditions were recorded nonetheless. In 1924 she subjected the area to its first subzero Christmas in more than fifty years; on May 25, 1925, she sprinkled the valley with snow; in July 1929, she carpeted parts of Columbiana County with frost; and, for an encore, shook the area the following month with an earthquake felt in five states.

According to published reports, the administration of Mayor Fred Warnock as the decade dawned was notable for "relentless attacks on bootlegging & vice" and a campaign to raise more funds for the city, with council favoring the taxation of single men.

A Reform-Minded Grocer Becomes a Mayor, but Briefly

In 1921 a frustrated electorate selected a new mayor for the city, a man of whom THE VINDICATOR said later: "While he lasted, he was known the world over." The man was George Oles, a grocer by trade, who served in office a scant six months after running as an independent and defeating the incumbent Warnock.

Oles' platform, broadcast by means of the advertisements for his popular grocery store, had been the cleansing of local politics. However, the reform movement was shortlived. Discouraged

EARLY TWENTIES: Peddlers hawk produce and goods along the Mahoning River.

and frustrated, Oles resigned in June 1922, after having tried to suspend the police chief, having hired a bodyguard, having briefly joined the race for Ohio Governor, and having offered to help "clean up" the City of Pittsburgh.

In 1923 the city adopted a form of government known as home-rule charter. The charter originally provided a four-year term for mayor and a council president elected from within the body.

Mayor and councilmen were elected in nonpartisan elections, for which nominations were made by petition. Other positions were then appointed by the mayor afterward. Consequently, the position of mayor was one of power under the new system.

At about the same time, the Ku Klux Klan, a secret society revived in the South in 1915, rose to prominence in the Midwest. The fraternal organization pushed white supremacy, nativism, and anti-Catholicism and furnished an outlet for the militant patriotism engendered by World War I.

Although the Ku Klux Klan claimed to be apolitical, its candidates won the mayoral elections in Youngstown, Niles, Warren, Girard, and Struthers

1921: George Oles, shown with his daughters, became Youngstown's reform mayor but quit in frustration after six months. Oles owned a popular downtown market.

in 1923, while also carrying the Youngstown Board of Education and the majority of Youngstown City Council. As a result a Klansman, Charles F. Scheible, became Youngstown's first charter mayor.

Frequent Violence in Niles Leads to a Klan Showdown

Because the Klan frequently took extralegal measures, especially against those it considered its enemies, the region's immigrant and black populations were terrified by that development.

The Klan bought a four-hundred-acre farm near the Canfield Fairgrounds, gathered the Konklave here for parades, "celebrated" holidays of importance to immigrants by exploding bombs and burning crosses, and demanded of various boards of education that only American teachers be employed.

Predictably, the Klan came to blows several times with the Irish and Italian residents of Niles in the summer and fall of 1924. When Youngstown native Clyde Osborne, the Grand Dragon of Ohio, called a tri-state meeting for November in Niles, the resulting riot had to be put down by the National Guard

1924: KKK rally in Niles.

and led to a declaration of martial law.

Such provocation and rampant lawlessness led inexorably to the ruin of the Klan's political empire well before Youngstown elected its second charter mayor in 1926, Joseph Heffernan, an Irish Catholic, but the ordeal had alienated many of the Mahoning Valley's people one from another.

Though the Youngstown YMCA had offered educational opportunities for decades and classes in law since 1908, higher education formally arrived in the valley in February 1920 when the YMCA for the first time granted bachelor degrees to law students who had completed a college curriculum.

In June the school celebrated its first commencement. That same year the school played host to Sen. Warren G. Harding as he began his run for the U.S. presidency. The YMCA School of Commerce won college accreditation in June 1924 and three years later opened its Day College of Liberal Arts.

From a South Side Porch, The First Radio Broadcasts

The beginning of regularly scheduled radio programs for the United States came in Pittsburgh in 1920 with the opening of KDKA by the Westinghouse Electric & Manufacturing Company. In the early twenties the program schedules printed daily in THE VINDICATOR included such stations as KDKA, WJZ Newark, KYW Chicago, WGY Schenectady, and WOC Davenport.

Youngstown got its first radio station when, six years after KDKA's start, WKBN began intermittent broadcasting from the home of Warren P. Williamson, Jr. In November 1926 THE VINDICATOR sponsored the broadcast of election returns over WKBN from an enclosed porch of the Williamson home.

By July 1920 a day without an automobile accident was considered newsworthy, and that Octo-

IN THEIR SPARE TIME...

IN THE REALM of entertainment, the development of talking movies spelled the beginning of the end of genuine stage shows in Youngstown, both legitimate attractions and vaudeville.

The Hippodrome, which booked Will Rogers, Jack Benny, and dozens of other greats, had given way years earlier to the Palace, where more of vaudeville's renowned appeared.

THEN THE Palace, too, gave way, yielding to the motion pictures, although orchestras and supporting variety acts continued to appear on occasion. Color films came to town in 1928. Southern

Exterior and interior views of the Keith-Albee Palace, which opened in 1926.

Park was also a popular place to go. Crowds would gather to dance at the hall or enjoy auto, horse, or greyhound races. Throughout the decade, people disagreed and debated whether the sabbath should include vaudeville, carnivals, basketball, music in theaters, shoe shines, dancing, gas sales, and flower sales.

IT WAS THE DECADE that brought about the evolution of the dance marathon, and Youngstown had its share of participants. THE VINDICATOR carried a report when Albert Kish and Helen Clark were eliminated from the Madison Square Garden dance-endurance contests in June 1928 after 168 hours. That month, the paper also carried calculations showing that the winners of a marathon at the Rayen-Wood Auditorium earned thirty-nine cents an hour for the 122 hours they spent shuffling around the ballroom floor.

Canfield Fair, 1922.

1928: Air mail service at the Lansdowne Field, the first municipal airport.

ber the police chief ordered a crusade against reckless driving. The Mahoning Valley lost thirty-six people to auto accidents that year, leading the entire U.S. in auto fatalities.

Progress followed on several fronts, with completion of a new concrete road to New Castle in 1921 and a new antispeeding ordinance in 1922 that included a jail sentence in the penalty.

Auto Fatalities and Speeding Bring Calls for License Law

However, the city made unflattering headlines again in 1927, ranking first in auto deaths among seventy-six principal U.S. cities. By the end of January 1928, speeders could expect to spend time in the county jail—five days for each mile over thirty-six miles per hour. By October 1929 city and county officials were advocating a licensing process for drivers to curb auto accidents.

The increased reliance on automobiles—and on jitneys, their taxi-like counterparts—cut deeply into streetcar ridership, fares for which had risen to nine cents by June 1920. The rails, especially those of the Youngstown & Suburban, recovered some of their importance, however, when freight connections established with the Montour Railroad at Negley made it possible to haul coal to Youngs-

town from Pittsburgh Coal Company mines in western Pennsylvania. And moving around the city became a lot easier during the twenties with completion of the first grade-elimination project at Belmont Avenue in 1924.

Other critical improvements to the city's transportation network included construction of the Lanterman's Falls bridge in 1920, the Oak Street bridge in 1922, and the South Avenue bridge in 1928.

As for the skies, the Great War had proved a boon to the infant air industry. After the war came barnstorming pilots in Curtiss Jennies and Standards. Early aviators quickly became accustomed to engine failures, stalls, and bumpy landings in rough cattle pastures. Bernard Airport on U.S. 422 was one of the city's oldest, and many air-minded Youngstown residents made their first flights with Alton N. Parker, a pioneer aviator who flew from Dead Man's Curve field and farmers' pastures.

In 1925, when the area experienced the

Oil was discovered in Mahoning County in 1921. A geologist estimated an oil reservoir of 12 billion barrels.

beginning of night mail, a VINDICATOR headline stated, PLANES PASS NEAR CITY, and Youngstown played host that year to the biggest air show in the country.

The following year, Lansdowne Field (sometimes called Bird Airport) opened when the federal government's decision to fly the mail provided an opportunity to join the Cleveland-Pittsburgh air mail route. Youngstown thereby became the second city in Ohio to have a municipal airport. The first service on the Cleveland-Youngstown-Pittsburgh line took place April 21, 1927, just a few weeks before an unknown pilot named Charles Lindbergh flew alone across the Atlantic Ocean to Paris.

In August of that year, the city celebrated when Lucky Lindy flew overhead. Perhaps thus inspired, twelve thousand locals were reported to have taken to the air for the first time in 1928. By the onset of 1929 plans were afoot to light the Cleveland-Youngstown-Pittsburgh airway for night flying. By May the route was reported to be the fastest growing and most profitable in the United States. While talk of a Lake Erie-to-Ohio River canal continued with no movement toward construction in sight, the A.M. Byers Company. of Girard erected a new wrought iron plant in 1925 at Ambridge, Pennsylvania (named for the American Bridge Company, which had set up shop

JAMES CAMPBELL

along the Ohio River at the turn of the century). That eventually spelled the end of the Girard plant, and all operations moved to Ambridge to be near cheap water transportation.

Geological Survey Fuels Oil and Gas Exploration

Although the decade saw no tangible progress on the canal, development of other resources did progress.

In February 1921, a petroleum geologist, Charles E. Nevin, declared that twelve billion barrels of oil underlay Mahoning County. Soon wells were being drilled throughout the district, and in April of that year, a well in North Lima was producing thirty thousand cubic feet of gas per day.

In the late twenties the Ohio Water Service Company built a series of reservoirs, one of which replaced the one that had previously been at Dry Run; the result was McKelvey Lake. The Mahoning Valley Sanitary District, organized in 1927, built Meander Reservoir, with a capacity of 10 billion gallons, to provide water for domestic use by its member cities, Youngstown and Niles.

For the steel industry, the twenties came to be known as the "merger years" as those in charge tried to balance, preserve, and sustain the growth that came with the first world war.

Youngstown was now home to six large producers—Carnegie, Sheet & Tube, Republic, Brier Hill Steel, Trumbull Steel, and Sharon Steel Hoop—and many smaller ones, too. Among the problems confronting the local steel indus-

try were increasing freight rates and the westward movement of steel consumption with development of the country.

As the twenties began, Chicago had already supplanted Youngstown as the second-largest steel center in the country. The first proposed solution was to merge nine companies—two in Chicago, three here, one in Cleveland, one in Buffalo, and two in Johnstown, Pennsylvania—into the North American Steel Corporation, rivaling U.S. Steel Corporation in size. The group wanted Jim Campbell to be the man in charge. Campbell's enthusiasm, however, was muted, and without his unqualified support the deal fell through.

In December 1922, however, Campbell's own Sheet & Tube acquired Brier Hill Steel, then a few weeks later bought Steel & Tube Company of America for $33 million. That gave Sheet & Tube the Chicago district plants it desired. The biggest steel merger in a quarter-century, it made Sheet & Tube one of the leading independents.

Sheet & Tube Consolidates, Builds, and Updates Facilities

Campbell and his associates set about increasing efficiency and consolidating operations. They got rid of the Empire and Thomas Sheet plants at Niles and dismantled the Western Reserve Mill at Warren. Sheet & Tube built an eight-inch sheet mill at Brier Hill and updated the Chicago-district plants, rebuilding blast furnaces and installing finishing units.

In December 1929 Frank Purnell succeeded Campbell as president of Sheet & Tube. Campbell stayed as board chairman until his retirement on February 4, 1932, having been the dominant personality at Youngstown Sheet & Tube for more than thirty years and a force to be reckoned with in the U.S. steel industry.

IN THIS DECADE

1921 BUYING GUIDE

Men's union suit, $2.98.

Men's work and dress shoes, $6.00 to $6.50 a pair.

Ladies' dresses, $8.75 each.

Ladies' suits, thirty dollars to seventy dollars.

Fur scarf, $39.50.

Turkish towels, fifty cents each.

Woolen blankets, fourteen dollars apiece.

Ivory soap, ten bars for seventy-seven cents.

Coal, one ton for eight dollars.

Sugar, one pound for nine cents.

Flour, five pounds for a dollar.

Oleomargarine, two pounds for sixty-five cents.

Peanut butter, one pound for twenty-five cents.

Coffee, three pounds for eighty-nine cents.

Uneeda biscuits, ten cents a box.

Preserving kettle, $2.69.

Leather traveling bag, eighteen inches long, $17.45.

Wilton rug, nine-by-twelve feet, $195.

Phonographs, $300 to $2,100.

Phonograph records, $1 to $1.50 each.

Used cars, $300.00 to $560.00.

Alcohol fuel for automobiles, per gallon, $1.25.

Suburban home built on a 50-foot by-175-foot lot; six rooms and bath. Price: eight thousand dollars.

Park Theater admission charges:

Fifty cents to $1.50 for Saturday matinee.

Seventy-five cents to two dollars for Saturday night.

News from the Mahoning and Shenango Valleys

1930

MAY 4: Botanist Ernest Vickers and a crew transplant to Mill Creek Park twenty-five thousand bluebells and other wildflowers doomed by the filling of Meander Dam basin.

JULY 6: Few blooms and no rain add up to a smaller honey crop in Mahoning and Columbiana counties. American foulbrood disease leaves some areas without bees.

OCT. 10: Six thousand people flood Rayen-Wood Auditorium for the final day of the Jessie Marie DeBoth VINDICATOR Cooking School. Police turn away one thousand. Nearly as many men attend as women.

OCT. 19: A section of the Erie-to-Pittsburgh Perry Highway being built north of Sheakleyville in Mercer County transforms itself nightly into a lake up to twenty feet deep, frustrating construction engineers.

DEC. 23: The New York Clearing House Association will no longer publish daily figures on bank closings, starving an illegal lottery that relied on those numbers. The "boys who peddle clearinghouse bets are sad of eye and heavy of heart," THE VINDICATOR reports on page one.

1931

MARCH 3: A blast and fire at the Lincoln Theater on Himrod Avenue injures twenty. Officials blame the same arson mob responsible for sixty percent of Youngstown's fire loss over the previous year.

APRIL 7: The Garden Forum will furnish garden plots "to help the unemployed help themselves."

JUNE 3: N.E. Wilson reports that 16,106 men bedded down at the Friendly Inn "flophouse" in Haselton Jan. 1–April 30. Through April 20, the inn served 24,903 meals.

NOV. 20: Nine carloads of apples ship to Pittsburgh from Greenford, highlighting the exceptional fruits and berries grown in Mahoning and Columbiana counties. The Packer, a national periodical, calls the area a leader in quantity and quality.

DEC. 13: Christmas shoppers use up stashes of large bills that went out in 1929, perplexing merchants whose cash registers have been rebuilt for the new small currency.

1932

JUNE 11: The Mahoning County Medical Society invites Judge J.H.C. Lyon to compare its fourteen-to-seventeen-cent jail menus with the "exorbitant" fifty-five to sixty cents Sheriff Adam Stone spends daily.

JUNE 16: Police Chief Leroy Goodwin sanctions the new brassiere swimsuits, saying Youngstown is no "hick town"–what's OK in Miami Beach and Hollywood is OK here.

SEPT. 20: National, state, and county offices will appear on one ballot for the first time in Ohio.

SEPT. 25: Home-canning passion sweeps the county, says C.F. Shipton of Growers Club Market, Pyatt Street; produce at bargain prices.

OCT. 7: Mahoning and Trumbull farmers watched their income drop to $175.00 last year; Mercer County farmers averaged even less, $152.27.

1933

MARCH 10: Macrae Smith Co. will publish "Strong Enchantments," a novel by Mary Schumann, Youngstown College instructor of English and voice culture.

APRIL 7: Prohibition ends: "Beer was legal and a fact in Youngstown today as thousands of cases [arrived] at local distributors' warehouses and were sent out immediately to Youngstown homes," THE VINDICATOR reports.

MAY 20: Output rises to forty-two-percent at Republic Steel. The Ohio Works has eleven open hearths lit for the first time since 1929; Youngstown, New Castle, Sharon, Warren, Mercer, Salem report sizable gains.

AUG. 1: Employers file into the Post Office to get the Blue Eagle insignia of the National Recovery Administration, the program expected to lead the U.S. out of the Depression.

NOV. 20: The government orders Youngstown and Mahoning County to move 4,913 men from relief lists to pick-and-shovel jobs in the new national civil-works program.

1934

MAY 28: The worst invasion of locusts since 1916 leaves Wick Park pitted as the insects emerge a year behind schedule.

AUG. 18: Pennsylvania dedicates Pymatuning Lake, its largest inland body of water. Gov. Gifford Pinchot leads a motorcade inspection.

OCT. 22: G-men corner Charles ("Pretty Boy") Floyd, Public Enemy No. 1, behind a Sprucevale farm corncrib in Columbiana County. "Outlaw Floyd Dies Like a Rat," THE VINDICATOR headline reads.

NOV. 11: Defeat of a 1.5-mill tax has Girard facing suspension of streetlight service. It owes Ohio Edison more than eight thousand dollars.

1935

JAN. 11: Poland households urged to donate five books to the new public library. A committee wants at least fifteen hundred volumes to ensure the library's timely opening.

JAN. 11: On her ninety-ninth birthday, Emma McAllister of New Castle recalls when she was enslaved on a Kentucky plantation.

FEB. 1: Housewives complain of sediment ruining their laundry. "When the water is put in the bathtub it looks like mud," one fumes. Water Commissioner Dan Parish knows the reason: new water pipes.

OCT. 28: Simply Sybil's Pallas, a cow from Hugh W. Bonnell's Cranberry Run Farm, wins national honors at two stock shows.

NOV. 11: Recount likely in Campbell. Totals show the incumbent mayor, John B. Ross, winning by forty-two votes instead of losing to Michael J. Kovach, as first announced.

1936

MARCH 5: Fire causes five hundred thousand dollars damage at Cold Metal Process, Mahoning Avenue, destroying a completed mill and three under construction.

MARCH 6: Youngstown city workers are glad to receive a month's pay, even in scrip; it is their first paycheck since last October.

APRIL 1: U.S. Steel and Carnegie Steel oppose a Lake Erie-Ohio River canal, saying it would take business from their railroad customers and increase their tax burden.

JUNE 30: Police recover hijacked liquor worth five thousand dollars at a farm northeast of North Lima. The cases were buried in straw.

1937

FEB. 9: Three city hospitals and the TB sanatorium remain off-limits to visitors even as the flu epidemic eases. Health Commissioner W.W. Ryall still urges "common sense cautions" and avoidance of crowds.

MAY 10: An advertisement for the movie "Shall We Dance?" includes a promise of the "first complete pictures of the Hindenburg Disaster."

MAY 28: Social fallout from the steel strike: A bridegroom working in the Sheet & Tube office will miss his wedding tomorrow; other June weddings will likely be postponed.

JUNE 2: In Warren, a plane making a food drop to those under siege at Republic Steel crash lands into a boxcar. The pilot escapes injury.

NOV. 7: On display at the Auto Show at Stambaugh Auditorium: Buick, Cadillac, Chevrolet, Chrysler, DeSoto, Dodge, Hudson, LaFayette, LaSalle, Lincoln, Nash, Oldsmobile, Packard, Plymouth, Pontiac, Studebaker, Terraplane, and Willys.

1938

JAN. 16: Clyde Singer of Malvern, Pennsylvania, wins first prize of two hundred dollars in the New Year Show at Butler Art Institute. His oil painting, "Rush Hour," shows young women heading home from work.

MAY 18: The suffragist Harriet Taylor Upton, a former valley historian, writes from California of her amusement over an erroneous reference to her death in the special VINDICATOR issue of March 27.

AUG. 6: With a special election two days off, THE VINDICATOR runs a ribbon above its flag: "Unite, Youngstown, for a better city! Forget your petty differences! Awake to your opportunity to do a fine thing for your city." Multiple bond issues passed, but a school issue failed.

DEC. 3: East Liverpool police arrest a West Virginian for possessing lottery tickets. He had moved to West Virginia last summer when the Columbiana County grand jury "turned on the heat."

1939

JAN. 1: The Better Business Bureau hails a city ordinance regulating going-out-of-business sales. Merchants face penalties if they restock merchandise not listed in pre-sale inventories filed with the city.

JUNE 2: Crews from the Works Projects Administration clear the Vienna site of Youngstown's new airport. A force of four hundred doubles in the next four days.

SEPT. 1: Firefighters rush to Fairgreen Avenue and Covington Street only to find a man mistakenly trying to mail a letter in the alarm box.

SEPT. 9: For the first time, people attend a live broadcast from the new WFMJ station. The 275-member audience hears Paul Whiteman, the Modernaires, and Clark Dennis.

Chapter

1930 **4** **1939**

CRASH & CONSEQUENCES

1930: A Youngstown Municipal Railway bus boards passengers at the Mahoning County Courthouse. For many, buses were the only affordable means of transportation during the Depression. Youngstown Muni was the forerunner of today's Western Reserve Transit Authority. Youngstown Dry Goods, a Market Street fixture, had been in business since 1882 but did not survive the Depression.

For those who would be summoned only too soon to fight another great war, the Great Depression became the proving ground in how to cope with adversity.

From the stock market crash of October 1929 to the end of World War II, the citizens of Youngstown and Mahoning County faced many disruptions in their everyday lives…. The loss of jobs, homes, and security damaged the psyche of residents who had worked hard all their lives and now could not provide for themselves.

FREDERICK J. BLUE ET AL
MAHONING MEMORIES

1932: West Federal Street changed little as business, industry, and the people rode out the economic storm. One notable transition that did take place occurred at Federal and Hazel streets: The Liberty Theater became the Paramount.

THE COUNTRY FACED DIRE economic conditions in the wake of the 1929 stock market crash. For the Mahoning Valley, with its overwhelming dependence on steel and related industries, and relatively little in the way of diversified employment, what came to be known as the Great Depression had devastating consequences.

At the start of the 1930s, Youngstown, whose population had increased 273 percent since the turn of the century, was a city of 170 thousand. The decades of geometric growth were over, however; before this new decade ended, Youngstown's population would fall to 168 thousand.

Unlike the first quarter of the twentieth century, when wave upon wave of men had come to the valley from Europe and the American South on the promise of employment and better lives, the realities of the stock market crash and the chain-reaction economic devastation meant that the mills and other businesses and government offices were now forced to shorten work weeks and lower wages. Families suffered as

TIME ON HIS HANDS: Joblessness and home foreclosures were pandemic. Families doubled up and shared what little they had.

JUNE 1937: Striking steelworkers and members of their families queue up in a bread line maintained for their benefit by the Congress of Industrial Organizations (C.I.O.).

jobs were lost and homes and farms were forfeited. In ailing communities throughout the area, small banks failed and people fell delinquent on their taxes. Many school districts were unable to pay their teachers, and some teachers were reported to be starving.

The Rescue Mission, Friendly Inn, and Shantytowns

Pride and independence were sacrificed as many who had never done so before found themselves accepting charity to survive. Many homeless turned to the City Rescue Mission; others showed up at a former police station that had been converted to the Friendly Inn by Mayor Joseph Heffernan. Still others ended up in shantytowns.

As production rates slumped, the steel companies subjected employees not only to shorter hours but also to payment in scrip, just as the City of Youngstown had begun to do in 1930. In an attempt to help as best it could, Youngstown Sheet & Tube in 1932 provided 650 laborers with lots of one-eighth of an acre each to use for growing vegetables; included in the bargain was transportation to and from the fields.

Soon after the decade began, so did a drought, but northeast Ohio was spared much of the disaster that would turn Oklahoma and other states in middle America into a dust bowl. THE VINDICATOR named the summer of 1931 "one of the finest on record" and later noted that 1932 was "one of the best years in weather history." But in March 1936 the eastern United States experienced flooding that saw Pittsburgh's Golden Triangle submerged beneath eight feet of water. Floods in February 1938

were even worse. March and April 1937 brought dust storms and news reports that they were carrying dirt all the way to New Jersey from Colorado and Kansas.

Putting up fruits and vegetables—a lifeline for many—entailed planning, so the Garden Forum provided seeds for eleven hundred families in 1932. Those whose circumstances left them with little or no food found sustenance in the soup kitchens that blossomed around Youngstown. Six were in operation in 1932, and that July 900 thousand meals were served out of them, prepared at a cost of a penny a meal.

Milk and Postage Prices Fall; Romance Takes a Holiday

Bridal statistics paint a vivid picture of how the economic situation influenced lives: in June 1930 marriages recorded in the city had declined more than twenty-five percent from a year earlier. Even day-to-day expenditures reflect the turmoil shoppers faced: in 1933 the price of a quart of milk dropped to eight cents, and two-cent postage returned.

Unemployment begat a populace with time on its hands. Peo-

DECEMBER 1939: The Ohio Works streetcar makes its last run across the Spring Common Bridge. The line was abandoned in favor of trackless trambuses.

ple found diversion in jigsaw puzzles, Sunday comics, marathon dancing, miniature golf, chain letters, baseball, and radio, as well as gardening and canning fruits and vegetables as a hedge against leaner days. In the ten months from November 1933 to September 1934 the cost of living went up 22.5 percent. When families could spare some change, Idora Park provided good entertainment for the money, as did the Butler Art Gallery, which opened a new addition in 1931.

Edward VIII and the Dionne Quintuplets Make Big News

And although tough times gave rise to increases in crime and violence, they also inspired a period of tent revivals and Christian righteousness, and the recognition of Mary Baker Eddy, founder of Christian Science, as one of the country's outstanding women in a national poll in 1933.

Still just three cents daily and ten cents Sunday by the end of the decade, THE VINDICATOR offered a healthy return of information and entertainment for a small investment. It linked the area to the outside world, reporting on such history-making events as the birth of the Dionne quintuplets in May

WHAT IN THE WORLD: The Rotogravure pictorial section, printed in sepia ink, carried local, national, and international features.

1934 in Carbell, Ontario.

It was a time of sensational news happenings, and Youngstown's own Esther Hamilton wired first-person reports to THE TELEGRAM from Flemington, New Jersey, when Bruno Richard Hauptmann went on trial for his life for kidnapping and slaying the Lindbergh baby.

Another news event of intense, almost obsessive, interest in the 1930s revolved around the love affair between England's King Edward VIII and commoner Wallis Simpson, which led eventually to the king's abdication.

A popular daily feature was the day's news in pictures from round the country and the world, showing anything from international leaders to dog shows to fashion to army maneuvers and the lives of celebrities like Shirley Temple and Mae West.

ESTHER HAMILTON
Reporter and columnist

In 1934 THE VINDICATOR held its first spelling bee for schoolchildren. In 1935 it introduced a peach-colored late edition for sports fans that carried the freshest scores. The sepia-toned rotogravure—"roto" for short—was well on its way to becoming a Sunday favorite and would remain so for generations. The newspaper also provided area residents the opportunity to buy a six-volume set of the Wide World Illustrated Encyclopedia for ninety cents per book, plus sales tax. All VINDICATOR readers had to do was clip and send in coupons from the newspaper to collect each of the six gold certificates required for the six volumes.

Can't-Miss Comics: Orphan Annie, Dick Tracy, the Gumps

Other daily diversions provided by the newspaper included recipes from Alice Bradley, principal of Miss Farmer's School of Cookery, and the hottest comics of the day—Dick Tracy, Little Orphan Annie, Apple Mary, Gasoline Alley, Moon Mullins, Dixie Dugan, the Gumps, Secret Agent X-9, Bringing Up Father, and "Cap" Stubbs.

Jiggs could coax out a chuckle on even the gloomiest day in "Bringing Up Father."

Atwater Kent cathedral radio, 1933.

Warren P. Williamson, Jr. founded WKBN Radio in 1926 and pursued a television-station permit as early as 1930. THE VINDICATOR would later establish WFMJ, but in the early years of radio it teamed up with WKBN to broadcast election returns.

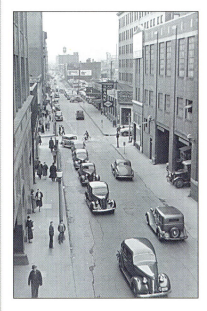

▲ MARCH 1939: Brick-paved Commerce Street was a bustling thoroughfare when this westward exposure was made from Wick Avenue. By 1939, the Depression was beginning to ease and the area was getting on its feet again.

———◆———

ON THE GO: East Federal Street as it appeared in 1938. Automobile travel had become a way of life, impervious even to the straitened circumstances of the Depression. Federal Plaza East occupies that location today.

▼

Come 1935, Ohio Edison and others began to introduce the public to the wonders of air conditioning. Every weekday afternoon for several weeks that summer, the Ohio Edison auditorium would be open so people could go in and feel the difference. And by 1936 prices of automobiles and electrical appliances had begun to come down. As the nation's economic crisis began to ease, people realized that such items, formerly viewed as luxuries, had become necessities as their lifestyles changed.

competition presented by the new medium that they refused to carry program listings, except as paid advertising.

People's lives were also affected by several developments in medicine over the course of the decade. An outbreak of smallpox was checked by inoculations in 1932, but an epidemic of polio in September 1933 led to the closing of the city schools.

Williamson, Jr. Looks Ahead To Television; WFMJ on Air

Looking to the future, Warren P. Williamson, Jr. began to pursue acquisition of a television station permit in 1930, while radio hit its stride and gained fans across the country.

Before decade's end, in 1939, WFMJ Radio took to the Youngstown airwaves. Throughout that summer, construction of a steel radio tower more than two hundred feet tall commanded the attention of passers-by in downtown Youngstown.

As radio carved itself a larger and larger niche in the 1930s, many newspapers so feared the

BITS AND PIECES OF VALLEY LIFE IN THE DEPRESSION

AS THE DECADE drew to a close and Europe drew closer to war, economic recovery appeared on the horizon at last. Meanwhile, progress at home brought new diversions: The Canfield Fair held its first "Pig Iron Derby" in 1938, and the Youngstown College Band made its debut that fall, just a few weeks before the college held its first homecoming. In 1939 THE VINDICATOR introduced its Mummers Parade, with huge, gas-filled balloons of comic strip characters and other personalities.

ENVIRONMENTALLY, seeds of concern that would grow to flourish in the decades ahead took root in the Mahoning Valley in the 1930s. As the decade began, estimates held that smoke emissions cost Youngstown $6 million annually. When the Mahoning froze in December 1932, it was, amazingly, a newsworthy event, a phenomenon brought about by work slowdowns and the coldest December day in eight years. THE VINDICATOR routinely ran ads for coal and coke yards, a boon to homeowners who were trying to balance heavy heating needs against pocketbooks lightened by the Depression.

MILL CREEK PARK gained much of its infrastructure—things like embankments, buildings, pavilions, walkways, parking lots, and insect and disease control—through the establishment of a Civilian Conservation Corps work camp there in 1935.

Appreciation of nature gained an additional foothold in 1938 when the area popularly known as "Poland Woods" became the first municipal forest in Ohio.

The next year, when Dr. Harry E. Welsh retired after forty years as health commissioner, a review of the advancements in health care over the course of his career showed that the incidence of typhoid had fallen dramatically to an average of ten cases per year; that the city's mortality rate for scarlet fever had dropped from 139 to three per year; and that the measles mortality rate had fallen to less than two per year.

Diseases of Childhood Yield To Advances in Medicine

The death rates for children from typhoid, smallpox, and diphtheria now totaled only thirteen per thousand, and the year after Dr. Welsh's retirement, community leaders could be found discussing the pros and cons of a mental-health hospital.

The battle against infantile paralysis, better known as polio, continued, however; in 1937 the valley suffered an epidemic of the terrifying disease, for which hospitalization and therapy in iron lungs were the standard means of treatment. The ongoing war against tuberculosis led schools to introduce chest X-rays in 1938.

As individuals found themselves awash in the day-to-day battles generated by the national economic situation, municipal governments throughout the Mahoning Valley struggled to maintain even the most basic services for their citizens. Youngstown's tax collection, for example, fell twenty percent short in 1930.

The city adopted a four-day work week in an effort to make a dent in the unemployment rate,

BEST OF THE BEST: The Warner Theater on West Federal Street was the most elaborate of the theaters in downtown Youngstown. It is now Powers Auditorium, home of the Youngstown Symphony.

APPEAL: Tax collections collapsed during the Depression, so a billboard urges everyone to ante up. The building, a branch library, replaced a fountain on Central Square.

OCTOBER 27, 1937: One might have stayed dry that day by ducking into the Crystal Lunch, or sneaking into the Cameo to watch the lurid "Ten Days in a Nudist Camp" and "Slaves in Bondage." Somehow, the titles always promised more than they delivered.

and later encouraged employees to work on rotating schedules as another means of providing additional work. In 1931 the city instituted a three-day work week as a means of affording one hundred additional employees.

When Mark E. Moore succeeded Joseph Heffernan as Youngstown's mayor in 1932, more and more people found their water supplies cut off for nonpayment of bills, and the city made plans to install community water fountains for public use.

For Some Workers, Payday Was a Thing Remembered

Calculations in 1931 showed that Mahoning County's tax values had increased twentyfold in thirty years, the largest gain in Ohio, but that did not ease the county's monetary woes. In 1932, for example, Mahoning County workers faced forty-two months

without pay. Interestingly, despite the hard times, complaints were already being voiced that the new courthouse was overcrowded.

Throughout the first half of the decade, as the Depression dragged on without any sign of surcease, THE VINDICATOR repeatedly published stories of good works and survival. For example, the Mahoning County Sheriff's Department, at no cost to taxpayers, distributed hundreds of bushels of potatoes to needy families in 1935.

With governing bodies striving to tighten their belts, cuts were made in police and fire departments, and gamblers and liquor runners capitalized on the shortage of manpower. In 1930, the mayor's son found a bomb in the yard of the family home, and gang warfare took on a life of its own.

The region found itself in the national spotlight in 1934, when G-man Melvin Purvis shot and

killed Pretty Boy Floyd, Public Enemy Number One, near East Liverpool. Purvis, head of the FBI's Chicago bureau, fifteen other G-men, and a posse of one hundred combed the woods south of Lisbon, finally cornering Floyd behind a corncrib on a Sprucevale farm. By the time THE VINDICATOR's City Edition went to press that day, its headline read, OUTLAW FLOYD DIES LIKE A RAT.

Depression or Not, Gamblers and Racketeers Find a Niche

Racketeering flourished during the Depression. Numbers slips and "hitting the bug" made frequent headlines in 1934. "Liquor joints" and other dives, many salted with slot machines and other games of chance, became popular hangouts. Capitalizing on the struggles faced by democratic government, area communists made occasional headlines, as in

A NEW AIRPORT, BETTER ROADS, AND RIDING THE RAILS

BY 1930 Lansdowne Airport had become outmoded, made obsolete by the advent of bigger and better aircraft (a development, THE VINDICATOR reported in January 1950, that left such "a bad taste in the mouths of a lot of Youngstown people [that] even today, some feel that expenditures for airport developments are 'a waste of money.' "). With no airport expansion plans on the horizon, the city was dropped from airmail routes in 1931.

YET, THE DESIRE for airplane connections to the outside world continued to grow. Five years after Lucky Lindy successfully soloed across the Atlantic, headlines heralded Youngstown's first aviatrix, eighteen-year-old MaryAnn Campana, when she made her first solo trip, having successfully completed lessons that totaled four take-offs and landings. For a time, it appeared that Youngstown, Warren, Niles, Hubbard, and Sharon might get together for joint construction of a tricounty airport, but by 1938, the idea having failed to jell, Youngstown set out to build its own airfield in Vienna, a $2.6 million proj-

APRIL 1930: A bridge and grade-elimination project answered the problem of interminable tieups at the Fifth Avenue railroad crossing, a source of irritation for years.

ect conducted by the Works Progress Administration.

THE LAND was obtained with help from the publisher of THE VINDICATOR, William F. Maag, Jr., and construction began round-the-clock in June 1939. The city celebrated the opening of its new airport in summer 1941. Ease of getting around on the ground also improved. The Perry Highway from Youngstown to Pittsburgh opened in 1930, railroad grade eliminations were completed at Fifth Avenue in 1930 and Wick Avenue in 1936, and Hazel and Phelps streets were designated one-way thoroughfares in 1932 to lessen traffic congestion. Trambuses were introduced in 1936 and welcomed by passengers because they could be steered to the curb for boarding, unlike their streetcar predecessors, which couldn't

leave their tracks.

In 1938 the Works Progress Administration invested more than $3 million in improvements to Mahoning County's roadways. Because national legislation dictated that public-works projects be under way by January 1, 1939, to qualify for federal funding, a special election was held in August 1938.

YOUNGSTOWN VOTERS faced five issues: park and playground improvements; street improvements; bridge building; public buildings; and a school bond issue. All but the school issue passed; however, because it failed by less than 2.5 percent, the board of education determined to proceed anyway and pledged the necessary money to qualify for federal participation, making possible additions to a dozen city schools.

The 1930s also brought tales of the golden age of luxury trains, and of hoboes, unable to find work, hungering for the open road, riding the rails. Passenger traffic on the railroads would decline significantly by 1938 owing to the rise of other forms of transportation; nevertheless, when fares were lowered to two cents a mile that year, passenger counts once again increased.

The elegant Pierce Arrow. Some could afford it.

1932, when they staged a demonstration before starting a "hunger march" to Columbus.

As representatives of the people debated how to maintain services, they considered myriad options: how much money would six-month school terms save? Should street lights be turned off? Should services at city hospitals be curtailed? Should playgrounds close? In one cost-cutting misstep, late payment of bills by the City of Youngstown nearly forced Youngstown Hospital Association to close its South Side unit in 1934. Fortunately, the threat was recognized and the bills paid.

While financial challenges grabbed headlines, an amendment to the city's home-rule charter was adopted in November 1933 providing for the election of a council president. The public approved that and other charter changes after a contentious campaign in which the Youngstown Federation of Women's Clubs led the charge for the amendments, working with the city's civic, fraternal, and social organizations.

Voters Adopt New Provisions For Civil Service and Parks

The approved changes included amendments creating a three-man civil service commission and a park and recreation commission to assume duties formerly handled by the city council-controlled park department; requiring council's approval of water commission and board of control purchases over five hundred dollars (as was already required for other city departments); allowing political parties to endorse candidates on the city's nonpartisan ballot; and creating the elective position of council president.

By 1936, the worst of the financial crisis appeared to be over and a sense of relief prevailed when the City of Youngstown ended the year with a balanced budget.

As the Depression lingered,

RING THE GOOD OL' BUGLE, BOYS... : Though the ranks were thinning, the Grand Army of the Republic mustered enough Union veterans of the Civil War in the thirties for a get-together at Hotel Pick-Ohio on West Boardman Street. The GAR dissolved in 1956. The hotel went on to become Amedia Plaza, a low-rent apartment house.

many of those who could afford to do so retreated from the dismal job market to the college classroom and considered how best to prepare for the future.

Although the YMCA decided to drop its course offerings in law in 1931, it appointed Herbert O. Jones of Hiram College to the position of assistant general secretary in charge of all educational activities. Three years later, the YMCA celebrated its golden jubilee, and in 1935 it graduated its last high school class, one hundred strong, concluding that fifty-year-old program. That same year the Jewish Federation of Youngstown was organized.

While the exploits of pilots like Charles Lindbergh, Wiley Post and Amelia Earhart made national headlines, local youngsters became fascinated by aviation and the stunt pilots who traveled the country sharing thrills and taking risks barnstorming.

The dangers of stunt-flying made news in 1934 with the death of a man as he performed near Unity. The skies also were home to dirigibles; disasters like the crash of the Akron in New Jersey in April 1933 and the Hindenburg in May 1937 grabbed headlines and

imaginations as well.

Additionally, the 1930s witnessed the infancy of professional football, Babe Ruth's every home run as a news event, and the thrill of the 1936 Olympics in Berlin, Germany, where Cleveland native Jesse Owens, educated at Ohio State University, repeatedly broke world records.

Steel Companies Campaign For Lake-to-River Waterway

Access to and availability of water cropped up often in local news. In 1932 the Ohio River resembled a highway to Youngstown as YS&T coal shipments began to arrive by that route. That same year, the water-treatment plant at Meander went into full operation, and two years later, officials dedicated Pyma-

tuning Dam across the line in Pennsylvania. Talk of a Beaver-Mahoning canal reached a fever pitch during the decade. In 1932 the railroads went on record opposing such a project, but the National Rivers and Harbors Congress gave its approval two years later.

In May 1935 THE VINDICATOR announced that Youngstown would get $5 million in federal money for the canal, with work to begin by that July. Opposition forces blocked progress, however, even as the valley's steel companies pledged to pay the cost of constructing local docks. The issue would continue to appear in the headlines well into the 1940s.

Valley steel production made national headlines when directors of the Youngstown Sheet & Tube Company approved a plan in March 1930 to sell the company to Bethlehem Steel Corporation. THE VINDICATOR termed the proposal "a billion-dollar deal," but trouble arose at that April's stockholders' meeting, where detractors contested proxie voting and questioned the investment practices of some of the principals.

Government Scuttles Merger Plan by S&T and Bethlehem

Youngstown officials and City Council opposed the merger, and the federal government soon began an investigation of possible antitrust violations amid concerns that the marriage of Sheet & Tube to Bethlehem would form an illegal monopoly.

Between the sickly national economy and the legal wrangling caused by the merger talk, Sheet & Tube's losses for 1932 totaled nearly $13.3 million. The company developed work-share programs in 1933, an effort that helped to keep eighty percent of the steelworkers on payrolls.

Not until summer 1933, for the first time since the economic col-

SEEMS LIKE OLD TIMES: Soup kitchens that sprang up in the early thirties returned in 1937 to help steelworkers and their families during the month-long Little Steel Strike.

lapse, did mill schedules finally begin to increase; that July, fifty-one of the district's eighty-three open hearths were operating.

In 1934 mill operations were as high as they had been in early 1929, and Sheet & Tube, Republic, and Carnegie Steel began to move plans from drawing boards to construction sites, enlarging existing mills and erecting new ones.

In its role as a national company of some stature, Sheet & Tube made news when it announced that it would build a Steckel hot-strip mill at its Indiana Harbor works. In 1936, as the economy began to roll again in earnest, the productivity of Sheet & Tube's continuous-strip mills at the Campbell and Brier Hill works outstripped expectations.

For labor, that year also saw formation of the Congress of Industrial Organizations (C.I.O.) and confirmation of the official status of the Steel Workers Organizing Committee. President Frank Purnell, meanwhile, organiz-

ed the Youngstown Sheet & Tube Chorus, and as the year drew to a close, hopes were high for the future of worker-employer relations.

Union Activists and Steel Management at a Crossroads

Because basic steel was the Youngstown district's primary commodity, however, the Mahoning Valley was a critical locale for the development of labor relations, and as the S.W.O.C. worked nationwide to unionize the entire steel industry, and as the C.I.O. gained momentum, the fears and desires of the parties involved in both management and labor

SUPPLY DROP: A biplane loaded with food for Republic Steel's Warren plant crash lands. Air drops were commonplace at strikebound mills during the Little-Steel strike.

▲ MARTIAL LAW: After the June 19 riot, the governor dispatched the National Guard to help the steel mills reopen.

◀ READY FOR ANYTHING: National Guardsmen manning a water-cooled machine gun.

came to the fore. Whereas some in labor merely wanted recognition in the form of organization and bargaining strength to increase wages, hours, and safety, others yearned for change of revolutionary dimensions.

National Steel Strike Triggers Riots in Youngstown, Warren

Against such diverse demands, the reactions of those in management ranged from stubborn recalcitrance to anxious alarm at the thought of communist uprisings. And while waves of new immigrants had for generations ensured manpower for the mills, as the tide of immigration began to recede, management had to accept the fact that workers were no longer expendable.

At midnight May 26, 1937, a national strike began at the companies called "Little Steel," including Bethlehem, Sheet & Tube, Republic, and Inland. In the weeks that followed headlines told of pickets, tear gas, arrests, interference with rail shipments to the mills, and planes mak-

ing food drops into the plants. In Warren, a thousand strikers fought 250 policemen at Republic, resulting in one death and fourteen injuries.

Then, on June 19, a riot at Stop Five on Poland Avenue in Youngstown killed two and injured fourteen (including a VINDICATOR photographer). Ohio's governor reacted by sending in the National Guard. By June's end, the workers had returned to the mills. Complete victory had eluded them, but changes were definitely in the air.

International events shifted the focus in 1939. As tension mounted in Europe with the rise of Adolf Hitler and his invasion of Poland on September 1, local mills went to work at record levels and power consumption hit an all-time high.

RIOT: A battle between striking steelworkers and the police at Republic Steel Company in Youngstown left two dead and fourteen injured.

News from the Mahoning and Shenango Valleys

1940

JAN. 14: Westlake Housing Village, largest federal project to date, will be home to twenty-five hundred people in 618 apartments. By eliminating slums, low-cost housing will "reduce juvenile delinquency," Mayor William B. Spagnola says.

APRIL 25: F.H. Waring, Ohio Health Department chief engineer, says reservoirs should be built in Berlin Township and on Mosquito Creek in Trumbull County to ease Mahoning River pollution and flooding.

OCT. 3: A throng estimated variously at fifteen, twenty or thirty-five thousand jams Central Square to greet Wendell L. Willkie, Republican presidential candidate.

DEC. 1: THE VINDICATOR invites readers to contribute to a Christmas party and gift fund for one hundred-fifty Youngstown national guardsmen training at Camp Shelby near Hattiesburg, Mississippi.

DEC. 9: Campbell officials welcome a new electric bus service; it replaces the last city rail lines, except for the Youngstown & Suburban.

1941

FEB. 14: One hundred pounds of dynamite turns up in a vacant farmhouse on Youngstown-Poland Road. The house has been vacant for years, but a Pennsylvania car has been in the vicinity recently.

MAY 16: The Cleveland chapter, American Institute of Architects, will survey how long it would take to evacuate Cleveland in wartime.

JULY 1: Thousands attend the dedication of Youngstown's $2.6 million airport in Vienna. The first airmail flight in eleven years arrives.

DEC. 8: "Instead of people buying flags or labels...to put on their cars to say they are Americans, now is the time for them to prove they are Americans.... It is the duty of every American, whether in the plants or in the army, to give one hundred percent support to his country."–U.S. Rep. Michael J. Kirwan on the bombing of Pearl Harbor.

1942

JAN. 3: Ray G. Hagstrom, tire-rationing coordinator, says Mahoning County will be divided into six rationing districts, each under a committee. Tires for ordinary passenger cars will not be available, he warns.

FEB. 23: Sixty air-raid wardens are briefed at the YMCA before teaching a school for twenty-five hundred new Youngstown wardens.

APRIL 27: A one-week sugar freeze takes effect at midnight, after which consumers must present rationing stamps to buy their allowances of one pound a week.

DEC. 16: An Associated Press poll picks Youngstowner Frank Sinkwich number one male athlete of 1942. The Georgia halfback outpolls Ted Williams and Don Hutson.

1943

MARCH 14: Members of the Junior League perform wartime service as nurses' aides, hospital receptionists, motor corps drivers, radio operators, and Red Cross workers.

MARCH 24: A blast detonates at the Ravenna Arsenal as workers move bombs from a storage igloo to a truck, killing eleven.

JUNE 23: A mother of five gets six months in jail for hiding her newborn son in a dresser to keep his birth a secret from her husband.

JULY 27: A B-17 bomber buzzes the South Side, accidentally dropping a seven-pound weight through the roof at 39 East Avondale Avenue and causing an uproar.

1944

JAN. 2: Crime and politics held the local spotlight in 1943. A recount of Youngstown's mayoral race gave Ralph W. O'Neill a thirteen-vote win over Republican Arthur H. Williams. In the war on crime, eight racketeers drew sentences as authorities cracked the $10-million-a-year gambling racket, closed bordellos, and put bookie joints out of business.

MARCH 14: An eleven-year-old boy dies of rabies, the third death from dog bites in eight months.

JUNE 6: The paper reports D-Day in a slim extra edition. "Faced with the imperative necessity of saving paper...THE VINDICATOR publishes this invasion extra in skeleton form [to supply] all the facts available up to press time," it explains.

OCT. 1: Elizabeth G. McLeod, nineteen-year-old Irish stowaway, says she was engaged to twelve servicemen in an effort to get into the U.S. "I always wanted to come to America. I determined to marry an American boy so that I could."

1945

APRIL 13: Youngstowners are asked to give five pounds of cloth-ing for war victims, but the collection so far yields only a little more than one ounce per person. "Are you proud of that record?"THE VINDICATOR asks in a front-page notice.

APRIL 29: Radio announces Germany's surrender, but Youngstowners recall the premature armistice in 1918 and hold their elation in check. They're right, it wasn't true.

MAY 7: An EXTRA! edition announcing the German surrender contains a World War II chronology, maps, a mayoral proclamation, a list of major postwar problems, and a pictorial, "The Road to Victory."

JUNE 5: Counterfeit summer: "Partly cloudy and continued cool today and tonight with danger of frost..."

NOV. 18: In a broadcast by WFMJ, the Quiz Kids play to a full house at Stambaugh Auditorium. The show sells $365 thousand in war bonds.

1946

MARCH 28: Otis Elevator does the first postwar escalator installation in the world at the G.M. McKelvey Company, a $300 thousand job.

JULY 7: The area endures its most "meatless Sunday" yet; Oles Market shuts its meat counter. Butter is up thirty to thirty-five cents a pound to a high of ninety-five cents.

OCT. 31: Thirty thousand tour Carnegie-Illinois Steel Corporation, Youngstown Sheet & Tube Company, and Republic Steel Corporation.

NOV. 11: On Armistice Day, THE VINDICATOR reflects: "Americans are the privileged of the earth. This did not simply happen. It came because generations worked and planned and fought and died to make it so. We, too, have an obligation to build well for those who come after us."

1947

JAN. 4: On page one, THE VINDICATOR says basketball scores are available by calling 7-2016. But "please dial it carefully...a slip on the number may disturb someone who is ill."

JUNE 8: A tornado kills six and injures hundreds. Six hundred families are left without shelter by the tornado, which swept south of Warren and Vienna and into Sharon.

AUG. 4: A queen bee loses her way in downtown Youngstown, disrupting West Federal Street traffic until she and her swarm come to rest on the marquee of the Bus Arcade.

OCT. 7: Mickey Schuster, twenty-eight, who has been fed through a tube inserted into his stomach since he was two, can eat normally after a series of operations.

1948

JAN. 26: Gambling equipment is removed from the notorious Jungle Inn at Hall's Corners and from other spots in advance of a Trumbull County grand jury investigation that has summoned mayors, police chiefs and marshals of all Trumbull County cities and villages.

FEB. 5: Crews make way for the new Spring Common Bridge, razing old buildings along Mahoning Avenue and the old Pennsylvania Station. A new Pennsy station will be built where Smith Brewing stood.

JUNE 27: AT&T lays telephone-television cable along U.S. 224 as part of a coast-to-coast hookup. The cable can carry fourteen hundred long-distance calls and two TV programs at the same time.

SEPT. 17: A Convair B-36, the world's largest bomber, flies over the Mahoning Valley on National Air Force Day. The plane sweeps in from the north below two thousand feet on a simulated bombing run.

SEPT. 24: Washingtonville residents, distressed by accidents at "Suicide Crossing," take their fight for signals at the Erie's Route 14 grade to Gov. Thomas J. Herbert.

1949

JAN. 2: Christmas mail: Nearly seven thousand letters landed in the dead-letter office in December, and the post office destroyed twenty-one thousand third-class pieces with flawed addresses.

JAN. 13: To get children out of "barrooms, where they go to see television," provide them with playgrounds, Detective Ted O'Connor tells Hayes Junior High School PTA.

APRIL 22: The city will stay on Daylight Saving Time five months, in line with New York, Washington, Pittsburgh, and Cleveland, but not with Columbus and Cincinnati.

JULY 25: A whiskey still found in Cleveland contains these ingredients: grain mash, garbage, potato peels, coffee grounds, and several pairs of old socks. One of two men arrested claims to be a minister.

5

WAR & PEACE

SEPTEMBER 1948: With six backward-facing propeller engines and four turbojets, the B-36 Peacemaker was an impressive sight over Youngstown. The largest bomber ever built, it served postwar America and never saw combat. The B-52 replaced it in the late fifties.

They stand taller than the rest–a remarkable generation whose remarkable deeds let us enjoy the fruits of democracy today while taking them for granted.

German dictator Adolf Hitler

It was a period marked by radical innovations in the economic and political structure of this nation…. The catalyst of the transition was two wars occurring in close sequence, one hot, the other cold. Together, they changed the face of the world.

CABELL PHILLIPS
THE 1940S: DECADE OF TRIUMPH AND TROUBLE

REPUBLIC STEEL 1943: Due to the shortage of working men, women begin working the mills to help the war effort. Florence Reed, one of the first women to ever work in the Republic Steel tube mill, puts the finishing touches on pipe for an Army contract.

A S THE WAR THAT RAGED IN Europe spread to the Pacific, and with the December 1941 bombing of Hawaii's Pearl Harbor finally drawing in the United States, the entire country found itself in the midst of life-altering sacrifices for the war effort. With its industrial capacity, the Mahoning Valley gave tremendously to that effort due in large part to the fortunate timing of Youngstown Sheet & Tube's construction of a continuous-strip mill and adoption of the cold-metal rolling process in the mid-thirties. Republic and U.S. Steel having followed suit, the Mahoning Valley was prepared to contribute significantly to the country's wartime needs.

An economic and industrial survey early in the forties warned that the valley needed to strive toward diversifying its output beyond basic steel to the manufacture and fabrication of goods that could be sold directly to consumers. However, in a twenty-four-hour production economy fueled by the war and the immediate needs of the military, the need to

LOOSE TALK CAN COST LIVES

▲ PROPAGANDA POSTERS—collector's items today—appealed to Americans' sense of patriotism and duty to country.

OPPOSITE PAGE: American GIs advance ▶ through the devastation of Cologne, Germany, in March 1945.

diversify did not seem compelling. The population within the City of Youngstown had fallen to 167,720 by 1940, but the larger metropolitan area covering the Mahoning Valley still ranked third-largest in Ohio. Hence, the focus of the people was too narrow, and the comfort zone too wide, for cautions about a single-layer economic base to evoke any more than fleeting interest. It was an oversight—neglect, if you prefer—that would reap a whirlwind less than forty years later.

The stark reality of the Second World War touched everyone's life. Even before the U.S. entered the war, the country's production levels rose in response to the needs of the British and other forces in Europe, and its young

WASTE NOT: Rubber-tired buses had replaced trolleys, so the steel tracks were torn up and channeled into the war effort. This is West Federal Street near Spring Common.

men were registering under the Selective Service Act, a peacetime draft that went into effect in September 1940. Then, as the nation absorbed the shock of Pearl Harbor, it greeted a new year, 1942, that would bring rationing, shortages, transportation problems, the uncertainty of the draft, and bittersweet farewells to those going off to foreign lands. A record 2,665 couples tied the knot

in Mahoning County that year, inspired by such diverse hopes as to settle one thing in an unsettled world, or to become draft-proof, a strategy that was not always successful.

Rationing began in April of that year as well. It was a means for the Office of Price Administration, one of the many government agencies that sprang into existence to manage the war effort, to control the distribution of sugar, fats, meat, gasoline, tires, cigarettes and countless other everyday items that had previously been taken for granted. Ration stamps, coupons, and tokens were issued with assigned point values for various commodities.

Depending on supply, demand, and shortages, older stamps and coupons were retired and new ones issued with higher point values, a frustrating occurrence if one had been saving points in an effort to make a special purchase.

Black Market Profiteers Exploit Shortage of Goods

Throughout the war, therefore, black-market trade thrived; soldiers and civilians often worked side deals for everything from silk to "fags"—that day's slang for cigarettes. Even rationing coupons were traded, and in 1944 local authorities uncovered a ring that produced counterfeit gas coupons.

Concerns arising from the war engaged everyone. While wave after wave of young men went into the armed forces, women were drafted to fill the positions that had been vacated in the factories and on the production lines. Like everyone else, THE VINDICATOR felt the strain of the war effort.

Washington classified newspapers as "essential" industries for their communications (and propaganda) value, but "essential" was a word subject to interpretation. If paper rationing was a curse to thorough news reporting, then the manpower shortage was calamity itself, for newsprint benefits mankind only if there are people to bring it alive with news and photographs. Through the war, the paper's acting managing editor (the managing editor was in the Navy) typed letters—each more desperate-sounding than the last—seeking deferments for reporters and other editorial employees summoned for induction into the armed forces. The correspondence, found half a century later, did not reveal a single letter of approval.

Factories throughout the country converted their facilities for war production. The Youngstown Rubber Company made life preservers.

Women recruited to shore up the work force often did not stay, gravitating to the war effort as nurses or joining the women's branches of the armed forces. In 1942 people could buy defense stamps for a dime or a quarter as a means of contributing money to the cause, and companies raised funds on location in a nationwide "Name a Bomber" drive in 1943. However, by 1944 the need for money to finance the war was so critical that local War Loan drives were undertaken, exhorting people to "Buy Till It Hurts." The war became so all-consuming that Labor Day 1943 came and went without parades.

Even with Candy in Short Supply, the Show Goes on

Like so many valley routines, Esther Hamilton's Alias Santa Claus Show made sacrifices for the war. The show, in which prominent citizens wearing butcher's aprons coaxed audience members to buy candy as a way of raising holiday money for the needy, had been started in 1931 by Miss Hamilton when she was a reporter for THE TELEGRAM, and she brought it with her to THE VINDICATOR when the papers merged in 1936. When the shortage of sugar, and therefore candy, became acute in 1943, the "candy butchers," as the VIPs were known, rose to the occasion and peddled Animal Crackers instead, ensuring the program's suc-

VALUED AGENCY: United Service Organizations catered to servicemen's social, educational, and religious needs. The Central Square library, background, was the USO information center.

AT HOME, OTHER TRIALS AND TESTS

MOTHER NATURE, too, made memorable impressions on the citizenry. In summer 1944 the area endured an infestation of Japanese beetles; June 1945 brought frost. When the war ended, Mother Nature didn't notice.

IN MAY AND JUNE 1946 THE VINDICATOR reported flooding that damaged four hundred homes, closed roads, and flooded downtown Youngstown, with losses above $100 thousand.

A year later a tornado ripped through Trumbull and Mercer counties, killing six. The paper told of hundreds left injured and homeless by the storm, property damage from which totaled $1.5 million.

JANUARY 1948 was so cold that water froze in fire hydrants and two people froze to death in Youngstown. Lacking gas to run heaters, many families had to leave their homes, and industrial gas supplies were cut in half. As if that weren't enough, a seventeen-inch snowfall, worst in the area since 1901, crippled transportation at month's end.

AT THE END of the war, Europe faced massive reconstruction and the possibility of famine. Across the United States, the government was promoting "meatless Sundays" by 1946 as a way to conserve food. The next year brought broad American concern about the need to rebuild Europe, formalized in the Marshall Plan instituted at the Paris Economic Conference in July 1947.

cess by continuing to claim, as they had in years past, that they could not make change for their customers. Besides shortages of just about everything, wartime produced campaigns for scrap metal, wastepaper, and tinfoil. Those commodities were recycled for production of military materials, becoming such items as containers for food and plasma, protectors for shell casings, and cartridges for gas masks. As the war dragged on, labor shortages and absenteeism worsened; leaflets were sometimes dropped from airplanes urging those not already doing so to get jobs related to the war effort.

With the United States fully involved in and committed to the war, civil defense became a universal concern. Schoolchildren were subjected to air-raid drills, and sirens were erected on buildings throughout the valley. Because of fears that such a highly industrialized area, with all it was providing to the Allied war effort, might be a target of Axis bombs, Mahoning County began to enforce blackout conditions in 1943. During those brief times when they could detach themselves from the war effort, soldiers from the Army's Shenango Replacement De-

pot—it became Camp Reynolds in 1943—looked to Youngstown and environs for their entertainment.

To the USO Falls the Task Of Shoring Up GI Morale

The United Service Organizations also worked locally to entertain the servicemen, including staging a Christmas Eve open house at the USO Club in 1943, and in 1944 working to find rooming for visiting servicemen in private homes.

With traditional values turned upside down by wartime necessities, the community grew increasingly alarmed by the expanding number of unwed mothers and the moral fiber (or flowering lack thereof) of women in their late teens and early twenties who were allowed to socialize unchaperoned with servicemen. By the end of the decade, for example, the bishop of Youngstown would issue an order imposing curfews at Catholic school dances and banning strapless gowns.

While 1944 ended with the Battle of the Bulge, 1945 began with fuel shortages across the country. Every last resource was commit-

NATURE'S WRATH: In 1947, a tornado killed six and dispossessed six hundred families in Trumbull and Mercer counties.

ted to bringing the war to a victorious conclusion. To preserve fuel, communities were urged to close schools and libraries, if possible. That winter authorities imposed curfews, and brownouts were frequent as well.

As the final days of World War II approached, the newspaper tradition of publishing "extra" editions drew to an end as well. Among THE VINDICATOR's last were the announcement of the death of President Franklin D. Roosevelt on April 12, 1945; an eight-page issue on May 7, 1945, consisting of a chronology of the war up to and through the German surrender; and an eight-page edition on August 14, 1945, detailing Japan's surrender and inviting people to dance in the streets at home.

In Reporting the Day's News, Subtle Changes in Approach

Even before the war, radio could broadcast breaking news faster than a VINDICATOR compositor could set a line of type, and television would soon beam the news directly into the living room. As exciting as they may have been to the people who wrote and edited them, extra editions were no more going to outrun the airwaves in 1945 than horses were going to prevail over motorized vehicles in 1922.

For THE VINDICATOR and other papers, World War II marked a watershed, a philosophical shift that placed less emphasis on speed and more on comprehensive reporting and analysis, areas in which newspapers excelled.

As absorbing as the war effort was, Greater Youngstown experienced changes during the decade unrelated to the ongoing international crisis. When the nineteen forties began, police and fire departments had become fully radio-equipped. In January 1940, Westlake Housing Village, the first federally authorized low-income

housing in the country, was dedicated. Its construction pricetag was $3,180,000, and residents paid rents of $19.00 to $22.50 a month, which included all utilities except telephone.

Eleven months later the last streetcar made its final run, and the following year the city pulled up many of the old rails and sold them to the local mills as scrap for the war effort.

In 1943 the Court of Appeals for the Fifth District confirmed a decision of the Trumbull County Common Pleas Court directing the city of Youngstown to extend Fifth Avenue through the Henry Stambaugh Golf Course; in January 1944 the state Supreme Court concurred in that decision.

That same month the area noted the death of Ida Tarbell, one of the most famous of the country's muckraking journalists. The muckrakers (so termed by Teddy Roosevelt because of their propensity for "raking filth") exposed the abuses of business and political corruption in the first decade of the twentieth century.

Miss Tarbell, a native of Erie, Pennsylvania, gained her knowledge of the American industrial machine during the two years she spent in the eighteen eighties as lead teacher at the private Poland Union Seminary School. She brought that knowledge to bear in her 1904 "History of the Standard Oil Company," which is considered a masterpiece of investigative reporting.

SEPTEMBER 21, 1940: Westlake Terrace Gardens opens. The federal housing project on West Federal Street (now Martin Luther King Boulevard) was the first of its kind in the U.S.

A wide range of news events on the home front filled the headlines, too, as in March 1946, when the G.M. McKelvey Company introduced Youngstown's first escalators to the public and, over the course of that same year, a rash of fires struck Hotel Pick-Ohio, first in January, then again in March, a third time in May, and a fourth time in July.

Home Savings Becomes A Beacon on the Skyline

One high point was the installation of a new lighting system on the Home Savings & Loan's downtown building in celebration of the financial institution's fiftieth anniversary in 1949; the installation quickly became a highlight of Youngstown's nighttime skyline.

The newspaper also reported personal tragedies indicative of the times, including the death of a woman who was electrocuted when a radio fell into her bath in June 1948, and the fatal fall of a Salem youth from the Wildcat roller coaster at Idora Park later that summer.

Strike by Operators Curtails Long-Distance Phone Service

In an era when local telephone numbers were dialed on rotary phones and contained only five digits, THE VINDICATOR often ran notices on its front page inviting readers to call the sports desk for the latest scores. But because calls to companies with more than one extension or long-distance calls often required the assistance of switchboard operators, a walkout by 750 telephone employees in April 1947 was understandably big news. Only emergency long-distance service was provided until the Ohio Bell Telephone strike ended on May 18.

Medically, the forties brought tremendous advances, in no small part because of the military crisis. In 1944 Youngstown's hospitals were made depots to handle penicillin, which had been proven effective by English doctors only three years earlier for the treat-

FEBRUARY 1948: This view from Spring Common looks north up Fifth Avenue, with West Federal Street intersecting. The WRTA bus terminal occupies that corner now.

ment of bacterial infections.

But also in 1944, rabies descended on the Mahoning Valley and became such a problem over the next few years that by June 1948 the Mahoning County Health Department ordered the inoculation of all dogs except those in the incorporated areas of Youngstown, Campbell, and Struthers. By July those three communities were forced to follow suit as well, and the health commissioner ordered all the city dogs quarantined.

Even during the war, gambling and racketeering continued to flourish, so rampantly in fact that

bug writers worked shifts at the gates of factories and steel mills.

Raids on Gambling Joints And a State Investigation

Bookie joints provided a refuge for slot machines and other forms of gambling. In 1943 headlines reported raids on two such haunts, "The Big House" and "The American House," as well as a state investigation and indictments.

Youngstown's first Italian-American mayor, William B. Spagnola, was sworn into office for a four-year term in January 1940, and in 1941 the City Charter was amend-

FOR YoCo, A SURGE IN ENROLLMENT

THE FORTIES produced important changes to the structure, curriculum and enrollment at Youngstown College. In 1941 the college, now with an enrollment of 1,750, took over Warren's Dana Musical Institute. Then, during the war, on the advice of the college president, Dr. Howard Jones, the board of trustees pulled the college away from its long association with the YMCA.

THAT MOVE enabled the institution to gain accreditation from the North Central Association. In 1944 the college won approval to issue bachelor of engineering degrees, and in August 1946, due in large part to the GI Bill of Rights and the edu-

cational benefits it made available to returning veterans, the college's enrollment jumped dramatically when more than twenty-seven hundred freshmen signed on, bringing the census to 3,460.

ed again, this time to allow for party primaries. When Spagnola's Democratic successor, Ralph W. O'Neill, took office in 1944 as the first partisan mayor since 1923, he ordered an end to gambling on the numbers lottery, but the effort was unavailing.

The Jungle Inn, among the most notorious of gambling joints and mob hangouts, opened in June 1947 at Halls Corners, an incorporated crossroads in Liberty Township.

By Any Other Name, Still The Notorious Jungle Inn

Popular with bookmakers, card sharks, slot-machine addicts, and craps shooters, the Jungle Inn was closed down in January 1948, only to reopen two months later under the front of Army-Navy Union Garrison 504. Everyone still called it the Jungle Inn, however, and the slot machines, headline stories, and other troubles continued. That October Youngstown's police chief, Edward J. Allen, cut off the joint's phone service.

An amendment to Youngstown's charter in 1945 provided for the election of a mayor every two years and permitted his re-election. Two years later, the city elected a Republican, Charles P. Henderson, to the mayor's office and a major war on racketeering began in Youngstown.

There were plenty of spots worthy of investigation in and out of the city, including the State Line Club near Sharon and Green Acres in Struthers. In May 1948 the police shut off the racing wire service used by a bookie joint called the Empire News Company.

Despite the soaring productivity generated by the war, property values east of Central Square in downtown Youngstown declined steadily through the forties, so by 1948 Mayor Henderson began to lobby for fairer distribution of state tax money to cities.

GAMBLING MECCA: The Jungle Inn ran wide open in southeast Liberty Township during the postwar years, shrugging off token raids and brief shutdowns. It took Gov. Frank Lausche and a squad of state liquor agents to close it down for good in August 1949.

Even before the war's end, predictions were forthcoming that a building boom would follow in the war's wake, and by 1947 the valley found itself challenged to find emergency housing and build homes for its returning veterans. By 1948 a campaign was afoot to provide good low-cost homes for them.

Three Councilmen Lie Low To Block GOP Appointment

In January 1947 THE VINDICATOR repeatedly carried headlines of a scandal brewing on Youngstown City Council.

The trouble came to light when three Democratic councilmen boycotted a council meeting to block Republican Party efforts to name one from its own party to the Third Ward seat vacated by State Sen. Nicholas P. Bernard. Not quite a week later, the paper reported that the three missing councilmen had been "found in Florida in the company of Jack Lombard, alias Napolitana, former operator of the old Savoy Club."

As one example of the outrage expressed locally, the paper reported a week after that the call from a valley preacher, the Rev. Ronald A. Luhman, pastor of First Reformed Church, for the "impeachment of the itinerant councilmen."

In 1948 the valley's voters gave a seventh term to their long-time representative in Washington, D.C., Congressman Michael Kirwan. Kirwan had drawn national attention earlier in 1948 when he

19TH DISTRICT REPRESENTATIVE: Michael Kirwan's service in Congress encompassed the administrations of six presidents.

NOT SINCE THEN... : Cleveland's Bob Feller, one of the greats, fires his fast ball against the Boston Braves on the way to the Indians' World Series championship in 1948.

was unanimously elected chairman of the National Democratic Congressional Campaign Committee, becoming the first northerner ever to hold the post.

Dwight ("Dike") Beede, Youngstown College's football coach, made a remarkable contribution to the game in 1941, evidence of which is visible every time referees take to the field even today.

It was Beede who first suggested that attention be called to penalties not by horns, which tended to disrupt the action, but rather by bright fabric squares that could be thrown by the referees as soon as they saw an infraction. That fall the first penalty flags were introduced in Youngstown at a game between Youngstown College and Oklahoma City University.

Baseball, a perennial favorite, continued to engage valley sports fans throughout the war as THE VINDICATOR annually reported on Youngstown's playing host to the National Amateur Baseball Federation tournament.

Professional ball made many sports headlines as well, the most frustrating of which for local fans came as the Cleveland Indians headed to the World Series in 1948. Valley residents sent more than 3,700 letters asking for series

DWIGHT ("DIKE") BEEDE

tickets; unfortunately, thousands were disappointed by the letters of regret they received in return.

An event of tremendous importance to the valley's large Roman Catholic population took place in 1943 with the Vatican's designation of the See of Youngstown. That July the church filled the bishopric with the Most Reverend James A. McFadden in an investment ceremony in Saint Columba Cathedral.

Other headlines involving the church included the report of a pontifical mass conducted at the cathedral in March 1946 by Edward Cardinal Mooney after his return from the consistory in Rome.

During World War II, school funding was tight, but THE VINDICATOR reported in May 1947 that a $5.4 million school-bond issue swept to victory with a plurality of sixty-nine percent.

The close partnership between school and community that existed in those days came into sharp focus in 1948 when the Youngstown superintendent of schools ordered the confiscation of comic books in the schools. In support of the school administration, drugstores stopped selling comics, and the mayor named a twelve-member committee to

monitor and censor them.

The Youngstown Board of Education, mirroring prevailing attitudes in the postwar years, barred the hiring of married women in 1949; those already on staff, however, were allowed to remain.

Larger, Faster Planes Again Leave Muni Airport in a Fix

The new Youngstown Municipal Airport officially opened in Vienna on July 1, 1941, and the Civil Aeronautics Administration authorized two major airlines, United and Pennsylvania Central (later to become Capital), to make Youngstown a scheduled stop.

As had happened with Lansdowne Field in 1930, however, Youngstown once again found its capacity to welcome air traffic threatened by newer, larger planes. Vienna's runways were long enough for twin-engine DC-3s and C-46s, but they were not considered adequate for the four-engine DC-4s that were aloft by 1944.

The Youngstown Chamber of Commerce took the lead in promoting the airport's expansion to accommodate larger planes, and a $600 thousand improvement program was approved in 1947.

Returning War Veterans Swell Ranks of Aviation

The city and federal government shared the cost of lengthening runways and enlarging the administration building, and the expanded facilities were dedicated in September 1949.

Local aviation received a lift from the country's being at war insofar as hundreds of the area's young men learned to fly in the training programs of the U.S. Army Air Forces and Civil Aeronautics Administration. Others earned pilot's licenses through flight training under the GI Bill of Rights.

The GI training helped to subsidize aviation in the postwar pe-

JULY 1, 1941: The grand opening of Youngstown Municipal Airport packs them in.

Youngstown and Leetonia.

Throughout the war, manpower was so tight, and the need for military materiel so great, that in 1943 the War Manpower Commission, another government agency created to manage the war effort, ordered steelworkers to work forty-eight-hour weeks. As wave after wave of men left their jobs to enlist or answer the draft, "Rosie the Riveter" stepped into the void and became a familiar sight in Mahoning Valley factories and mills, just as she was elsewhere in the country.

Mills and Factories Turn Out Varied Products for Warfare

Items produced locally for the war effort included Mae West life preservers; disposable fuel tanks of thin sheet steel for fighter aircraft; half-track gun platforms used for fighting enemy aircraft; leather products for gloves, boots and thermal clothing for high-altitude fliers; short lengths of lightweight pipe to supply gas and water to the Allied invasion forces as they moved forward; sheet-metal ammo belts for fifty-caliber machine guns; shipping crates; and munitions of all kinds from the nearby Ravenna Arsenal.

No matter how diminished the pool of workers became, it seemed

riod and kept alive much enthusiasm that might otherwise have withered and died.

With United and Capital Aboard, Airport Thrives

In 1949 United Airlines and Capital Airlines provided the Youngstown airport with daily service. Over the course of that year, forty-two thousand passengers used commercial airline service in and out of the airport, and thousands of others made noncommercial flights. Flight operations in 1949 totaled 78,724. On January 29, 1950, in a special issue of THE VINDICATOR looking back over the first half of the twentieth century, a reporter observed:

A silver DC-4 streaked down the runway and into the skies over Youngstown Municipal Airport in Vienna. Its 50 passengers settled back in soft reclining seats and resumed conversation as the giant of the airways swept gracefully over the dull gray Mahoning Valley. Far below, scarcely an eye turned skyward to watch the big four-engine plane pass overhead. An airliner was as commonplace as an ordinary housefly.

The popularity of automobiles, meanwhile, led by the end of the forties to the installation of radar equipment on many county highways and city streets throughout the Mahoning Valley, and tales of violations often appeared in print.

As automobile ownership rose, the census of railroad passengers dropped to the point where, by the end of the decade, the Public Utilities Commission of Ohio allowed the Youngstown & Suburban to discontinue passenger service, which had dwindled to a handful of runs daily between

1943: Mosquito Reservoir was built as part of the war effort to increase the industrial water supply. It also improved flood control and gave Warren a better water source.

as if it were always becoming more so. When the Battle of the Bulge began in December 1944, for example, the Ravenna Arsenal ran continual advertisements in THE VINDICATOR for additional workers.

The government turned a deaf ear to tub-thumping for construction of a Lake-to-River canal as critical to national defense, but the need for a stable, constant water supply to bolster wartime production did lead in 1943 to federal approval to dam Mosquito Creek in Trumbull County.

As Hostilities End Abroad, New Ones Flare Up at Home

Construction of the Berlin and Mosquito Creek reservoirs, combined with Lake Milton, gave industries up and down the Mahoning Valley access to more than seventy-five billion gallons of water. It couldn't happen too soon: VINDICATOR reports in 1944 told of water shortages hindering the war output of the district's steel mills.

While the war raged, management and labor had been unified in their focus. Although all welcomed the war's end, it

OCTOBER 1942: Berlin Reservoir adds another link to the water supply for industrial production. From all sources, industry has access to seventy-five billion gallons.

meant new realities: veterans looking for jobs, return to regular working hours, no more frenzied push to supply the war machine.

Nineteen forty-six, therefore, produced strikes by steelworkers, trainmen, brewery workers, coal miners, and truck drivers—disruptions that often caused a domino effect from one industry to the next. For example, a two-day railroad strike that May threw fifty thousand out of work in various district industries. Headlines on January 21, 1946, reported that seventy-five thousand had been idled by a steel strike. With the mills shut down, the Mahoning River froze. The steel strike ended by mid-February, only to be followed in April by a coal-mine strike that choked off supplies to Youngstown steel mills, forcing production cutbacks and idling more than fifteen thousand work-

ers initially. By May, Carnegie-Illinois Steel had to shut down entirely, affecting twenty-five thousand workers, and Republic followed quickly; Youngstown Sheet & Tube, meanwhile, cut production to thirty percent.

Coal Strike Cuts Domestic Supplies, too; 40,000 Idled

By May 21, THE VINDICATOR was reporting that the coal pinch had idled forty thousand in the district. In November, the coal strike again forced mills to cut back to save fuel. By November 24, domestic coal had dwindled to a four-day supply; two days later, Niles schools, their coal supplies exhausted, closed their doors.

Not until December 7 would the newspaper be able to report that the coal strike had finally ended and that the various em-

RESOLVE: Posters accentuate work ethic and productivity, urging those at home to do their best for our fighting men abroad.

▲ ON THE LINE: Strikers idle away the hours in one of a series of work stoppages that plagued industry almost as the last gunfire was dying down overseas. Strikes proliferated in the mid-forties as labor discarded its wartime truce with industry.

TANNERY: The Ohio Leather Company ▶ of Girard was an early war contractor, receiving a $100 thousand Navy order in 1941 for shoe leather. By 1943, the company was processing eight thousand calfskins daily for the war effort. The company, founded in the early 1900s, closed in 1971.

bargoes and brownouts were over, too. Even with the work slowdowns, however, THE VINDICATOR estimated that thirty thousand people attended Halloween open houses at the steel mills in 1946.

Concerns about the environment became paramount when, in 1948, a terrible five-day smog moved into the mill town of Donora, Pennsylvania, upriver from Pittsburgh, resulting in five deaths; experts advised that under certain weather conditions, such an event could happen in the Mahoning Valley.

In September of that year, Republic Steel announced that it would electrify its Bessemer plant downtown, thereby cutting smoke and noise annoyances. Downtown smoke pollution was further reduced in 1949 when the Pennsylvania Railroad replaced its entire switching fleet with diesel-powered engines, and the Erie Railroad helped additionally by introducing sixty diesel-powered locomotives of its own.

By 1949 the Youngstown district ranked nineteenth among the country's industrial markets, but the state of the steel industry persuaded President Harry Truman to ask a fact-finding board to look into its wage and price structure.

1941 BUYING GUIDE

Men's work shirts, eighty-nine to ninety-eight cents.

Ladies' dress shoes, $6.75.

Ladies' girdles, $3.50.

Girls' spring frocks, $1.19.

Girls' coats, $5.98.

Beer, large glass, five cents.

Sunday dinner, full-course, one dollar.

Apples, seven pounds, twenty-five cents.

Potatoes, thirty pounds, thirty-nine cents.

Eggs, two dozen, forty-three cents.

Butter, two pounds, sixty-five cents.

Lipstick, Max Factor, one dollar.

Deodorant, Arrid cream, thirty-nine cents a jar.

Cigarettes, carton of ten packs, $1.40.

Wedding rings, fifteen dollars plus.

Engagement rings, fifty dollars plus.

Replacement watch crystal, nineteen cents.

Music lessons, fifty-five sessions, $1.25 each.

Hot water bottle, $1.50.

Heating pad, $4.95.

Venetian blinds, thirty-five cents per square foot.

Cedar chest, Lane, $27.95.

Living room suite, three pieces, $199.

Radio, RCA Victor, $99.95.

Washer, Speed Queen, $64.95.

Hot water tank, $15.75.

Refrigerator, Westinghouse, $177.95.

Sandwich grill and waffle iron, automatic, $11.95.

Buick Special, four-door sedan, $1,021. White-side-wall tires extra. State tax, optional equipment, and accessories extra.

▲ MAY 1949: A blast furnace explodes at Republic Steel, sending a plume of dense smoke over the East Side of Youngstown. Fortunately, there were no injuries.

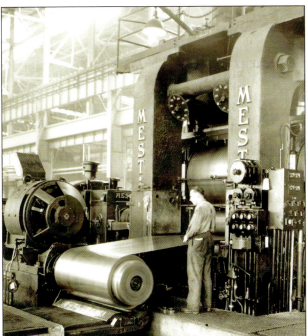

HOT STRIP MILL: ◄ Sheet steel rolls off the line at the Youngstown Sheet & Tube. Mesta Machine, a Pittsburgh company with a facility in New Castle, was an important engineering company for the steel industry.

The third nationwide steel strike in twelve years began in October 1949, and with laborers not receiving their wages and the mills not producing any goods, the effects were felt by the railroads, office personnel, retail workers, and many others in the Mahoning Valley. The Red Cross stepped in to assist steel-working war veterans who had been idled by the strike.

News from the Mahoning and Shenango Valleys

1950

APRIL 19: At a Warren junkyard, a wrecking ball destroys one hundred Jungle Inn slot machines from the closed Halls Corners den.

SEPT. 25: Smoke from Canadian forest fires darkens the area for two hours. Midnight-in-midafternoon triggers thousands of calls to THE VINDICATOR, the police, radio stations, and the weather bureau.

NOV. 28: Record twenty-eight-inch snow paralyzes the area, beginning without warning the Friday of Thanksgiving weekend. Snow damage and days of lost industrial production and retail trade cause a loss of nearly $20 million. THE VINDICATOR doesn't publish till Tuesday.

DEC. 31: Looking back on November's storm, THE VINDICATOR notes: "Entry for understatement of the year: On November 24, the Friday the Big Snow began, the weather report read 'Snow flurries...' "

1951

MAY 31: The "Man on the Monument," the seven-foot Civil War memorial on Youngstown's Central Square since 1870, falls forty-seven feet from its pedestal Memorial Day morning when firefighters bump it while decorating for the parade.

JUNE 21: In Columbiana County, more than 250 people jam a hearing to protest state plans to relocate U.S. 30, bypassing Lisbon.

OCT. 3: A ribbon of concrete finally extends from the Ohio line to Philadelphia, the first completed link of the Pennsylvania Turnpike between those two areas.

OCT. 30: A portable radar meter becomes the ally of the Youngstown Police Department in enforcing speed laws.

1952

MARCH 30: In the first "surprise" air alert, mill workers are called off the job and others are roused from bed to man Youngstown's civil-defense observation post atop the courthouse. Housewives, shopkeepers, and farmers man posts in Canfield, North Lima, and Ellsworth.

JUNE 24: Paddy Deskin, thirteen, saves Mary Ann Boyle, also thirteen, from drowning in Pleasant Valley Lake north of Church Hill. A modest hero, he keeps silent two days. Finally, he tells Mary Ann's mother when he delivers the paper.

AUG. 5: Air protection for the industrialized Mahoning Valley arrives with fifteen jet fighters of the 166th Fighter Interceptor Squadron at Youngstown Municipal Airport.

AUG. 30: Negotiators make their first deal for Ohio Turnpike right-of-way in Mahoning County–a quarter acre at the end of the Pennsylvania Turnpike. The owner, Arthur R. Koch, may get two hundred dollars.

1953

APRIL 8: Limited nighttime programming will begin in a week on WKST-TV (Channel 45) in New Castle.

SEPT. 22: The G.M. McKelvey nine win the National Amateur Baseball Federation Championship, beating Birmingham 4–0.

OCT. 1: Youngstown holds its biggest parade ever to close Ohio's five-day sesquicentennial celebration. Gov. Frank J. Lausche joins the 125 thousand who jam downtown.

OCT. 2: An electrical problem causes an F84 Thunderjet from Youngstown Air Base to accidentally strafe buildings and cars with machine-gun bullets in Farrell, Pennsylvania. No injuries.

1954

AUG. 20: Abram P. Steckel, whose development of cold-rolled and hot-rolled steel in the 1930s led to streamlined cars with solid roofs, dies at his Crandall Avenue home.

SEPT. 3: Lightning strikes Saint Columba Cathedral, causing a general-alarm fire that guts the fifty-year-old Wood Street structure and causes a loss of $1,250,000.

OCT. 22: Walter H. Sammis, Ohio Edison president, dedicates a $35 million power plant near Niles as part of the diamond jubilee of light.

1955

JUNE 12: A week-long celebration follows dedication of Youngstown's $700 thousand Jewish Community Center, already in use nearly a year. Fund drives for the North Side center began in 1944.

AUG. 11: A gas explosion and fire in Andover kills twenty-two people, injures twenty others, and causes $500,000 damage to six buildings.

AUG. 17: FBI agents and state police nab Charles (Little Mosco) Falzone, one of the FBI's ten most-wanted, in New Bedford, Pennsylvania. His wife turned him in after seeing his photo on an FBI flyer.

1956

APRIL 15: Building of the Saint Lawrence Seaway raises the possibility that Cleveland and Pittsburgh would support a Lake Erie–Ohio River waterway. A new canal appraisal would be worthwhile, THE PITTSBURGH SUN-TELEGRAPH writes.

MAY 18: State Health Director Ralph E. Dwork calls the twenty-miles of the Mahoning River from Warren to Lowellville the state's most backward area on pollution. Youngstown is the main offender.

JULY 17: NBC's "Home" show calls Youngstown a "yeasty, lusty slice of America-in-transition," with steel as its "lifeblood." The show, seen on WFMJ-TV, features Arlene Francis.

JULY 24: The Youngstown Board of Education waives a thirty-year rule barring employment of married women. Too few single women for teaching positions and other jobs, says Superintendent Paul C. Bunn.

NOV. 19: Capitalizing on a strike at the three Cleveland newspapers, thieves steal 400 VINDICATORS, 1,392 Akron papers, and 250 Canton papers, and sell them to Clevelanders for up to three dollars a copy.

1957

FEB. 8: Executives of Sharon Steel Corporation dedicate a $14 million slabbing and blooming mill at the company's Roemer Works in Farrell.

APRIL 13: Police Chief Paul H. Cress forms a seven-man squad, headed by Lt. Frank Watters, to investigate Youngstown bombings.

MAY 23: Surgeons at North Side Hospital successfully separate the Siamese-twin sons of Mr. and Mrs. William Freeman.

JULY 13: Robert S. Hay, civil defense chief, demands to know why Youngstown wasn't alerted for an imaginary bombing of the city Friday. A hydrogen bomb "hit" Youngstown at Wick and Rayen avenues in the nationwide exercise, but "take-cover" sirens didn't sound until six minutes afterward.

JULY 26: Hydrogen-sulphide gas from Youngstown Sheet & Tube and Republic Steel coke ovens discolored paint on more than forty homes in Struthers and the Colonial Home Development, says Walter I. Rauh, city air-pollution engineer.

AUG. 19: Three men escape death when single-engine planes collide in an airborne accident at Southern

Airways on U.S. 224 in Boardman.

1958

MARCH 10: In only two tries, a helicopter plants the cross on the tower of the new Saint Columba Cathedral.

APRIL 5: William R. Stewart, Youngstown's first Negro lawyer, dies at ninety-three. Stewart, born in New Castle in 1864, came to Youngstown in 1865, graduated from The Rayen School in 1883, and opened his law practice in 1886.

JULY 7: Saint Elizabeth Hospital is the scene of the first Caesarean section locally in which the mother was placed under hypnosis.

SEPT. 3: Youngstown Sheet & Tube's Bessemer plant pours its last steel after fifty-two years' service.

SEPT. 17: Traction Commissioner James W. Cannon predicts a $1 million outlay for Youngstown Transit Company buses by 1960 and elimination of trolleys within five years.

NOV. 12: Elizabeth Hauser, national leader of the women's suffrage movement and an organizer of the League of Women Voters, dies at eighty-five at her Girard home.

1959

JAN. 27: Sheet & Tube and Bethlehem Steel end a thirty-year effort to merge. The Justice Department killed proposals in 1931 and 1956.

JULY 14: A photo of three striking steelworkers at Youngstown Sheet & Tube's Campbell Works appears over a caption asking, "How Long?" Answer: 116 days. The strike idled fifty thousand workers in all.

JULY 23: Cleveland Raceways stockholders agree to sell Thistledown and Cranwood tracks to Edward J. DeBartolo, the plaza tycoon.

SEPT. 10: Mr. and Mrs. Paul Laughlin, Youngstown, drift on Lake Erie three days in a fourteen-foot boat. "Scared and hungry," they are rescued twenty-seven miles offshore.

SEPT. 19: U.S. Sen. John F. Kennedy testing the presidential waters, addresses a fund-raiser at Idora Park honoring U.S. Rep. Michael Kirwan.

NOV. 18: A day thick with tragedy: Four young men die in a two-car crash near Cortland; J. Fred Thomas, ex-Sharon mayor and state senator, and his stepdaughter die of carbon monoxide fumes; a car kills Edna Giffin, widow of Niles's first municipal judge.

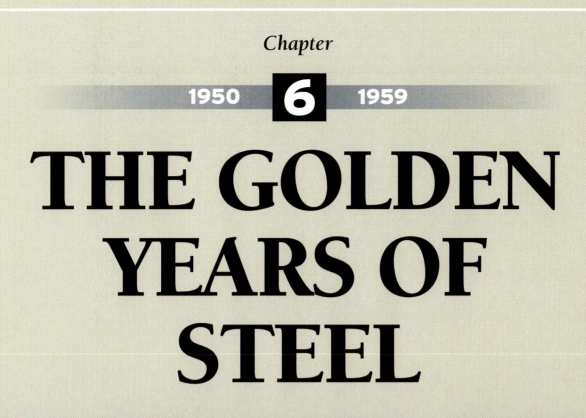

1950 **6** **1959**

THE GOLDEN YEARS OF STEEL

The Campbell Works open-hearth plant of Youngstown Sheet & Tube. Photographer Walter A. Bartz turned the photo into an oil-tinted mural fourteen feet long by seven high. Sheet & Tube presented it to Mahoning County, which had no artwork depicting steelmaking.

The red menace, civil defense, and a dirty little war in the Far East were much in the news. The steel mills boomed—when they weren't strikebound.

In mid-1954 Bethlehem Steel announced that it had proposed a merger with Youngstown Sheet & Tube, fifth largest firm in the industry…. Eisenhower's Department of Justice felt the steel industry was already too highly concentrated…. In December 1958, a federal court ultimately agreed.

PAUL A. TIFFANY
THE DECLINE OF AMERICAN STEEL: HOW MANAGEMENT, LABOR AND GOVERNMENT WENT WRONG

SEPTEMBER 1952: An aerial view shows how the steel industry and downtown Youngstown developed cheek by jowl in the Mahoning River basin. At right, Republic Steel's Bessemer plant; to the left of the Market Street Bridge is United Engineering & Foundry.

THE FIRST FIFTY YEARS OF the twentieth century in the United States had heralded the invention of the airplane, the coming of age of the automobile, the rise and fall of travel by electric street car lines, the birth and growth of truck and bus lines, the evolution of gigantic transportation networks, the advance of railroads with the streamlining of trains and development of diesel engines, and the transformation of most dirt and cobblestone streets into smooth highways of concrete and asphalt.

With the arrival of the 1950s, as the world recovered from the ravages of World War II and as the Korean war took on a life of its own, the day-to-day concerns of Americans included a growing awareness of civil defense. Additionally,

KOREAN WAR: American troops fought the communist invaders of South Korea from 1950 to 1953 as part of a U.N. task force.

A TREND TO WATCH: After the war, suburban Youngstown grew in earnest. That's Market Street in the foreground of this 1950 picture, looking west; the wishbone street is Cadillac Drive in Boardman. As the decade opened, Youngstown's population was just under 170 thousand, but the metropolitan area had grown significantly, now totaling more than 525 thousand. The city's population would fall more than forty percent by 1990.

many people grew to believe, as stated by Gen. Omar Bradley to Youngstown's Industrial Information Institute in 1950, that the U.S. must stay strong both politically and militarily to combat communism's determined worldwide fight to destroy American freedom.

In the Mahoning Valley, logical progressions from such concerns filled the 1950s, and the area capitalized on the advances of the first half century, realizing remarkable gains in the areas of communications, transportation, medicine, education, and industry.

As the decade opened, Youngstown's population, just under 170 thousand, was about the same as ten years earlier, and THE VINDICATOR reported that Youngstown's rank among the one hundred biggest U.S. cities had dropped eight places to fifty-seventh from its 1940 ranking. Still, the metropolitan district's population had grown to more than 525 thousand, a trend that showed no sign

of abating. The seeds of suburbia had been sown, and as everyone's means of communicating and getting around improved, suburbia's roots took hold not only in the soil but also in the hearts of much of the population.

Electronic Communications Advance on Every Front

As the decade began, some areas were still not a part of the telephone dialing system. North Jackson, for example, did not receive dialing capabilities until 1952. In 1953 the dialing system of two letters and five numbers was introduced, however, and three years later, Ohio Bell put direct-distance-dialing systems in operation.

As it had done since the 1920s, radio continued to connect the valley to the world beyond. In December 1951 WFMJ became an affiliate of the National Broadcasting Company and nationally syndicated programs became part of the station's regular fare.

Each evening, listeners could

read that night's radio offerings in THE VINDICATOR, and the listing of radio programs was as long as (and occasionally longer than) the television listings. Some favorites included "Fibber McGee and Molly," "The Lone Ranger," "The Lawrence Welk Show," "Truth or Consequences," "Can You Top This?" and "America's Town Meeting." Daytime radio provided such diversions as

WFMJ's transmitter tower. In 1953, it broadcast over UHF Channel 73. Channel 21 came later.

IN THE BEGINNING: Television began daily broadcasts in the Mahoning Valley in 1953. By the mid-fifties, the valley had four stations. Much of the programming was live in those days.

"The Arthur Godfrey Show," "Queen for a Day" and "The Guiding Light" (later to become one of TV's longest-running soap operas). Sports broadcasts were always popular, as were such local programs as columnist Esther Hamilton's "Talk of the Town" and Marjorie Mariner's cooking broadcast.

Better Technology and Access Ensure Television's Future

Real growth in communications came, however, in the television industry, which progressed during the 1950s through infancy and childhood. Locally, the area's fringe-area reception and status ended on the last day of 1952, when Youngstown generated its own television picture for the first time. WKBN-TV's Channel 27 televised Dwight D. Eisenhower's presidential inauguration in early 1953, and only days later, WFMJ televised its first test pattern on Ultra-High-Frequency Channel 73. Its first program, "Who was Stalin?," aired March 8.

That May WFMJ-TV sponsored the city's first TV election party, reporting returns of the primaries, and in July offered the first man-on-the-street show. On September 28, 1953, WFMJ became the city's first full-time television station, coming on air at 7 a.m. with Dave Garroway's "Today" program and signing off with a newscast at 12:05 a.m. September 29. Less than a year later, WFMJ completed its tower on the city's South Side, which the newspaper called "awe-inspiring," and moved down the dial to Channel 21.

By September 1954, WFMJ was testing color equipment in preparation for handling NBC color broadcasts, and in November, for the first time in the city's history, the three local radio stations and two TV channels combined forces to carry "Six Important Years," a program about Mayor Charles P. Henderson's years in office. WYTV appeared not long after, and for a few years, the city had a fourth television station as well, WXTV.

The fifties brought geometric growth to the transportation infrastructure throughout the country with the federal highway system. While the Mahoning Valley benefited from the road construction in Ohio, even before that it thrived on the development of a toll road in western Pennsylvania.

The day after Christmas 1951, area residents were able to roll onto the new western extension of the Pennsylvania Turnpike, and if they wanted to, they could follow it all the way to Philadelphia. Over Memorial Day weekend 1952, headlines were generated as eighteen thousand cars and trucks jammed feeder roads to the turnpike. Only a few months later, over the Labor Day weekend, an estimated eighty thousand cars clogged U.S. 224 between the Pennsylvania Turnpike and the Canfield Fairgrounds.

Ohio Turnpike Under Way; Mahoning Stretch Opens

Only a few days before the Labor Day traffic snarl, negotiators had purchased the first parcel in Mahoning County, farmland near Petersburg, for construction of Ohio's turnpike. Work began in 1953, and at the December 1954 ceremony heralding the opening of the Mahoning County portion of the highway, participants celebrated what THE VINDICATOR termed "the firmer linking of the district with rich commercial areas in the East and eventual superhighway ties with the North, South and West." By October 1955

1950: The west section of the Pennsylvania Turnpike connected Irwin, Pennsylvania, to Petersburg in Mahoning County.

JULY 20, 1956: A lone Civil Defense policeman crosses Federal Street during an air-raid drill. As the siren sounded, vehicles pulled to the side and pedestrians took cover.

the Ohio Turnpike's full length had opened, and more than a million cars had passed over its Eastgate section.

In 1956 the valley learned that the auto would have an even greater impact on day-to-day life beyond providing transportation: the manufacture of Chevrolets at a General Motors plant to be built in Lordstown would provide thousands of jobs and strengthen the economy. The announcement provided incentive to voters, who approved a bond issue that year to help finance plans for a highway innerbelt for Youngstown.

Water Services Develop Fast, But the Canal Proves Elusive

The region's access to water for transportation and domestic use also improved in the fifties, although still not in the form of the Lake Erie-to-Ohio River canal for which so many had worked and hoped for so long.

Throughout the decade, communities put in sewage-disposal systems, and in 1951 and 1952 the Mahoning Valley Sanitary District authorized the installation of equipment to add fluoride to the drinking water from Meander Reservoir. Preparations began in 1955 for a $4.9 million harbor expansion at Ashtabula in readiness for the 1959 opening of the Saint

Lawrence Seaway.

The dark side of the water equation manifested itself in January 1959 as the Youngstown district endured the worst flooding it had experienced since the catastrophe of 1913. When the Mahoning and Shenango rivers and their tributaries overflowed, the surging waters caused some $20 million in losses, left thousands homeless and temporarily idled from jobs, and led to states of emergency in Warren, Newton Falls, Leetonia,

JANUARY 24, 1959: The worst flood since 1913 hits Youngstown. On Andrews Avenue, a stranded worker gets a lift to dry land.

CIVIL DEFENSE ON LAND AND IN THE AIR

DEVELOPING skyways were also making their mark throughout the country, and defense concerns in the 1950s led to construction of a ten-million-dollar air base at Youngstown Municipal Airport in Vienna, as well as civil-defense training and preparation at every level of the population. On occasion, mock air raids were conducted in conjunction with statewide alerts.

IN 1951 General Fireproofing announced plans to build a $1.5 million addition to its plant to produce parts for jet fighters and bombers. Such developments were embraced by a populace that had just learned that twenty-four men from the Youngstown district listed as missing in action in Korea were, according to the North Korean communists, being held as prisoners of war.

FIVE YEARS after the Air Force opened its base, headlines heralded the first Delta Dagger to arrive there, flying in from Dayton's Wright-Patterson Air Force Base in only fifteen minutes. Such neighbors also brought risks, however: In April 1959, an F102A Delta Dagger from the Youngstown base crashed into Lake Erie, killing the lieutenant aboard, and again in June a Dagger crashed, that one on take-off from the air base. Although the two crewmen escaped injury in that accident, the Air Force announced in October that the squadron would be deactivated.

BOARDMAN PLAZA, 1959: High water overflows into the plaza parking lot.

Sharon, and New Castle. Meadville, too, experienced hard times as French Creek overran its banks.

Out of the flood waters, however, came a positive development for the future: the final impetus for the successful congressional fight by U.S. Rep. Michael J. Kirwan to include in federal legisla-

tion money for the West Branch Reservoir and Shenango River Dam. The allocations came through a public-works bill that passed over President Eisenhower's veto, the first Eisenhower veto to be overridden by Congress.

In 1955 the trustees of Youngstown College, desiring to keep

pace with the institution's continuing departmental expansion, voted to change its name to Youngstown University.

Two years later, the university decided to discontinue its School of Law upon the graduation of the current students.

That program, one of the first of the collection of classes that eventually evolved into Youngstown College (popularly known as YoCo), had begun under the auspices of the YMCA nearly forty years earlier. By the end of the decade, the university had added the School of Education to its menu of offerings.

The Mahoning Valley's steel mills and supporting industries found themselves very busy as the decade began, but, as in the past, the availability of coal, industrial gas, trains, manpower, water, and customers, whether because of cold or strikes or drought or de-

MEDICINE: A SCOURGE VANQUISHED

AS THEY HAD for generations, mothers and fathers dreaded the arrival of July as the fifties began because it was the month that generally ushered in the year's first cases of poliomyelitis.

In the summer of 1951, Youngstown recorded seventeen cases of the scourge, the highest in city history, and Mahoning County registered fifty-four cases, likewise an all-time high. Three of the afflicted died, the first polio deaths in the district in six years. In 1952 polio took the life of yet another victim. In August 1953 the district recorded its first case in years of the virulent bulbar strain of polio, and four people succumbed to the disease that year.

FAMILIES REJOICED In 1955 to learn that a vaccine developed by Jonas Salk had proved safe, and that April the first doses were administered locally. Although isolated cases were reported over the next few years, the threat of infantile paralysis would never again terrify people

in quite the same way.

New research in cancer was focused in Youngstown in 1955 as three researchers developed a test based on the optical density of blood serum.

ALONG WITH THOSE positive developments, the decade brought growth to the area's hospital facilities. Woodside Receiving Hospital, named for Probate Judge Clifford M. Woodside, opened in 1952 with Gov. Frank L. Lausche performing as master of ceremonies at the dedication. Over the course of the decade, Saint Elizabeth's and the Youngstown Hospital Association built additions to their facilities totaling more than $7 million. None of which suggests that people no longer took ill. In October 1957 an epidemic of Asian flu laid people low. Some schools re-

1955: The microbiologist Jonas Salk in his Pittsburgh laboratory.

ported more than fifty percent of their students and teachers under the weather. Parochial schools were ordered closed, and police received orders to chase children from downtown.

▲ LONG STRIKE: Morris J. White, Jr., Frank Wilson, and Stephen Sanders wait out the 116-day steel strike of 1959 at the Campbell Works of Youngstown Sheet & Tube.

⋙⋘

JULY 1956: Picket duty at Republic Steel. ▶ That year's strike targets also included Sheet & Tube, Truscon, Commercial Shearing, General Fireproofing, Westinghouse, Bessemer Cement, and WKBN.

mand, affected the day-to-day operations of the steel mills. Such fluctuations often swelled the ranks of the unemployed.

On April 8, 1952, the first volley of a Ping-Pong match between labor and Washington began as leaders of fifty-five thousand C.I.O. steelworkers completed their plans for a strike, only to have President Truman announce the next day that he was seizing the mills, an action that meant area employees of the basic-steel industry had to troop back to work.

Trapped Between the Union, A President, and the Courts

Three weeks later, a judge in Federal District Court ruled Truman's seizure unconstitutional. The following day, however, the Federal Court of Appeals voted to once again restore government control of the industry. On June 2 the steelworkers left the plants for the third time in two months after the United States Supreme Court upheld the initial ruling, and the mills were yet again returned to private ownership.

In July, four thousand applica-

tions had been filed for unemployment benefits. The fifty-four-day strike ended with an agreement July 26. There would be many other strikes in the decade; the longest, 116 days, in the summer and fall of 1959, would end when President Eisenhower invoked the Taft-Hartley Act and the Supreme Court upheld his injunction.

SOUTHWARD BOUND: A long train leaving Youngstown Sheet & Tube in 1955 carries pipe destined for Venezuelan oil fields.

Although World War II was by now old news and the Korean conflict would come to an uneasy peace in 1953, the defense industry was already growing into big business, and steel needed for defense jobs rolled out of valley mills whenever they were operating.

In the Mid-Fifties, Booming Mills, Industrial Expansion

Frank Purnell, Sheet & Tube's chairman of the board and a company man from way back, announced March 6, 1953, that he would resign April 28. Honored on March 10 by an estimated 850 people as Youngstown's Foremost Citizen, he died March 19 at the age of sixty-six, 5½ weeks before his scheduled retirement.

What THE VINDICATOR termed "record prosperity" came in 1955. That year, signs of prosperous times were repeated in page-one stories from month to month as more and more companies announced expansion programs, the steel rate climbed, unemployment decreased, and the city's capital-improvement projects began to take shape. The Youngs-

SEPTEMBER 1955: Kimmelbrook Homes brought to the East Side low-rent housing on a par with Westlake Housing Village, opened on the Northwest Side fifteen years earlier.

town Sheet & Tube Company reported that 1955 was its best year in history in earnings, sales, production, and shipment of steel products. The good fortune spilled over into the Youngstown Community Chest's annual collection for charity, which exceeded its goal for only the second time in nearly a decade.

Unions Strike Steel Plants, Commercial, and Others

The good times lived closely with the bad, however. The valley's hold on fourth place in steel production slipped in 1955 to eight percent of the national total, compared with 8.8 percent a year earlier. Strikes were a frequently used means of protest.

During 1956, for example, strikes hit Youngstown Sheet & Tube's Campbell Works, Commercial Shearing & Stamping, General Fireproofing, Westinghouse Electric in Sharon, Truscon Steel Division of Republic, Bessemer Limestone & Cement (the first strike in that company's history), many of the building trades, and WKBN Broadcasting.

On December 11, 1956, Sheet & Tube and Bethlehem Steel announced that they would merge, the result of ongoing talks that had first come to the public's attention more than two years earlier, and during which Sheet & Tube had indicated that such a

merger would put $150 million into district Sheet & Tube plants.

Immediately, the U.S. Justice Department moved to block the consolidation as a violation of antitrust laws, and nearly two years later, on November 20, 1958, a U.S. District Court judge in New York City rejected the proposed merger. Sheet & Tube, meanwhile had moved its corporate offices out of the heart of the steel valley, over a ridge and into a new building in Boardman.

REPUBLIC STEEL 1959: Flames from a Bessemer converter bathe the converter building in an unearthly glow. Republic's Bessemers produced nearly one hundred tons of steel hourly. Specially built rail cars took molten iron from the blast furnaces to the converters through a tunnel beneath a maze of railroads.

The last few years of the decade, right up to the last months, were marked by high unemployment in steel and related industries.

At one point in 1958, a lack of orders slowed production at U.S. Steel and elsewhere to forty-seven percent, and in March of that year claims for state unemployment were the highest since World War II and among the highest in history. But then in November 1959, ironmaking rose to its highest level in three years as Sheet & Tube put the seventh of its seven blast furnaces into production.

Two Tornadoes, a Drought, And the Snow of Snows

Colorful and splintering accents to this whole mosaic of life in the Mahoning Valley of the nineteen fifties were provided by the people, weather, recreation, social issues, and, of course, crime and politics.

Tragedies could be found almost daily in the paper. A random selection from 1953 includes THREE GIRARD CHILDREN BURN IN HOME AS MOTHER WATCHES FROM STREET; 13-YEAR-OLD SHOOTS HIS SISTER AND SELF IN THEIR LONELY HOME NEAR GUILFORD LAKE; 10-YEAR-OLD GIVES BIRTH TO FIVE-POUND, 14½-OUNCE BABY AT FLORENCE CRITTENDON HOME; and BRIDE OF TWO MONTHS FOUND STRANGLED IN HER HOUSE; HUSBAND DIES SIX HOURS LATER OF SELF-INFLICTED WOUNDS.

Weather, too, disturbed the peace on occasion. The record-breaking twenty-eight-inch snow of November 25, 1950, marked the only time, excepting the 1964 strike, that THE VINDICATOR went unpublished. The snow paralyzed the entire region for nearly three days and imposed a loss of $20 million from structural damage, business closings, and curtailment of industrial production.

A flooding rain in May 1953 was followed by a drought that reduced farms, gardens, and lawns to almost rock-like hardness by Au-

PHELPS STREET 1950: Cars weren't going anywhere in twenty-eight inches of snow.

gust, THE VINDICATOR reported.

The drought also ushered in the longest heat wave in twenty years. When the rains finally came the following April, they raised the level of Meander Reservoir 15½ inches in twenty-four hours.

In March 1955 three tornadic storms blasted through the region in twenty-two days—one on the city's East Side, a second in rural Columbiana County near Leetonia, and the third through Poland, Struthers, rural Mahoning, and Columbiana counties, and the Ravenna Arsenal. The loss for three weeks of calamity: nearly $3 million. In August 1956 two more tornadoes blasted across Mahoning and Trumbull counties, and that time two persons died.

FRANK R. FRANKO

The newspaper often carried stories of bank robberies, safecrackings, robbers, and people bound and gagged in their own homes while intruders looked for money. Bombings and mysterious explosions peppered the local and national news (sixty-five over ten years, thirty-two in 1954 alone), with reports of racketeering, gambling, and organized crime lurking in the shadows, as in POLAND COUNTRY CLUB PADLOCKED, and CLUB 18, NOTORIOUS BOOKIE JOINT, ORDERED CLOSED.

Perhaps the most curious political figure of the decade was Frank R. Franko, a municipal judge. In 1957 the Mahoning County Bar Association sought disciplinary action against him on allegations of violating the judicial code of ethics.

Among other offenses, it was alleged that Franko did not mark violations on driver's licenses to obtain political favors. The Board of Commissioners on Grievances and Discipline recommended that Franko be suspended indefinitely from practicing law, and the Ohio Supreme Court adopted that recommendation. In 1959 the Supreme Court of the United States refused to hear Franko's appeal, causing him to lose his judgeship.

Interestingly, come November 1959, Youngstown witnessed one of the most acrimonious campaigns in its history when that very same Frank R. Franko, having campaigned on the Democratic ticket, emerged as the new mayor of Youngstown.

News from the Mahoning and Shenango Valleys

1960

FEB. 9: The State Water Pollution Board refuses to renew Youngstown's permit to dump raw sewage into the Mahoning River.

AUG. 11: Vincent Innocenzi, 29, a key suspect in safecrackings and underworld unrest in Youngstown, turns up dead in an Akron woods.

SEPT. 26: First United Presbyterian Church, oldest in the Western Reserve, dedicates $1,160,000 building on Wick Avenue at Wood Street.

OCT. 10: From atop the Tod Hotel marquee, John F. Kennedy, Democratic presidential candidate, pushes his "New Frontier" in a speech to thousands on Central Square.

OCT. 22: Fire damages the paint and finishing departments of General American Transportation Corporation's tanker plant in Masury.

OCT. 29: An Arctic Pacific charter that had transported the Youngstown University football team earlier in the day crashes on takeoff later in the day in Toledo, killing twenty-two, including members of the California Polytechnic football team.

1961

MAY 26: A gas well drilled on a Smith Township farm in Mahoning County may produce 2.5 million cubic feet daily. At 8,031 feet, it is the deepest ever drilled in Ohio.

MAY 27: U.S. Rep. Michael Kirwan is one of three hosts for a birthday party for President Kennedy, who turns forty-four May 29.

JULY 17: A bomb kills racketeer Vince DeNiro when he switches on the ignition of his 1961 convertible on busy Market Street.

AUG. 3: U.S. Atty. Gen. Robert F. Kennedy, "very familiar" with Youngstown crime, promises action on the wave of gangland bombings.

AUG. 26: Five engines and thirty-seven cars of a Pennsylvania freight derail in East Palestine. Several land on Royal China Company.

NOV. 22: Niles hails its state champion football team, the McKinley High Red Dragons, with a parade.

1962

MAY 4: U.S. Steel Corporation to lay off 550 workers, twenty percent of its McDonald force. Customers hedging against a strike cancelled big orders when it didn't take place.

MAY 21: The Youngstown Board of Education appoints the city's first

Negro principal, James Ervin, to head Hillman Junior High School.

SEPT. 27: A state probe of Youngstown's 1960-61 payroll unearths a phantom water-department worker. The invisible man never missed a payday in fourteen months.

SEPT. 29: Ex-president Harry Truman addresses a Democratic Party rally at Idora Park. The next morning, he has to hitch a ride to the airport with a VINDICATOR reporter.

NOV. 30: The Renner Company, Youngstown's only brewery, suspends operation under an agreement with Old Crown Brewing of Fort Wayne, Indiana.

1963

FEB. 3: Intruders set a $702 thousand fire at the Youngstown Club in the Union National Bank Building. WFMJ-TV televises the fire live.

JULY 15: "None of us can afford to ignore the pressing problems of minority groups," U.S. Atty. Gen. Robert F. Kennedy tells Slovak Catholic Sokols at Hotel Pick-Ohio. Kennedy cites THE VINDICATOR'S record for morality and right.

SEPT. 22: In remarks for a Jefferson-Jackson Day dinner at Beaver Local High School, Vice President Lyndon B. Johnson says U.S. "leadership depends not only upon our strength but upon the example we set for the rest of the world."

SEPT. 24: Dr. Homer J. Holier, a scientist who worked on the atomic bomb, dies at seventy-three in Canfield. An expert on corrosion, he developed cathodic metal protection.

OCT. 24: Youngstown is one of 177 U.S. centers for an illegal auto-repair scheme, the U.S. Justice Department says.

1964

JAN. 16: Dropping the time of day from postmarks February 1 should save many man-hours, says Chester W. Bailey, Youngstown postmaster.

MARCH 2: The rush by speculators to collect oil and gas leases in rural Trumbull County continues unabated. Acreage under lease doubles.

JUNE 8: One hundred thirty-three boys and girls open summer Fresh Air Camp on Wilkinson Avenue.

SEPT. 2: Police, Youngstown officials, school administrators, and school board members plan to fight rowdyism on football nights.

OCT. 9: Vatican Council change:

Diocesan priests may now celebrate Mass facing the congregation, Bishop Emmet Walsh says.

NOV. 12: More than three hundred at the Pick-Ohio help Youngstown Rotary celebrate its fiftieth year.

1965

JAN. 12: The first bargaining meeting since November 19 takes place between THE VINDICATOR and the Youngstown Newspaper Guild.

JAN. 15: At the Pick-Ohio, industry and business thank General Motors Corporation for forty-eight hundred jobs and $5 million in new income.

FEB. 11: The L.A. Beeghlys give their Market Street homestead and $1 million in foundation money to Youngstown Hospital Association.

MAY 10: Randall Gardner walked away from an Alabama prison camp in 1943, but he has lived a normal life since. Judge Don L. Hanni lets him go, citing his fine work record.

NOV. 21: S. Sgt. Robert G. Wright, son of Mrs. Virginia Wright, becomes the first Youngstown serviceman killed in the Vietnam war.

1966

FEB. 21: Her role in "A Patch of Blue" wins ex-Youngstowner Elizabeth Hartman an Academy Award nomination for best actress.

APRIL 26: The Chevrolet Division of General Motors rolls its first car off the Lordstown assembly line.

MAY 22: The Coitsville Township home of William H. McGuffey will be a national historic landmark.

JULY 20: The state summons Youngstown's National Guard unit to Cleveland to help suppress racial rioting in the Hough district.

1967

FEB. 16: A single-engine plane crashes at Youngstown Municipal Airport, killing two Illinois men, the airport's first fatalities.

MARCH 16: Trumbull County dairymen dump milk into fields as the National Farmers Organization withholds milk to force a price rise.

APRIL 17: Franz Bibo, past conductor of the New York City Symphony and Oberlin College Orchestra, becomes conductor of the Youngstown Philharmonic Orchestra.

SEPT. 26: Under police escort, two trucking-company convoys pick up steel at Youngstown Sheet & Tube's Campbell Works, igniting sniper fire

in Mahoning County and leading to the arrest of three independent steel haulers in Trumbull County.

1968

FEB. 8: The Warner Theater will close Feb. 21. It opened in May 1931 as a Warner family hometown memorial to Sam Warner, founder of Warner Brothers Hollywood studio.

APRIL 10: Fire-bombings, window-smashing, and the wounding of a thirteen-year-old boy mark Youngstown's second night of civil unrest after the April 4 killing of the Rev. Martin Luther King.

SEPT. 27: Joe Flynn, star of television's "McHale's Navy," speaks of life and friendships in his hometown at the kickoff of the United Appeal at Hotel Pick-Ohio.

NOV. 11: Rose Mary Wood, formerly of Sebring, will continue to serve as Richard Nixon's secretary when he becomes president.

NOV. 14: The 184-room Tod Hotel closes its doors, a casualty of urban renewal, after nearly one hundred years on Central Square.

DEC. 3: Dr. Samuel H. Sheppard's resignation from Youngstown Osteopathic Hospital last Nov. 21 is announced as news breaks that his second wife is suing for divorce. In 1966, a court-ordered retrial absolved the surgeon of the 1954 killing of his first wife, Marilyn.

1969

MARCH 14: With approval of a $120 thousand guiding permit, Youngstown State University may have its FM radio station on air by June.

SEPT. 20: A Hubbard ironworker, John J. Sawaska, 26, is killed during labor strife at the building site of the Fisher Body plant in Lordstown.

SEPT. 21: The restored Warner Theater reopens as the Youngstown Symphony Center with a presentation of "Die Fledermaus" by the Youngstown Symphony Society.

OCT. 28: Members of the Fraternal Association of Steel Haulers confront a Teamster truck escort at the Poland Avenue gates of Republic Steel and burn the car of John Angelo, Local 377 secretary-treasurer. One Teamster is shot to death.

NOV. 22: Two hundred Negroes storm New Castle City Hall after a teen dance at the YM/YWCA was prematurely closed due to "minor incidents." Fourteen are arrested.

1960 **7** 1969

DEATH BY UNNATURAL CAUSES

OCTOBER 1960: Thousands packed West Federal Street, straining against police lines, as John F. Kennedy brought his presidential campaign to Youngstown. Kennedy was in a fierce race with Republican Richard Nixon, and the valley's Democratic vote was crucial.

The post-industrial age had arrived, and service industries were on the rise. Changing markets at home and abroad spelled trouble for the industrial giants.

1960: American physicist Theodore H. Maiman demonstrates first successful laser.

• Soviets shoot down Gary Powers and U-2 spy plane.

1961: Bay of Pigs invasion.

• Construction of Berlin Wall.

1962: School prayer violates First Amendment, U.S. Supreme Court rules.

1963: JFK assassinated.

• Medgar Evers, NAACP leader, assassinated.

• Martin Luther King's "I have a dream" speech.

1964: U.S. surgeon general declares cigarette smoking a health hazard.

• Gen. William Westmoreland appointed to command U.S. forces in South Vietnam.

1965: Nicolae Ceausescu becomes leader of Romania.

• Malcolm X assassinated.

• Medicare and Medicaid established.

1966: Edward Brooke of Massachusetts becomes first African-American elected to U.S. Senate.

• American Surveyor I makes first soft landing on the moon.

1967: U.S. astronauts die on launch pad.

• First successful human heart transplant performed.

• Radio astronomers locate first pulsar.

1968: MLK assassinated.

• RFK assassinated.

• Viet Cong launches Tet Offensive.

1969: Americans ▶ Neil Armstrong and Buzz Aldrin are first men to land on the moon.

American life in the…1960s displayed a new face. It featured plastics and Pampers, suburbs and supermarkets, environmentalism and ecology, aerobics and robotics. It was an age of interstate highways and fast-food restaurants, motels and discount houses, television and computers, nuclear power and aerospace exploration, shopping centers and health spas.

EUGENE MURDOCK
THE BUCKEYE EMPIRE:
AN ILLUSTRATED HISTORY OF OHIO ENTERPRISE

DOWNTOWN: Youngstown's Central Square as it appeared in the summer of 1968.

AS EVIDENCE THAT the 1950s shift to suburbia had made its mark on the Mahoning Valley, Youngstown's population ranking slipped from fifty-eighth to seventy-fifth among U.S. cities as the 1960s began. Yet in the previous ten years, Columbiana County's population had increased nearly eight percent, Mahoning County's nearly fifteen percent, and Trumbull County's nearly twenty-five percent, and the populations of Austintown and Boardman townships had doubled. The post-industrial age had arrived, and "service" industries were on the rise. Changing markets

VIETNAM 1969: A helicopter deposits a 155mm howitzer on a Vietnamese hilltop during a war that divided the U.S. almost as badly as Vietnam itself.

GM—THE EARLY DAYS: Construction of the Lordstown plant of General Motors was the economic high point of the sixties, and the automaker would become the preeminent Mahoning Valley industry as the sun set on the steel mills a decade later. The first car rolled off the line April 28, 1966. The valley was proud the next year as the Lordstown work force completed its 500,000th Pontiac Firebird.

at home and abroad spelled trouble for the industrial giants.

As interstates continued to spread across the country, the downtown areas of cities began to wither as more and more people chose to shop closer to their suburban homes. Criminal activities earned Youngstown the nicknames "Little Chicago" and "Murdertown," and raids on the high-stakes Turkish dice game barbut, numbers booking, and bombings repeatedly splashed across THE VINDICATOR'S front pages.

The Industrial Landscape Changes in a Promising Way

Yet despite such turbulence, the Mahoning Valley rejoiced because General Motors was building a car plant at Lordstown and projecting eventual employment of fifty-seven hundred.

The tumultuous sixties were under way: after the stands for civil rights, the assassinations of John and Robert Kennedy and Martin Luther King, Jr., the anti-war demonstrations, the Apollo 11 mission to the moon and countless other events, the country and the Mahoning Valley would never be the same.

Tough economic times, meanwhile, meant a decade sprinkled with urban-renewal projects and federal grants. By 1969 welfare problems had produced demands from recipients for more and better services; the protests came in typical sixties fashion: sit-ins.

In 1965 the newspaper reported the first deaths of regional boys in the Vietnam War; Youngstown, like the rest of the nation, found itself facing turmoil brought on by opposition to the war and a new social awareness that zeroed in on civil rights, desegregation, and women's liberation.

After the assassination of the Rev. Martin Luther King, Jr., in April 1968 Youngstown's South Side exploded with such violent civil unrest for three days that the Ohio National Guard was called in

▲ **APRIL 10, 1968:** A woman passes by under the watchful eyes of national guardsmen who were sent in to restore order after blacks rioted on Youngstown's South Side.

◄ **JULY 17, 1969:** Youngstown's South Side erupts in violence a second time. Rioters overturned this car and set it afire.

BULLETS, BOMBS, AND BAD GUYS—AND EVIDENCE THAT GREW LEGS

THE VINDICATOR reported in 1960 that crime had "surged ahead thirty percent during the year," twenty percent beyond the national increase.

THAT YEAR, gangland guns roared, killing a rackets kingpin, S. Joseph ("Sandy") Naples, and his girlfriend, Mary Ann Vrancich, on the porch of her home; wounding gambler Joseph Romano on Tod Lane; and liquidating a Coitsville hood, John ("Big John") Schuller, as he fixed a purposely deflated tire near Vienna in Trumbull County. Later

SANDY NAPLES

on, in Warren, Mike Farah, a racketeer and gambling czar of long standing and considerable influence, took a direct hit from a shotgun blast one sunny Saturday morning as he chipped golf shots on his front lawn on the Southeast Side. In none of those killings was anyone ever brought to trial. In 1961, the newspaper reported that the district bombing

JULY 2, 1962: A derrick lifts the crumpled garage roof from a car still containing the body of William ("Billy") Naples, who was killed by a bomb on Youngstown's North Side when he switched on the car's ignition.

total had risen to seventy-six in ten years. Six more bombings occurred in 1962. There had been five bomb-related fatalities in the previous four years, one an eleven-year-old girl.

IN SEPTEMBER 1962, Joseph ("Little Joey") Naples, who would himself come to a bullet-riddled end years later, was among a group of men secretly indicted on thirty-three felony counts, mostly for booking bets in the illegal numbers lottery. A couple of months later, shortly after the gambling trial began, state's evidence in the case mysteriously vanished from the courtroom. Despite the setback, the prosecution

JOEY NAPLES

won, and Joey Naples was found guilty of receiving stolen goods and promoting the numbers game, although he was found not guilty of illegally possessing a submachine gun. Naples drew two terms in the state penitentiary, for two-to-seven years and one-to-ten years.

BY 1963 the U.S. Department of Justice had entered the fray, investigating racketeering and crime in Youngstown. The situation didn't improve as the decade progressed; the grand jury expressed "an alarm of urgency" in 1969 for an all-out war on narcotics in Mahoning County.

1961: Vince DeNiro, another of the city's journeyman racketeers, died when an ignition bomb shredded his car outside a bar in the Uptown district of Market Street one night.

1962: Pope John XXIII greets the auxiliary bishop of Youngstown, the Most Reverend James W. Malone, D.D., at the Vatican. In spring 1968 another pope, Paul VI, elevated the auxiliary to bishop of Youngstown.

and a curfew imposed. In the summer of 1969, violence flared anew, that time on the East Side as well as the South Side. The riot produced curfews, liquor bans, and martial law. When things died down, nine had been injured and twenty-six arrested. New Castle, Pennsylvania, had similar violence.

With the rest of the country, the Mahoning Valley endured a telephone strike in April 1968, and shortly thereafter a strike by the Youngstown Transit Company left the area without bus service.

Here as elsewhere, young people called for an end to the Vietnam war and held moratoriums, while others criticized the demonstrators and accused them of giving aid and comfort to the enemy. The area did enjoy some bright spots: in the spring of 1968 Pope Paul VI named the Most Reverend James W. Malone, D.D., the third bishop of Youngstown, and THE VINDICATOR changed to a larger typeface for improved readability.

The Hurly-Burly of Politics: Anyone Seen Frank Lately?

Nineteen-sixty was "a whacky year for local politicians," THE VINDICATOR said. Voting machines blew fuses at the primaries that May, and Democrats won all the seats on Youngstown City Council that November for the first time.

The lawyer Harry N. Savasten, a Republican, won Youngstown's mayoral election in 1961, ousting Frank R. Franko, who, having served only one term, found himself immersed in legal difficulties, trying to explain mysterious and questionable time he had spent away from the mayor's office. Although Savasten spent only one term in the office, he raised a curious issue by asking in March 1963 for an investigation of forty thousand parking tickets that went unpaid in 1962.

1960: John F. Kennedy, speaking here from the marquee of the Tod Hotel, visited the valley several times in his presidential bid.

OCTOBER 1960: Among the thousands packed into the square, Kennedy found receptive ears for his New Frontier platform.

1968: Vice President Hubert Humphrey brought his presidential hopes to town.

Making headlines in 1962 was a tax irregularity uncovered by a Canfield lawyer. Nils P. Johnson filed suit for his mother, asserting that the county budget commission did not follow the law and reduce tax rates in proportion to increases in property valuations.

The lawsuit followed protests by hundreds of taxpayers during collection of the first-half 1961 property taxes. Johnson estimated that the tax bill averaged nine percent too high for all of Mahoning County, with residents of some townships overcharged as much as forty percent.

Kirwan, in His Thirteenth Term, Still Pushes for Canal

In November 1963 the Democrats swept city elections, installing Anthony B. Flask in the mayor's office. Flask, a beverage distributor, would go on to win second and third terms. The Republicans rebounded in 1969, regaining control of Youngstown government with the election of Jack C. Hunter as mayor and a Republican majority to City Council.

For Michael J. Kirwan, 1960 produced a thirteenth congressional term. The following year, he asked that a survey for the Lake Erie-to-Ohio River canal be expedited and took time out from his official duties to play host to President John F. Kennedy's birthday party. Kirwan's persistence gained the canal project a recommendation from the U.S. Corps of Engineers in 1965,

and canal approval and appropriations were moving through Congress a year later. Believing his goals accomplished, Kirwan announced he would retire in 1970, after having been elected in 1968 to a seventeenth term.

Although its political prominence had diminished, the Mahoning Valley merited visits from several national figures as the 1968 presidential campaign progressed: Hubert Humphrey, the Democratic candidate; two vice presidential candidates, Edmund S. Muskie and Spiro T. Agnew; Humphrey's son, and a daughter of Richard M. Nixon, the Republican presidential candidate.

Elsewhere in the news, Channel 45, WXTV, went dark in 1962, the VINDICATOR spelling champion placed third in national competition in Washington, and Youngstown's Hotel Pick-Ohio closed its Purple Cow coffee shop because of "declining business and undesirable loiterers." Then, in 1963, the Voyager Motor Inn opened across from the courthouse, where old Westminster Church once stood.

In 1966 Gov. James A. Rhodes invited Youngstown University into the state system of higher education, and the school officially became Youngstown State University in 1967. Later that year, the uni-

versity dedicated its $1.75 million Ward Beecher Science Hall.

As the cost of private hospital rooms increased to thirty-four dollars a day from thirty-two dollars in 1966, a change in the landscape south of Youngstown loomed as L. A. Beeghly gave money and his Boardman estate to the Youngstown Hospital Association for development of a Boardman unit. By the close of 1968, YHA rooms had

1967: Youngstown University joins the state system of higher education, becoming Youngstown State University.

ILLUSTRIOUS PAST, NO FUTURE: In the early days, one could catch a vaudeville act there. After that, first-run films. Then, in summer 1964, the venerable Keith-Albee Palace on Wick Avenue came down to make way for a mall and Cinerama theater that were never built.

risen to forty-six dollars and fifty-three dollars a day.

The slipping economy and the migration of consumers away from Youngstown's central business district meant that public entities dependent upon city tax revenue suffered, especially the educational system.

Failure of School Tax Issues Produces Drastic Economies

By 1967 the starting salary for a teacher in the Youngstown Public Schools had increased to $5,800 a year, but a year later, a tax levy went down to defeat for the sixth time, causing the schools to close from Thanksgiving through Christmas because of financial difficulties. Other high schools in the region dropped spring sports when tax issues in their districts failed. The crisis in education prompted THE VINDICATOR to publish a front-page editorial on New Year's Day 1969 urging the public to pass a school levy.

In what the newspaper termed "one of the major philanthropic moves here in recent years," Mr. and Mrs. Edward W. Powers purchased the Warner Theater in September 1968 and presented the downtown treasure to the Youngstown Symphony Society for use as its new home.

GET YOUR KICKS... : Actors Martin Milner and George Maharis of CBS-TV's "Route 66" rolled into Youngstown in 1961 to film three episodes of the popular adventure series. Some townspeople got a moment in the sun as extras in the filming.

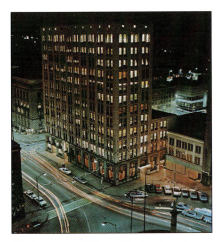

1960s: As population shifts to the suburbs, plazas and malls eat away at downtown commerce. This is southwest Central Square and the Mahoning Bank Building.

Earlier that year, on Valentine's Day, area residents had welcomed the opening of a seventeen thousand-square-foot skating rink and lodge house at the James L. Wick Recreation Area in Mill Creek Park.

At the end of summer 1964, THE VINDICATOR encountered problems of its own; a strike by newsroom, circulation, and classified-advertising employees lasted until April 1965. And in 1966 the valley struggled as garbage collectors, street and water crews, and city employees went on strike in July, as Youngstown teachers went on strike at Thanksgiving, and as nurses, policemen, and firefighters struck in December.

Labor unrest in September 1969 led to the shooting death of a Hubbard ironworker at the construction site of the Fisher Body stamping plant in Lordstown, and a Cleveland man was slain the following month as members of two Teamster factions clashed at the Stop Five gate of Republic Steel Corporation. The two deaths led to investigations by the federal government and a Mahoning County grand jury.

Addition of Two Reservoirs Achieves Flood-Control Goal

The decade also brought more water resources and better flood control. Ground was broken in 1960 for Mercer County's Shenango Reservoir and Sharpsville dam, and construction of the $14.5 million West Branch Reservoir in Portage County began in 1962. With those in place, the area had finally tamed the Mahoning and Shenango flood plains.

OCTOBER 1969: Hostility between the Teamsters union and Fraternal Association of Steel Haulers boiled over when FASH members confronted Teamster-driven trucks on Poland Avenue. One man was killed and eight were injured. No one was ever prosecuted for the killing, but ten men later received fines and suspended jail terms arising from the riot.

At the dawn of the 1960s, the local steel industry endured economically wretched conditions as the Mahoning Valley began to realize that its steel plants had grown obsolete in the face of declining markets. Growing foreign competition was blamed for causing a "steel recession" here.

Manufacturing Jobs Decline; Sheet & Tube, Lykes Merge

Although for a brief period in 1961 the operating rate of the steel mills hit sixty-eight percent, the highest in more than a year, unemployment hit ten percent the next year. As a result, the area received $3 million in federal assistance for public-works projects. For the twenty-seven-month period from May 1960 through September 1962, manufacturing jobs in the Youngstown-Warren market declined 19.6 percent.

THE VINDICATOR declared 1963 "a comeback year for steel" as it reported on the automakers' best year since 1955 and steel's best year since 1957. The Youngstown Sheet & Tube recorded a fifty-six-percent increase in earnings over 1962 at the three-quarter mark, the most profitable nine-month period in six years. Sheet & Tube again became the subject of merg-

er talk in 1969 as it was being courted by two different companies, Avnet, Incorporated, of New York and Lykes Corporation of New Orleans. Lykes opposed the idea of Sheet & Tube's merging with Avnet, and at first Sheet & Tube declined the invitation to merge with Lykes. But by May the issue had been resolved, giving birth to the Lykes-Youngstown Corporation. Construction of the Lordstown division of General Mo-

1966: Charging hot metal in an open hearth at Republic Steel. The sixties brought the unsettling realization that area steelmaking facilities were showing their age.

CROSSING THE MILES

NETWORK: The Ohio and Pennsylvania turnpikes, I-80/76, Ohio 11, and many beltways make the area a valuable transportation hub.

MOVING FROM town to town by automobile around the Mahoning Valley, and to and from the world beyond, became much easier during the sixties.

As the decade began, so did the building of the "Mahoning-Market Expressway," a part of what we know today as Interstate 680, and ground was broken in 1963 near Wheatland, Pennsylvania, for the "Keystone Shortway." Forty-seven more miles of Interstate 80, from Hubbard to Emlenton, Pennsylvania, were opened In 1967 by Govs. James A. Rhodes and Raymond P. Shafer.

TRAINS REMAINED critical to the movement of raw and finished materials to and through the valley, but sometimes accidents made headlines. In a two-week period in 1961, East Palestine was the location of three train derailments that involved sixty-eight railroad cars and five diesel locomotives.

In 1963 the Air Force expanded operations at Youngstown Municipal Airport in Vienna with the new 910th Troop Carrier Group. The strength of the carrier group was increased four years later, but people worried when plans to close it were discussed. The valley breathed a sigh of relief when those plans were dropped in 1968.

JANUARY 1961: Youngstown Sheet & Tube tests an oxygen-jet converter at its Campbell open hearths. Converters were cost-effective and efficient, but upped smoke emissions.

tors inspired consolidation and expansion of numerous area fabricators and manufacturers, and the first car rolled off the new assembly line on April 28, 1966.

The valley celebrated in 1967 as the GM work force completed its 500,000th Pontiac Firebird. In February 1968, however, the United Auto Workers union subjected Lordstown to a ten-day strike, even as expansion plans were being made for a stamping plant and a $50 million truck-assembly unit that would employ eighteen hundred.

EDWARD J. DeBARTOLO

On another front, far removed from the river valleys and the bustle of heavy industry, enclosed shopping malls developed by the Edward J. DeBartolo Corporation and the Cafaro Company were reshaping the landscape of retail merchandising at home and across the country. In 1968, Cafaro opened the Eastwood Mall in Niles. A $15 million building permit for another mall, to be built at Southern Park in Boardman, was issued to DeBartolo in July 1968.

1966: General Motors' Chevrolet Division rolls the first car off the Lordstown assembly line. The plant quickly reached its production goal of a car a minute and added a new Pontiac model to its array.

News from the Mahoning and Shenango Valleys

1970

JAN. 5: The Erie Lackawanna ends more than a century of Youngstown passenger service with a final run to Chicago by Lake Cities Express.

FEB. 4: Lykes-Youngstown earnings fall to $11,511,000 in its first year with Sheet & Tube, a deficit of twenty-three cents a share.

MARCH 2: Seventeen Penn Central cars derail in East Palestine, spilling two hundred new Chrysler cars.

MARCH 17: Patti Danko, a receptionist from Niles, drives the first Chevy van off GM's new truck line.

MAY 4: Sandra Scheuer, twenty, of Boardman, a bystander, is one of four Kent State University students killed as national guardsmen break up an unsanctioned antiwar rally.

SEPT. 15: The UAW strikes GM's Fisher Body unit as contract talks fail, idling nine thousand here.

1971

APRIL 12: Southern Airways on U.S. 224 closes; it will be replaced by Hitchcock Square, a $40 million housing and commercial complex.

JUNE 11: Sagging economy pushes Mahoning County welfare cases to a record 7,531 (16,104 recipients), up 20.5 percent from a year ago.

AUG. 31: It will take $336 million to clean the Mahoning River to federal standards, Consultant William Harnisch tells a hearing on pollution.

OCT. 24: Authorities arrest fifty-two and seize hashish, LSD, and amphetamines in Youngstown, Austintown, Boardman, and Poland.

NOV. 12: A car careers down a West Federal Street sidewalk, killing seven people and injuring eight.

NOV. 21: Fire guts the old New York Central terminal at Himrod and Penn avenues, consuming a two-month supply of VINDICATOR newsprint stored there.

1972

JAN. 11: Movers transport Saint James Episcopal Church six-tenths of a mile to Boardman Park from its Market Street location of 163 years.

MARCH 1: Commercial Shearing & Stamping Company, renamed Commercial Shearing, Inc., will sell 150 thousand shares of common stock.

APRIL 26: Saint Mary Home for the Aged, 278 Broadway, created by the Youngstown Diocese in 1952, will close; it has fifty-one residents.

JUNE 25: Hundreds from East Liverpool to Bellaire flee their homes as the Ohio River floods, swollen by rain from tropical storm Agnes.

DEC. 12: Searchers find the body of Dwight ("Dike") Beede, retired head coach of Youngstown State University football, who drowned in Little Beaver Creek near his Lisbon farm.

1973

FEB. 20: A newborn girl is found alive in a toilet in a United Air Lines plane at Youngstown Airport. Her mother, from Louisiana, gets two years for attempted manslaughter.

MARCH 17: Deputies book Earnest Holmes, Pittsburgh Steelers defensive tackle, for wounding a highway patrol helicopter pilot, Larry Myers, during a search for a man who fired on trucks along area interstates.

MARCH 27: In rural Berlin Center, Stanley, a three-hundred-pound lion, escapes his owners' barn and goes calling in the neighborhood.

APRIL 8: Thousands welcome the return of Navy Cmdr. Robert H. Shumaker, a New Wilmington, Pennsylvania, native, after eight years in a North Vietnamese prison.

APRIL 24: The board of the Mahoning County Tuberculosis Sanatorium advises county commissioners to close the hospital.

NOV. 24: Cardinal Mooney wins the state AAA football championship, defeating Warren Western Reserve 14-3 in the Akron Rubber Bowl.

DEC. 14: Independent truckers idle their rigs, protesting fuel prices and closely policed speed limits. As the strike turns violent, strikers force Penn-Ohio Plaza, near North Lima, to stop diesel-fuel sales.

1974

FEB. 7: Deputies burn a shanty used by striking truckers and reopen beleaguered Penn-Ohio Plaza.

FEB. 9: Lykes Youngstown's Sheet & Tube subsidiary reports income of $43,283,000; overhead continues to outstrip sales-price increases.

MAY 12: To ease a penny shortage, Union National and People's banks offer $1.10 for a hundred pennies.

JULY 7: Foreclosure action closes the Voyager Inn, opened on Market Street less than eleven years ago.

OCT. 5: Youngstown dedicates Federal Plaza, a $2 million revamp of Central Square. The islands go, but the Man on the Monument stays.

1975

APRIL 4: The Mahoning County Emergency Committee to Save the Babies from Vietnam seeks foster care or adoptive homes.

JUNE 30: Sixty thousand watch the Air Force Thunderbirds execute crossovers, trail rolls, and loops at Youngstown Air Reserve Base.

AUG. 6: Seven Erie Lackawanna cars derail at Youngstown's Westlake's Crossing, killing Alberta Ceryak in her van; an alcohol tanker ignites, creating an inferno.

AUG. 15: Science Hill Junior High will close, consistent with dropping enrollment in public schools. It was built on Youngstown's Northeast Side in 1920 as an elementary school.

1976

JAN. 4: In two days, seventy-six Amishmen dismantle a hundred-year-old barn south of Youngstown, coding the timbers for reassembly in New Wilmington, Pennsylvania.

JAN. 21: Two hundred tenants are evacuated and seven hospitalized when fire damages two rooms at Hotel Ohio; one later dies of burns.

APRIL 7: Private hospitals form the Mahoning Valley Community Blood Center to collect enough blood to meet round-the-clock needs.

MAY 31: Deputy sheriffs use tear gas to end holiday-weekend rowdyism by two thousand youths at Pymatuning State Park, Andover.

JUNE 21: Toxic smoke from burning hay in Kinsman sends one hundred fifteen people, many of them firemen, to hospitals for treatment.

AUG. 23: Six YSU students from Poland return home after canoeing two thousand miles in sixty-seven days to New Orleans via the Mahoning, Beaver, Ohio, and Mississippi.

OCT. 17: "Invest in your own future"–elect Jimmy Carter president, the Georgia Democrat tells seventy-five hundred downtown.

1977

JAN. 15: Conrail's No. 28 makes its final Cleveland-to-Youngstown run, erasing Youngstown from the list of cities with passenger train service.

MAY 5: Youngstown council finally authorizes the Board of Control to grant a cable television franchise.

MAY 19: Comedian Bob Hope, who got his start at East Palestine's old Overlander Opera House, gives a carillon to First Church of Christ.

JULY 19: The second mineshaft in two months opens up in Youngstown. The Kirkmere mine, forty feet across and fifty feet deep, is smaller than the 115-foot-deep Hylda Avenue mine that caved in June 13.

NOV. 26: Dr. Robert Foster, Salem, and two grandchildren are unhurt when faulty landing gear forces the former Youngstown orthopedic surgeon to belly-land his Cessna 210 at Youngstown Municipal Airport.

1978

JAN. 11: In Columbiana, fire destroys the seventy-four-year-old, three-story Union Bank building on South Main Street.

FEB. 7: Farmers in Mahoning, Trumbull and Columbiana counties incurred $1.1 million in losses to buildings, equipment, and livestock in January's blizzard.

MARCH 24: In Saint Columba Cathedral, worshippers ask God's help in reviving the Campbell Works.

APRIL 3: Struthers welcomes home its girls' basketball team as Ohio's AAA women's champion. The Wildcats defeated Middletown.

APRIL 15: Northeastern Ohio Universities College of Medicine is dedicated in Rootstown. A day of festivities precedes three open houses.

1979

FEB. 10: Fire destroys Bertram Builders & Supply Company, Leisure Homes, Inc., and Gateway Trucking on Logangate Road, Liberty.

MARCH 22: State employment offices area-wide take applications from twenty-five hundred people for work at General Motors' Packard Electric Division, five times more applicants than jobs available.

AUG. 2: Former A&P grocery stores on Belmont Avenue, Kirk Road and Boardman-Poland Road will reopen as Giant Eagle supermarkets.

DEC. 16: Gary Lee, a 1970 YSU graduate and business administrator at the Tehran embassy, is among fifty-six hostages held hostage by Iranian revolutionaries.

DEC. 27: What was once Youngstown Sheet & Tube's Furnace D makes its last cast of molten iron at J&L Corporation's Campbell Works. It is the last of YS&T's eight furnaces. Tomorrow, the last cast will become steel as the last three open hearths at the Brier Hill Works end their careers as well.

1970 **8** 1979

POWERLESS TO STOP THE FALL OF STEEL

FEBRUARY 1975: Republic Steel tears down its spike mill, which for years supplied fasteners for anchoring rails to railroad ties. In time, pictures like this would be the norm rather than the exception throughout the Steel Valley.

In September 1977, the company that began life in 1900 as Youngstown Iron Sheet & Tube moved inexorably toward the grave. The Rust Belt was its legacy.

EVENTS BEYOND THE VALLEY

1970: Apollo 13 crew returns safely after onboard explosion cripples command module.

• Boeing 747 jumbo jet airliner enters service.

1971: U.S. ends twenty-one-year trade embargo with China.

• Joe Frazier defeats Muhammad Ali for heavyweight boxing title.

1972: Burglary at Democratic National Headquarters, located in Washington, D.C.'s Watergate.

• Palestinian terrorists kill eleven Israeli athletes at Munich Olympics.

1973: Last U.S. troops withdraw from South Vietnam.

• American Indians protest at Wounded Knee, South Dakota.

1974: Richard M. Nixon becomes first U.S. president to resign from office.

1975: Exodus of Vietnamese boat people begins.

• Suez canal reopens to shipping after eight-year interruption.

1976: Viking space ▶ craft lands on Mars.

1977: Trans-Alaska Pipeline goes into operation.

• The first Apple II personal computer is marketed in the U.S.

1978: The first human test-tube baby is born in England.

1979: Nuclear accident at Three-Mile Island power plant in Pennsylvania.

• Fifty-six U.S. Embassy employees are taken hostage in Iran.

• The first case of AIDS, an acronym for Acquired Immune Deficiency Syndrome, is reported.

Many Ohio industries were still operating in their original plants, which were becoming obsolete.

EUGENE MURDOCK
THE BUCKEYE EMPIRE:
AN ILLUSTRATED HISTORY OF OHIO ENTERPRISE

THE DEATH IN July 1970 of Michael J. Kirwan, who had represented the Nineteenth Congressional District for thirty-two years, marked the end of an era. That blow fell on a community that had been stunned two months earlier by the shooting of four students May 4 at Kent State University in a confrontation between Ohio National guardsmen and antiwar demonstrators. One of the dead was Sandra Scheuer, twenty, of Boardman; deepen-

EPITAPH: A cross made from scraps of wood announces "5,000 jobs killed" at Stop 14 in front of Youngstown Sheet & Tube's idle Campbell Works on Poland Avenue.

ing the heartbreak was an investigation confirming that the young woman was not a part of the protest and was merely on her way to class at the time.

Later, guardsmen said they had responded to provocations by the war demonstrators that represented to them a clear and present danger.

Firebombings, executions, and arson continued as the age of rock festivals, rap sessions, and methadone-treatment programs dawned. Although the metropolitan statistical area was now home to more than 530 thousand, Youngstown had slipped to ninety-eighth largest city in the U.S., with a population of not quite 140 thousand. The city would slip further, to 114th, by the year 1977.

As the midpoint of the decade approached, hearts were warmed by the return home of newly released prisoners of war. But then, with the Watergate scandal draining the life's blood from the Nixon presidency, and an energy crisis absorbing everyone's attention, the Mah-

MAY 4, 1970: Four students died at Kent State University when the Ohio National Guard fired on demonstrators protesting the involvement of the United States in Vietnam.

CRIME IN HIGH PLACES: Facing impeachment in the Watergate scandal, Richard Nixon resigned in 1974. His secretary, a former Sebring resident, ▶ Rose Mary Woods, erased 18½ minutes of dialogue from White House audio tapes, which were a key body of evidence in the investigation of Nixon's involvement in Watergate.

oning Valley found itself enduring a slump in steel production, residential construction, and auto manufacturing.

Still, as the country faced the frustration of defeat that came with the end of the Vietnam War, the valley also found itself welcoming refugee South Vietnamese families here to make new lives for themselves, and in 1976 attendance at the Canfield Fair topped half a million for the first time.

Platform Shoes, Disco Fever, And the Shakeout in Steel

Those were the days of platform shoes, discos, and "Saturday Night Fever." The mid-seventies brought the country's bicentennial, Jimmy Carter, and swine flu, and for the valley, they also brought disaster.

It happened on September 19, 1977, one inglorious day that will be riveted in local memory for generations to come. That day brought the unexpected, the unbelievable, and the inconceivable: the announcement by the Youngstown Sheet & Tube Company that five

thousand employees would be let go by the end of the year; that the company's headquarters would move to Chicago; and that its Indiana Harbor Works would henceforth be the battleground of its fight for survival. The American steel industry, as Youngstown knew it, had lapsed into a coma from which it would not awaken.

Reflecting the stresses residents of the Mahoning Valley were facing before they had any idea of the devastation that would come to the local steel industry, 1972 found increasing numbers on the welfare roles, and a flu epidemic that January that limited routine visiting at all local hospitals.

Shoppers bade farewell to the retail name McKelvey's as the beloved institution became Higbee's in 1973, and the Youngstown Public Schools and the National Association for the Advancement of Colored People went to court in 1976 over desegregation, although the Civil Rights Act had passed a dozen years earlier.

Natural disasters provided challenges as well, like the tornados that hit New Wilmington in 1972 and Mineral Ridge in 1978, the above-average snowfall in January and February 1978, and the rains that came with Hurricane Agnes.

A report in March 1978 said property values in the Mahoning Valley had increased sixty-six percent since 1966, but that increase, unfortunately, was less than anywhere else in northeast Ohio.

Charles J. Carney, a Democrat who had served in the Ohio General Assembly, was elected to Congress in 1970 to succeed Mike Kirwan, and 1971 saw the reelection of Republican Jack Hunter, despite predictions that he would lose the Youngstown mayoralty.

Then, while the country immersed itself in the Watergate scandal, wondering what President Nixon knew and when he knew it, Hunter was elected to his third term in 1973, and city council retained a GOP majority.

Lyle Williams, a Republican, Wins Congressional Seat

With Hunter's reelection in 1975 came the challenge of working with an all-Democrat council. In 1976 Hunter gave the incumbent congressman, Carney, a scare in a close race for the district seat.

In 1976 the Supreme Court of Ohio reinstated Frank R. Franko, the former Youngstown mayor, to the practice of law, and in 1978 Lyle Williams, a Trumbull County commissioner, became the first Republican congressman from the area in forty-two years.

TRANSITION: In 1973 McKelvey's becomes a part of the Higbee's department store enterprise, ending a family-owned business that spanned ninety years of downtown-Youngstown shopping history.

NATURE UNTAMED: The Blizzard of 1978 may not have be remembered with the same I-was-there keenness as the Big Snow of 1950, but it was a doozy in its own right. The snow started at midmorning, whipped by gale winds. Temperatures bottomed out, depositing a glare of ice beneath the snow that made driving a thrill a minute.

The Youngstown public schools dedicated the Choffin Career Center in 1973, and Youngstown State University's enrollment hit 15,500 in 1975, the same year it named its new $6.06 million library for William F. Maag, Jr., late publisher of THE VINDICATOR.

As in the sixties, however, deficient funding continued to cripple school districts in the valley.

Money-saving efforts in Youngstown led to total confusion with the start of school in September 1974, when students were to be taken by the Western Reserve Transit Authority instead of by the familiar yellow school buses.

Three Districts Close Briefly In Response to Money Pinch

In 1975, lacking operating capital, Campbell schools closed on November 15, not to open again until January. Jackson-Milton schools closed on Nov. 10, 1976, for the same reason. In 1978 the schools that closed early for the winter holidays to save money, that time for only six days, were in Boardman.

As Boardman's retail district expanded and developed, the oldest Episcopal church in the Connecticut Western Reserve, Saint James, was relocated to a grassy vale in Boardman Park in January 1972, after 163 years on Market Street Extension, where it had overlooked the transition of Southern Park from open recreational space to enclosed shopping mall.

Major infrastructure developments of the area's roadways continued through the early 1970s, with new sections of Interstate 80 opening ten miles at a time and links of the so-called Youngstown Expressway becoming functional bit by bit; one link, then called the Boardman Expressway, opened from South Avenue to East Midlothian Boulevard in 1975. In December of that same year the valley's link to the rest of Ohio was strengthened by completion of the Ohio Turnpike. Those improvements were completed just in time to greet the devastation wrought by the collapse of the local steel industry in September 1977. Two years later, in a

ON THE POLICE BLOTTER

FIREBOMBINGS, executions, and arson continued to trouble the valley as the 1970s began. It was estimated in August 1972 that armed and unarmed bandits were "striking virtually at will in every part of the city," averaging one robbery a day since the first of the year, and THE VINDICATOR reported in 1973 that Trumbull County had been "rocked by 25 murders."

A BURGLARY RING was uncovered within the Youngstown Police Department in 1974, with details of department members committing break-ins and thefts while on the beat over a two-year period. The scandal resulted in the eventual resignation and conviction of thirteen Youngstown policemen and the suspension of several others who were not directly involved.

Despite that, however, the city's crime rate rose to only 9.6 percent that year, compared with the national rate of seventeen percent.

IN ADDRESSING criminal activities in its overview of 1976, the newspaper termed the local crime scene "bizarre," noting that two Austintown residents, a man and a woman, murdered their spouses that year and received life sentences; that a South Side brother and sister died a fiery ritualistic death in a murder-suicide; and that the underworld figure Philip ("Fleegle") Mainer turned up dead after an eighteen-month disappearance.

APRIL 4, 1972: A bomb demolishes a car at an apartment house on Brookwood Road in Boardman.

climate of economic uncertainty and a diminishing tax base, Youngstown learned from engineers that the Lake Milton dam required $5 million in repairs.

Conflicts between management and labor erupted year after year.

General Motors employees went on strike for more than two months in the fall of 1970, and Mahoning County sheriff's deputies struck on November 21 of that year, staying away until Sheriff

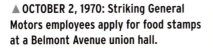

▲ OCTOBER 2, 1970: Striking General Motors employees apply for food stamps at a Belmont Avenue union hall.

SEPTEMBER 1976: Policemen and fire-▶ fighters strike the City of Youngstown for four days.

Ray T. Davis ran out of money to run the department on December 8. When Youngstown teachers struck in September 1973, the clergy arranged secret negotiations between the teachers and board of education. Campbell's teachers struck that fall, too. The next year, Sharon teachers struck, and the area's Catholic schools endured a one-day strike as well.

Strikes Hit General Motors, Steel Haulers, and Hospitals

The United Auto Workers union conducted a forty-five-day strike in 1974, and a violence-marred strike by independent truckers against steel-hauling companies required activation of the Ohio National Guard. At the end of that year, four hundred-fifty registered nurses struck the Youngstown Hospital Association in a dispute that would last fifty-three days.

Because the national energy crisis of 1974 adversely affected auto sales, General Motors furloughed nine hundred workers for three weeks, and the automaker's employees went on strike again the next year, that time over production standards.

Later in 1975 Campbell City police and firemen walked out for ten days, and library workers struck for six weeks. Even United Airlines workers went out on strike at Youngstown Municipal Airport. In September 1976, a strike by policemen and firefighters in Youngstown received na-

1974: Parts of Federal Street and Central Square were removed and reconfigured into Federal Plaza. This view looks west: at left, Central Tower; at right Union National Bank (Bank One today).

tional attention. The strike ended four days and a rash of fires later, with the strikers receiving a six percent raise negotiated with the city's Republican mayor and Democratic council.

Whatever problems the area's management and labor forces had faced so far, none could possibly compare with the closing of the steel mills that shattered the end of the decade. The possibility of a Lake Erie-to-Ohio River canal was all but forgotten with the death in 1970 of its greatest champion, Michael Kirwan.

Then, in 1972, Frank A. Nemec, who was chief executive officer of Youngstown Sheet & Tube, came up with a less-ambitious solution, a stub canal, in an effort to save the valley's obsolescent basic-steel industry and thousands of jobs. Although proposed, the idea didn't catch on, however, perhaps undermined by the progress implied by the corporate balance sheet. In February 1973 Lykes-

Youngstown, Sheet & Tube's parent company, listed income of $25,598,000 for 1972, up 176 percent over the $9,262,000 reported for 1971. Such apparent financial success enabled Sheet & Tube to begin addressing environmental concerns. In June 1973 the company announced that it would spend $20 million in the first year of, and eventually $50 million on, the Youngstown District's pollution-control program. By 1975, Sheet & Tube and the Ohio Environmental Protection Agency had agreed that the company would spend some $40 million for new facilities to control air pollution.

Lykes Drops 'Youngstown' From Name, Cuts Dividend

That serious trouble was afoot became apparent, however, when the Lykes Corporation dropped "Youngstown" from the company name in 1976, and the twenty-five cent dividend was reduced to ten cents a common share.

In that same year General Fireproofing, which had announced a $2.85 million expansion program just three years earlier, discarded those plans and decided to expand somewhere other than Youngstown. With Edward De-

▲ JANUARY 11, 1972: Specialists relocate Saint James Episcopal Church from the Market Street tract it occupied 163 years just west of Southern Park Mall.

—————◦>◦<◦—————

TOGETHER AGAIN: Steeple and structure ▶ are reunited at the historic church's new home in Boardman Township Park. Saint James is the oldest Episcopal Church in the Connecticut Western Reserve.

Bartolo now its majority shareholder, GF also eliminated dividends in the expectation of third-quarter losses. In Warren, meanwhile, Copperweld Steel had been acquired in 1975 by a French holding company, Societe Imetal, despite a unified effort by management and labor to block the takeover.

With so many clouds building on the horizon, the valley welcomed the few shafts of sunshine occasioned by General Motors' startup of Chevrolet Vega production at Lordstown in 1975, and its announcement in 1977 that Lords-

OCTOBER 1979: International Towers, a sixteen-story residence for the elderly, goes up where the Tod Hotel once stood.

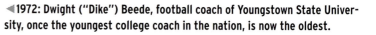

◀1972: Dwight ("Dike") Beede, football coach of Youngstown State University, once the youngest college coach in the nation, is now the oldest.

BEFORE THE FALL: Smoke and steam billow into the icy skies at Youngstown Sheet & Tube.

town would soon produce the Oldsmobile Starfire and Buick Skyhawk, as well as the Chevrolet Monza and Pontiac Sunbird.

A rush of steel orders in 1975 appeared to mirror a boom in the auto industry and other upticks in the national economy, which people accepted as a great boon to the Youngstown steel mills.

Then came 1977.

A seven-week cold snap that began in January dictated four-day work weeks at Youngstown Sheet & Tube because of low supplies of heating gas and electricity. The hard winter's curtailed production showed up as losses of $32.8 million in the Lykes report of first-quarter earnings.

September, 19, 1977: The Day the Music Died

Even so, steel operating levels hit seventy-four percent in April, and Sheet & Tube worked with the Mahoning County commissioners during the year on financing a study of how to clean up industrial and municipal wastes deposited in the Mahoning River.

But the most remarkable and desolate day in the Mahoning Valley in the twentieth century came September 19, 1977, with the announcement that the Sheet & Tube—as people had always called it—would be cutting five thousand jobs from the rolls. Just like that.

Even as the valley reeled from that blow, residents rallied in Washington, D.C., to take part in demonstrations at the White House and register their dismay. Back home, formal and informal coalitions sprang up in what would become a frustrating and fruitless effort to counteract the biggest industrial shakeout since the gasoline engine drove the carriage industry to oblivion. Adding insult to injury, the United Mine Workers union called a strike in 1978 that left Ohio Edison with only a forty-

day supply of coal at one point. That February Edison had to ask its customers to cut use of electricity twenty-five percent.

Government Allows Merger Of Sheet & Tube and J&L

In another development, Lykes and LTV, the parent companies of Sheet & Tube and Jones & Laughlin, reported net losses of $228.4 million. Three months later, Sheet & Tube asked Mahoning County for a fifty percent tax cut, equivalent to $8.7 million. Then, in November 1978, unemployment benefits began to run out.

In June 1978 the Justice Department approved the merger plans of Lykes and LTV, a bitter paradox

HAPPIER TIMES: Coils of steel awaiting transfer to General Motors in Lordstown jam the shipping dock of Youngstown Sheet & Tube's Campbell Works in November 1970.

considering how the same government had repeatedly torpedoed Sheet & Tube's efforts to merge with Bethlehem Steel earlier in the century.

Merger Joins Sheet & Tube With Jones & Laughlin

The merger, completed in December, married Lykes' Sheet & Tube, the country's eighth-largest steel producer, to LTV's Jones & Laughlin, the country's seventh-largest. Still, hope remained that somehow the community and the workers would figure out a way to buy and run Sheet & Tube locally.

But 1979 didn't get much better. Looking back, THE VINDICATOR called it "a bleak year." The closing of three more mills—U.S. Steel's Ohio Works and McDonald Mills and J&L's Brier Hill Works—were announced, meaning the loss of nearly five thousand more steel jobs. Bleak, indeed.

Washington Turns Deaf Ear To Save-the-Mill Proposition

The federal government, meanwhile, rejected an application from the Ecumenical Coalition of the Valley for $242 million in loan guarantees for a save-the-mills project, and the U.S. Commerce Department rejected a plan to establish a national steel research and development demonstration center in Youngstown. Finally, the U.S. Department of Housing & Urban Development blacklisted Youngstown for failing to meet federal rules governing low-

THE TREMENDOUS PRICE WE PAID

THE HARDSHIP FELT IN THE MAHONING and Shenango valleys in the late 1970s and early 1980s rippled through the economy. Youngstown alone lost $1 million in income taxes in 1979. In 1980, $448,000 in personal property taxes vanished after U.S. Steel's Ohio Works closed. The drain of personal income touched all businesses—everything from grocery stores to department stores to florists. All fringe spending stopped. Housing values sank. Attracting new businesses, never a snap, was even tougher. And the country was in the worst recession in history.

The exact number of jobs lost in steelmaking may never be known. Estimates ranged as high as fifty thousand. Some terminations were cut and dried. Others, just as final, masqueraded as layoffs. Company and union tallies sometimes differed, too, and reports from one news medium to the next varied as well.

Initial reports estimated ten thousand jobs lost over two years, but it is difficult to arrive at a reliable breakdown for the mills and their subsidiaries—U.S. Steel and its Ohio Works and McDonald mills; Sheet & Tube, which briefly continued as J&L, and its Campbell blast furnace; Republic's phaseout of Youngstown operations; and phaseouts at smaller mills as well.

From the authoritative Labor Market Review, however, there is this sobering post mortem: In 1977, jobs in primary metals in the Youngstown-Warren area averaged 39,000. By January 1979, that average had plummeted to 21,400, and by April 1982 it had tumbled further, to 13,200. Today, the area employs 5,800 in primary metals—a difference of 33,200 jobs in twenty-two years.

NOVEMBER 1979: Three hundred steelworkers picket United States Steel headquarters in Pittsburgh, protesting the company's closing of the Ohio Works, McDonald Mills, and fourteen other plants. No idea worked, no proposal bore fruit, no amount of talking made any difference. The Mahoning Valley was powerless to stop the fall of steel.

and moderate-income housing, leaving the city ineligible for Urban Development Action Grants.

Aircraft Projects Proposed, But Neither Takes Off

Attempts were made to bring two aircraft plants to the valley, but the first proposal, from ICX Aviation, failed, so hopes centered on Commuter Aircraft Corporation's plan to manufacture an airplane here. The death of that venture would come in the 1980s.

One final blow delivered in 1979 involved the expiration of special federal unemployment benefits for nearly two thousand former employees of Sheet & Tube. As the decade ended, many who had never imagined being jobless found that they had become dependent upon welfare or their forty-dollar payment each week from the unions' unemployment funds.

GONE WITH THE WIND: The open-hearth stacks that once sent smoky signals of prosperity and security aloft over Youngstown Sheet & Tube's Brier Hill steel works puffed their last in 1979. Sheet & Tube had lost some five thousand jobs between 1977 and 1979. Other companies, notably U.S. Steel, would soon restructure and add to the jobless rolls.

News from the Mahoning and Shenango Valleys

1980

JAN. 4: Ray. T. Davis, ex-Mahoning County sheriff, draws four five-year prison terms and a two-thousand-dollar fine for corruption in office.

JAN. 28: Five hundred steelworkers storm U.S. Steel headquarters on Salt Springs Road, demanding continued employment. USS officials will discuss a worker buyout.

JULY 31: The United Steel Workers union dissolves District 26, comprising Mahoning, Trumbull, Ashtabula, and Columbiana counties.

NOV. 4: Democrat James A. Traficant, Jr. defeats Republican Terrence Shidel for the office of Mahoning County sheriff.

DEC. 17: Charles D. Carabbia, one-time gambling boss of Struthers, is missing and may be the latest casualty in the war for mob supremacy.

1981

APRIL 10: Volunteer firefighters burn Poland's historic Carriage House for practice, finishing what an arsonist started last September.

AUG. 5: Three of eighteen striking air-traffic controllers return to work at Youngstown Municipal Airport under presidential threat of losing their jobs.

AUG. 23: Boardman Little League defeats Richmond, Virginia, 4-0 to win the World Series title for 13-year-olds in Taylor, Michigan.

OCT. 26: Hundreds pay last respects to John Litch, forty-three, a reserve deputy slain while driving a prisoner to jail from a hospital; he is the first local officer killed in the line of duty in some thirty years.

NOV. 5: A Piper Aztec plane with engine trouble crashes into the roof of the Sears Automotive Service Center in Niles's Eastwood Mall. The pilot, three passengers, and two people in the store are injured.

1982

FEB. 28: A two-week sales promotion by car dealers and banks in Trumbull and Mahoning counties drops interest rates to 12.9 percent.

OCT. 28: Idora Park, eighty-five years old, with a merry-go-round with a distinguished past, and one of the country's ten-best roller coasters, is for sale for $1.5 million.

DEC. 24: Forty-two hundred more were jobless in November, increasing Trumbull County's unemployment rate to twenty-four percent,

second highest in Ohio; Mahoning County's rate is 21.2 percent.

1983

JAN. 6: Youngstown Salvation Army expects to serve one hundred people a day at a new South Side soup kitchen.

JAN. 20: Workers at Valley Mould in Hubbard can get two-hundred-dollar bonuses for buying American cars or trucks within ninety days.

JAN. 26: NBC's "Today" show discusses joblessness and President Reagan's State of the Union address at Youngstown State University.

APRIL 6: In Bessemer, Pennsylvania, thousands line up for one hundred-fifty jobs at the soon-to-reopen SME Bessemer Cement Co.

OCT. 1: Bridgefest '83 celebrates the opening of the new Market Street bridge, officially named Vietnam Veterans Memorial Bridge.

OCT. 27: Cpl. Edward Johnston, Struthers, Lance Cpl. James E. McDonough, New Castle, and Lance Cpl. Stanley Sliwinski, Niles, are missing in the bombing of Marine headquarters in Beirut, Lebanon.

1984

FEB. 21: Three are injured when a bridge through Lincoln Park collapses into the Dry Run Creek gorge under the weight of a truck.

MARCH 5: An incendiary fire destroys the landmark Mansion restaurant on Market Street.

APRIL 26: A $2.5 million fire at Idora Park destroys the Lost River ride, part of the Wildcat roller coaster, and other areas; the park closes for good on September 2.

JULY 21: African Cultural Weekend opens at Youngstown's Star Theater with Muslim leader Louis Farrakhan.

SEPT. 26: Geraldine Ferraro, Democratic candidate for vice president, campaigns here, saying that President Reagan "let the valley rust."

OCT. 31: Hindu and Sikh residents agree that the Indian government's invasion of a Sikh shrine last June led to Indira Gandhi's assassination.

1985

MARCH 15: A run on Home State Savings in Cincinnati causes Gov. Richard Celeste to close for three days Youngstown's Metropolitan Savings Bank and seventy others in the Ohio Deposit Guarantee Fund.

MARCH 30: The Rayen Tigers win Youngstown its first basketball title, beating Columbus Linden McKinley 50-46 for Ohio's AA championship.

APRIL 15: A $500 thousand fire destroys the Starlite Cafe in Poland Township, leaving thirty-six jobless.

MAY 20: An illegal fireworks factory explodes on Western Reserve Road, Beaver Township, killing nine.

JUNE 7: A black bear is tranquilized and captured after entering a Packard Electric building in Warren.

SEPT. 8: At LTV Steel's deserted Campbell Works, a dynamite charge drops Big D, a blast furnace that set production records in World War II.

OCT. 10: Mahoning County's first known victim of AIDS, a former teacher, died last month.

NOV. 11: The last members of the Last Man Club, Leo Linberger, ninety-two, and Anthony Schaefer, eighty-eight, toast twenty departed World War I comrades with a forty-four-year-old bottle of champagne.

1986

JAN. 1: Ella Maag, retired VINDICATOR society editor, dies at eighty-seven. Her sixty-four years at the paper spanned the period when high society was a major newsmaker.

JUNE 27: Strouss-Kaufmann's, downtown Youngstown's last department store, closes; it opened in 1926 as Strouss-Hirshberg's.

AUG. 20: Gov. Richard Celeste chooses Ann N. Przelomski, VINDICATOR managing editor, for induction into the Ohio Women's Hall of Fame.

OCT. 2: The House Public Works and Transportation Committee authorizes a new study of a Lake Erie-Ohio River canal, but proponents must find $8 million to pay for it.

NOV. 28: Fires caused by a surge in gas pressure drive hundreds from their McDonald homes on Thanksgiving Day; thirty-one homes and two businesses damaged.

1987

MAY 24: The Rev. Jesse Jackson, verging on his second presidential run, asks Youngstowner Ron Daniels to head his Rainbow Coalition.

JULY 19: Giant Eagle, Valu King, Sparkle, and Foodland battle for local grocery dollars using double coupons and food giveaways.

AUG. 5: Pentagon security guards fatally shoot Dwain Wallace, a 1976 Cardinal Mooney graduate, when he

pulls a gun and bolts toward the National Command Center.

AUG. 24: County Commissioner Thomas J. Carney proposes a new Youngstown comprising Youngstown, Campbell, Struthers, Austintown, Boardman, Coitsville, and Liberty; provincial attitudes must yield to progressive thinking, leaders say.

DEC. 5: In Columbus, the Cardinal Mooney football team wins its fourth Ohio High School Athletic Association championship, hammering Thornville Sheridan High 30-7.

1988

MARCH 7: A University of Pittsburgh project finds above-average levels of cancer-causing radon gas in Mahoning and Shenango homes.

MAY 4: Mahoning County voters pass a 1.9-mill levy for Mill Creek Park, perpetuating their history of never turning away from the park.

AUG. 16: At Canfield Fairgrounds, grateful farmers welcome ten double trailers of hay sent by Maine to relieve suffering from the drought. Two years ago, farmers here sent hay to stricken North Carolina.

SEPT. 24: School officials may end night football between City Series teams after the arrest of nine minors and three adults in a brawl at the Rayen-East game September 22.

OCT. 28: Unimpressed by the Mahoning River's recreational potential, the Corps of Army Engineers refuses to dredge the river to remove pollutants.

NOV. 9: Beth Smith becomes the first elected woman judge in Mahoning County, defeating a sixteen-year incumbent, Fred Bailey.

1989

FEB. 3: Bill White, a graduate of Warren Harding High School and Hiram College, becomes president of baseball's National League; he is the first black to head a major professional sports organization.

FEB. 20: The Youngstown Center of Industry & Labor rises on West Wood Street; the center will focus on the area's steelmaking heritage.

APRIL 22: Abortion opponents block the Women's Center on Market Street; police arrest forty-four.

NOV. 13: Phar-Mor Inc. will sponsor two women's professional golf tournaments next year; one will be held at Squaw Creek Country Club.

Chapter

1980 **9** 1989

TOUGH TIMES... AND THEN SOME

APRIL 29, 1982: The era of smelting iron ore to make steel ended for good with demolition of U.S. Steel's Ohio Works blast furnaces.

The eighties ushered in disquieting times. As industry decayed, the area struggled to support too many people with too few jobs.

During the 1980s, jobs in America's basic industries were reduced by one-third…. Since health insurance was tied to employment, workers who lost their jobs stood to lose their insurance. If the company went out of business, they could lose their pensions as well.

SUSAN JONAS AND MARILYN NISSENSON
GOING, GOING, GONE: VANISHING AMERICANA

IN MANY RESPECTS, THE FInancial troubles endured by the valley's residents during the early 1980s resembled those of the 1930s, but in others the differences were worlds apart. As in the thirties, hardworking people who'd never expected to find themselves on public relief were just that, but unlike the thirties, no massive, nationwide public-works programs came about to allay the pain.

Unlike the Great Depression, this was a localized depression—the tailwind of a precipitate, but not unprecedented, change of direction in the industrial marketplace. For the steel companies, it was survival of the fittest, the free-enterprise system in basal form—sudden, lethal, and final.

Beyond the Rust Belt, however, life went on. The Mahoning Valley may have experienced incalculable change, but it would simply have to pull itself together and move on. Just as the South would never rise again, neither would the steel mills. It was a harsh reality to accept, and some never would, hoping against hope that history would reverse itself. Instead of chimneys belching smoke and sulfur, residents once again saw soup kitchens pop up and witnessed the last rites of the Youngstown steel district, known formally as "District 26," when the executive board of the United Steel Workers union voted its dissolution in July 1980. Welfare rolls were swollen with people who, in better times, would be considered "middle class."

Adding to the valley's woe was a general decline in population. The population of Youngstown plummeted twenty-eight thousand to 113 thousand in ten years, and Mahoning County's dropped 7.1 percent. Of slight consolation, Trumbull County's had grown, but only by two percent. From 1980 to 1988, the population of the Youngstown-Warren Metropolitan Statistical Area would decline nearly thirty thousand more.

Triple Whammy: Recession, Inflation, Unemployment

As the eighties dawned, the country found itself snarled in a recession and significant inflation, but few communities were dealing with the record unemployment levels found throughout the Mahoning Valley. For hundreds of jobless steelworkers, the new decade did not bode well as benefits began to expire. As the domino effect tumbled the steel industry and its soulmates, the area struggled to support too many people with too few jobs.

Sharp Drop in Property Value Counters a Statewide Trend

In June 1980 the area's unemployment was reported to have risen to between 9.5 and 9.8 percent, but federal statistics often understated the number of local jobless; unlike the Great Depression of the thirties, the ordeal of Youngstown and the Mahoning Valley was unique this time around.

When THE VINDICATOR reported in February 1980 that the total value of tangible personal property in Youngstown had decreased $21.3 million the year before, it

CHRISTIAN CHARITY: The kitchen at Saint Columba Cathedral hall feeds two hundred people daily and double that number at month's end.

also reported that the valuation for Ohio's other largest cities had increased. In October 1982 the Youngstown-Warren metropolitan area made national headlines when its 20.9 percent unemployment was reported to be the highest in the country for the previous August, and after those headlines, things only got worse.

Economic Meltdown Pushes Jobless Rolls to Record Levels

The Ohio Bureau of Employment Services reported that the unemployment rate rose in November to nearly twenty-two percent in Mahoning County and twenty-four percent in Trumbull County. The litany of corporate bankruptcies, company closings, and employee layoffs dragged on through the headlines in 1983. Not until July of 1985 would the jobless rate fall below ten percent for the first time since 1981; and for Lawrence and Mercer counties,

a ten-year low in the jobless rate didn't come till June 1989.

Residents grasped at every sliver of hope as small, diversified industries expressed interest in the area, often only to taste bitter disappointment as yet another plan melted away. In September 1981 the area rejoiced as Gov. James A. Rhodes officiated at the groundbreaking for the long-awaited Commuter Aircraft Corporation, only to have its spirits dampened a year later when foreclosure papers were filed.

Hope kindled anew in 1984 when there was talk of Ronneburg Brewery's building a plant in Youngstown, then fizzled when those plans were scuttled the next year amid missed deadlines for various applications. In 1985 the region prayed that it would be

chosen as the location for General Motors' new Saturn automobile assembly plant, only to be sorely frustrated when the Saturn went instead to Spring Hill, Tennessee.

As industrial property taxes dropped and personal income-tax withholding faded away, government at the local, state, and federal levels struggled to meet the needs of the citizenry.

Personal Computers, Smoke Alarms, and the Berlin Wall

American society first met and fell in love with personal computers and compact discs in the 1980s. Identification of the AIDS virus made international headlines in 1981, although the first local case wasn't revealed until 1985. Smoke detectors saved lives and radon gas levels in houses

OCTOBER 1982: Joblessness at 20.9 percent, and worsening. Thousands seeking jobs that aren't there, clinging to the tenuous lifeline of unemployment benefits.

LONELY TOWN: By the eighties, downtown Youngstown no longer teems with shoppers and commercial trade. How to reinvent the downtown will occupy many minds for many years.

THE TRAFICANT TALES: ELECTED, CHARGED, TRIED, ACQUITTED, ELEVATED

THE BIGGEST political story of the decade was the rise of James A. Traficant, Jr. from Mahoning County sheriff to United States congressman.

In 1982 he made front-page news as sheriff night after night, not only for his orchestrated raids for drugs, stolen goods, and gambling devices, and his use of profanity over live radio and television, but also for coming under indictment by a federal grand jury on charges of bribery and income-tax evasion.

THE FOLLOWING YEAR, serving as his own lawyer, Traficant won acquittal in Federal District Court, Cleveland. The charges derived from tape recordings made by the Carabbia crime faction during Traficant's election campaign. Traficant countered that campaign money taken from Mafia boss Jimmy Prato was part of his own strategy to set up the mob for criminal investigation. Traficant later lost a civil case and was assessed back taxes on the $163 thousand campaign stash.

Traficant continued to make headlines, battling with the FBI over its tactics and refusing to sign mortgage-foreclosure deeds. For that, he landed in jail on a contempt citation, serving two days of a one hundred-day term before agreeing to sign off on the deeds. That July, he raided area fireworks wholesalers in a move that cost the city its Independence Day fireworks display. The next year Traficant defeated the Republican incumbent, Lyle Williams, to win the congressional seat in what was now the Seventeenth District.

IN 1987 Traficant announced that he would run for president, hoping his campaign would focus attention on problems plaguing aging industrial cities. By the time the 1988 elections rolled around, however, the candidates to bring their campaigns to the valley were Michael Dukakis, the eventual De-

AUGUST 9, 1982: Special Agents Larry Lynch (left) and Robert G. Kroner, Jr. escort Sheriff James A. Traficant, Jr. from FBI headquarters for the trip to Federal District Court for arraignment on bribery and income tax charges. The government alleged that Traficant took $163 thousand illegally from organized crime.

BELOW: Having beaten the government's case, Traficant embraces Joe Christopher of Girard, foreman of the jury that acquitted him.

mocratic nominee; Dan Quayle, vice-presidential candidate on the Republican ticket; and the Baptist minister Jesse Jackson, who was then running against Dukakis on the Democratic side.

Earthy commentaries made the congressman popular with television news crews

> June 15, 1981
> Austintown, Ohio
>
> I, James Traficant, make the following free and voluntary statement to Robert G Kroner Jr and Mark S Swanger, Jr who have identified themselves to me as Special Agents of the Federal Bureau of Investigation. I realize, and fully understand, that I do not have to make this statement, and that it could be used against me at a later time. During the period of time that I campaigned for sheriff of Mahoning County Ohio, I accepted money from Orlando Carabbia, Charles Carabbia, Joseph Naples and James Prato. This money was given to me with the understanding that certain illegal activities would be allowed to take place in Mahoning County after my election, and that as Sheriff I would not interfere with those activities. I have read this statement consisting of this page, and it is true and correct.
>
> [signature] 6-15-81
> witness: [signature], SA, FBI, Youngstown, ohio 6/15/81
> witness: [signature], SA FBI, Youngstown, Ohio 6/15/81

Traficant said the FBI forged this confession, dated June 15, 1981.

briefly caught people's attention.

As it had during the close of the 1970s, the country continued to hang out yellow ribbons in acknowledgment of the U.S. Embassy hostages in Tehran, and rejoiced in January 1981 when they were freed, including a YSU graduate, Gary Lee; started to contemplate the Star Wars defense initiative in 1983; listened in 1985 as the Soviet Union's Mikhail Gorbachev preached glasnost and perestroika; wept over the space shuttle Challenger disaster in January 1986; and, as the decade drew to a close, cheered as the Berlin Wall, that tangible symbol of the Iron Curtain and communism, came tumbling down.

Downtown Shopping Fades To Black as Big Stores Close

In the valley, merchants left downtown Youngstown in droves. In September 1982 the city's oldest department store, Higbee's, formerly the G.M. McKelvey Company, left town after having been a mainstay at the heart of the city ninety-nine years. The decision of the Cleveland-based management left three hundred local workers without jobs.

Then, in June 1986, downtown Youngstown lost its last major department store with the closing of Strouss-Kaufmann's. Kaufmann's followed up in January 1987 by closing its stores in Austintown and Liberty.

In 1988 Youngstown Municipal Airport suffered a major setback when Continental Express discontinued passenger service.

The cost of a private hospital room increased to $115.00 a day at St. Elizabeth's and to $131.00 a day at the Youngstown Hospital Association's Northside and Southside units in 1980. Remarkably, in a headline

SEPTEMBER 1982: McKelvey's lasted only nine years under Higbee's ownership. Strouss-Kaufmann's pulled out four years later, leaving downtown Youngstown without an anchor store.

that might have been lifted from the teens or twenties, four patients with communicable typhoid fever were being treated at Northside in December of that year.

Strikes by unions marred the decade even further. One of two unions closed the Public Library

GARY LEE

JANUARY 21, 1981: Americans exult in their freedom after 444 days in captivity in Iran.

of Youngstown and Mahoning County for three months in 1980. In 1981 Ravenna teachers walked out in Portage County, as did their Youngstown counterparts.

A Nine-Week Strike Sours Voters on School-Tax Issue

The Youngstown strike lasted nine weeks, and when school resumed at the end of April, plans had to be made to continue the school year through June 30, including Saturday classes. Taxpayers, meanwhile, let their feelings be heard in the June primaries by defeating a 7.9-mill tax for school district operations.

In October 1981 the Western Reserve Transit Authority went on strike, stranding those who depended on public transportation, and Trumbull Memorial Hospital in Warren endured a twenty-week strike through the fall of 1982. Columbiana teachers struck for five weeks in 1986. Liberty teachers walked off the job the next year, and teachers in Lordstown the year after that. In 1989 instructors in the Warren schools and Youngstown State University staged strikes as well.

In the middle of the decade, in a nod to the revolutionary convulsions in eastern Europe and Lech Walesa's rise to power in Poland, a local labor group, Solidarity USA, sprang up to march in support of workers at several companies, including Weatherbee Coats and the new Boardman presence of the Pittsburgh grocery concern Giant Eagle.

A Favorite of Generations Plays Its Farewell Season

In a blow to more than three quarters of a century's worth of family entertainment, Idora Park went up for sale in 1982, survived a bad fire in 1984, suffered the indignity of diminishing attendance in its last season, and was finally dismantled and sold at auction in October 1984.

There were occasional bright spots and some interesting diversions, however. Three unidentified parachutists jumped from WKBN's fourteen-hundred-foot transmission tower in 1981.

In 1983 first-time home buyers were able to take advantage of

NOVEMBER 1982: A light plane with engine trouble hits the roof of Eastwood Mall, injuring the pilot and five others.

low-interest mortgage programs, and the United Way topped its $2.2 million goal. The International Peace Race, begun in the late seventies, came into its own with such success that it counted over one thousand participants by 1987. The next year, with dam renovations complete, engineers prepared to refill Lake Milton, which had been empty two years.

In 1988, the City of Youngstown was forced to cut its budget, and officials warned that additional layoffs and cutbacks were possible. Against that backdrop, citizens on the city's North Side mounted an effort to get their

neighborhood designated a Historic District, and concerned residents banded together to form the Stambaugh Pillars to restore and preserve a Fifth Avenue landmark, Stambaugh Auditorium. As for the matter of how to find reemployment for the valley's displaced labor force, Dr. Terry Buss, director of YSU's Center for Urban Studies, predicted that "the only way laid-off Mahoning Valley steelworkers will find jobs in the area is by starting their own businesses." As vital to reviving its economy, Buss stressed the need for a cooperative regional effort driven by the private sector, and resurrection of the valley's entrepreneurial traditions.

A tornado in June 1981 injured four at a campground at Berlin Reservoir, but that was eclipsed by a string of killer tornadoes that ripped through Trumbull County

END OF THE LINE: Idora amusement park served up thrills, chills, and unforgettable French fries to generations of Youngstowners. Fire damaged the park in April 1984. The owners opened the season on schedule, only to see attendance bottom out. It was the park's last hurrah. The Wildcat, Idora's nationally ranked roller coaster, was badly damaged in the fire.

and western Pennsylvania on May 31, 1985, and made national news. Looking back on that event, THE VINDICATOR reflected: "Within a few fast but furious moments on May 31, the year 1985 became the year of the tornado in the Mahoning Valley. It was an event that would dominate lives and local headlines for months to come." Winds of up to three hundred miles per hour flattened homes and reduced trees to kindling. Four days later, the newspaper reported the death count at twenty-two in northeast Ohio and ninety along a line from Pennsylvania into southern Canada.

Sensational Killings Scar The Decade's Second Half

Earlier in 1985, nine people had been killed when an illegal fireworks factory blew up in Beaver Township, and the middle to late eighties produced a bizarre series of killings.

In the fall of 1985, Warren residents were stunned by the torture-killing of twelve-year-old Raymond Fife. The boy's killer, Danny Lee Hill, was sentenced to death in Ohio's electric chair and at age nineteen became the youngest person on death row. Another sensational murder gripped the public's imagination in February 1988, when Kenmore B. Drake, a twenty-one-year-old Youngstown State Uni-

MAY 1985: Rescuers search for victims in the aftermath of a tornado that struck without warning, slicing through Newton Falls, Niles, Hubbard Township, and Mercer County, Pennsylvania. Four days afterward, the final death count stood at twenty-two in northeast Ohio and ninety along a line from Pennsylvania into southern Canada.

versity senior, was stabbed to death with a pair of scissors while house-sitting in Austintown for Timothy J. Lyons, Ph.D, dean of the Youngstown State University College of Fine and Performing Arts. Lyons resigned his deanship after it was revealed that the man charged in the murder was the dean's former lover.

In 1988 a Trumbull County resident, Maria F. Poling, was found guilty of killing her husband, Richard.

During the trial that summer, ghastly details emerged, including testimony by Mrs. Poling's alleged lover that the movie "Little Shop of Horrors" had inspired him to use an ax to cut the head from Poling's body.

Sebring Army Retiree Implicated in Spy Ring

The community of Sebring came under the spotlight in 1988 with a story of international intrigue. That August, West German authorities arrested a former resident, Clyde Lee Conrad, on suspicion of espionage.

Along with seven other people, the retired Army sergeant first-class was accused of involvement in a German-Hungarian spy network that for at least ten years had supplied secret U.S. and NATO documents to the Soviet Union.

THE VINDICATOR scored an exclusive interview with the sus-

MAY 1985: An illegal fireworks factory explodes on a Western Reserve Road farm in Beaver Township, killing nine people on the premises.

CLYDE LEE CONRAD

pect's wife from the couple's home in Bad Kreuznach, West Germany. She emphatically asserted her husband's innocence.

Although legalized in nineteen seventy-four by the outcome of Roe v. Wade before the U.S. Supreme Court, abortion became a local issue during the 1980s and would remain so into the next decade. The Most Rev. James Malone, Bishop of Youngstown, appeared on the NBC News program "Meet the Press," voicing the opposition of the Catholic Church to the practice, and in 1989 pro-life protests were conducted at an abortion clinic on Youngstown's South Side, resulting in dozens of arrests.

In '80, Presidential Hopefuls And Cost-Cutting Initiatives

The area's economic situation brought three national presidential candidates to the area during the 1980 election.

U.S. Sen. Edward M. Kennedy addressed three thousand at the Idora Park ballroom in May, then, although no longer a candidate, returned in October to appear at the Mahoning Country Club and in New Castle in support of President Jimmy Carter. Ronald Reagan also came to the valley in October, and President Carter himself conducted a town-hall meeting October 20 at WFMJ-TV.

During the first week of the decade, Ray T. Davis, former Mahoning County sheriff, was sent to prison, and ten months later James A. Traficant, Jr. became the county's newest sheriff.

With a withering tax base in 1980, Youngstown under Mayor George Vukovich was forced to cut department budgets and trim the work week to thirty-two hours in

1980: President-to-be Ronald Reagan meets the press at what by then was Jones & Laughlin's Campbell Works. At left, holding hard hat, is U.S. Rep. Lyle Williams, R-17th.

a bid to avoid deficit spending. Just before Christmas, Youngstown considered turning off some streetlights, calculating that the move would save $250,000 a year.

Mahoning County, on the other hand, took a different tack—a massive layoff of two hundred county workers shortly after voters killed a piggyback tax in November. The county commissioners had enacted the tax to offset a budget deficit predicted for the following year.

By 1986 many communities had such grave concerns about liability issues and the prohibitive cost of insurance that parks were closed as a money-saving measure, and in 1989 THE VINDICATOR reported that police in the area were beginning to arm themselves with semiautomatic pistols as drug-related violence grew at an alarming pace.

Political headlines were also made by State Sen. Henry Meshel, who was named president of the Ohio Senate in 1983, and Patrick J. Ungaro, who, as mayor of Youngstown elected in 1981 and reelected in 1984, 1987, and 1989, labored hard to put economic-development policies in place.

Youngstown's citizenry voted a

NO VACANCY: The Youngstown Hotel, a Boardman Street fixture since the 1920s, was torn down in the 1980s. In its heyday, it had a popular restaurant and Bert Rounds' busy barbershop.

DEFICIT BUDGETS
AND
DISORGANIZED CRIME

DIFFERENT PEOPLE had different thoughts about how to revitalize Youngstown. Mayor Vukovich launched a campaign in March 1981 to "brag a little about Youngstown."

As the city approached the November mayoral election, ten contenders stepped forward for consideration. But when a public meeting was held on the city budget, which called for a $6 million deficit, only one member of the general public attended.

ORGANIZED CRIME took several hits over the course of the 1980s. In 1983 the FBI arrested Orland Carabbia of Struthers on charges of marijuana-smuggling, and racketeer **Joseph ("Little Joey") Naples, Jr.**  was indicted that year for federal firearms violations and pleaded guilty. The two were imprisoned in 1984, the same year the FBI smashed a multimillion-dollar cocaine ring, sending ringleader Vincent J. Tisone to prison. In 1985, **Charles Carabbia,** the Struthers mobster who had been missing for years and was presumed dead, reappeared in the news as mob figure Angelo ("Big Ange") Lonardo gave the FBI chapter and verse on the underworld hit that took his life.

A FEDERAL INVESTIGATION led to the arrest of police officers in 1988. Lt. Michael S. ("Beef") Terlecky, former vice squad commander for the Mahoning County Sheriff's Department, and Joseph S. Rinko, former chief of the Beaver Township Police Department, were among eleven arrested by the FBI that April on charges of conducting illegal gambling businesses and obstructing state and local law-enforcement agencies. Terlecky was also alleged to have sold cocaine for a suspected drug dealer.

JUNE 1985: Once it was the El Dorosa Tavern in Poland Township. Then it was Sugar's Place. Then it was rubble after the bombers paid it an unwelcome visit.

black majority onto City Council for the first time in 1987, after a year of growing tension between the city's black community and its police force. Youngstown Police Chief Randall A. Wellington fired two patrolmen and suspended another in two racially related incidents.

Nineteen eighty-eight was termed "a watershed election year" by THE VINDICATOR as it reported the overturning of the old and the incoming of unprecedented new.

James A. Philomena, a Democrat, defeated his friend Gary L. Van Brocklin, the Republican incumbent, after a hotly contested race for Mahoning County prosecutor, and Attorney Beth A. Smith broke new ground by becoming the first woman elected to a Mahoning County judgeship.

Youngstown Voters OK First School Levy in a Generation

Atty. Charles ("Chip") Henry ended Thomas E. Carney's sixteen-year occupancy of the Ohio Senate, and Youngstown voters approved the first new operating levy for the city school district in nineteen years. At the end of the election season, Dr. William C.

Binning stepped down as long-time head of the Mahoning County Republican Party.

The issue of how to fund education appeared on ballots throughout the region. In the fall of 1988, eight of nine area districts passed school levies, a triumph THE VINDICATOR attributed to a unified front presented by each school district, its community, and area businesses.

City Schools Prevail in Tax Litigation; Villa Maria Closes

That same year, however, the Farmington district in Trumbull County merged with Bristol, and Columbiana High School couldn't field a football team because financial problems had caused the suspension of extracurricular activities. The Warren City School District's call for financial stability also went unanswered as residents continued to torpedo new tax proposals.

Youngstown schools, meanwhile, deflected a knockout punch when an antitax faction mounted a referendum to cut the recently passed 14.5-mill tax levy to one-half of one mill. After protracted court battles, the results of the November balloting were finally released, revealing that the reduction move had failed.

Private schools didn't necessarily fare any better. In 1989 Villa Maria, an all-girl Catholic high-school only recently turned coeducational, closed its doors permanently after nearly seven decades.

Sports captured the imagination of a public looking for any reason for celebration.

Boardman Little Leaguers Bring Home a Championship

In 1981 a Little League team Boardman sent to competition in Williamsport, Pennylvania, captured the World Series title for thirteen-year-olds, and Youngstown's Cardinal Mooney football team advanced to the Division II State Football Championship in the fall of 1982 and emerged victorious over Toledo Saint Francis. In 1985 the Rayen Tigers took the Ohio Class AA high school boys' basketball championship.

EDWARD J. DeBARTOLO, JR.

Although their team name spoke of California, the San Francisco 49ers earned a loyal following because they were owned by a hometown boy, Edward J. DeBartolo, Jr. The 49ers thrilled the Mahoning Valley each time they won the Super Bowl, in 1982 defeating the Cincinnati Bengals 26–21, in 1985 defeating the Miami Dolphins 38–16, and in 1989 defeating Cincinnati again, that time 20–16.

The Cleveland Browns' already-substantial following increased in April 1985 when the team hired a local talent, Boardman native Bernie Kosar, as quarterback.

Salem People Have Someone To Cheer for–Rich Karlis

Although the Browns lost their chance to take home the Super Bowl trophy in 1987, Salem residents cheered as their own Rich Karlis kicked the thirty-three-yard field goal that gave the championship to the Denver Broncos in overtime. The hopes of Browns fans were dashed again in 1988

BOARDMAN'S PRIDE: The Cleveland Browns added Bernie Kosar to their offensive roster in 1985. Kosar, who grew up in Boardman, forged a solid career as the Browns' starting quarterback, but the Clevelanders twice found their Super Bowl hopes dashed by John Elway and the Denver Broncos.

when the Broncos took home the Super Bowl trophy again.

Over the course of the decade, Raymond ("Boom-Boom") Mancini proved his mettle in the boxing ring, fighting as a lightweight, winning championships in two federations, and keeping local fans on the edges of their seats.

Among Mancini's memorable fights was a showdown with Jose Luis Ramirez in July 1981 in Warren. Mancini left the ring with his twentieth straight victory, taking home the lightweight championship of the North American Boxing Federation. Pitted against Alexis Arguello in October of that year, Mancini couldn't make the grade, losing the World Boxing Association championship in Atlan-

tic City on a technical knockout in the fourteenth round. Mancini rebounded in May 1982, however, winning the WBA lightweight crown with a first-round TKO over Arturo Frias. In November 1982 he successfully defended his world title, in Las Vegas, but that time, he and his opponent, Korea's Duk Koo Kim, boxed for fourteen grueling rounds. Kim ended up in a Las Vegas hospital with fatal injuries. When Boom-Boom geared up to defend his title in Johannesburg, South Africa, in 1983, he broke his collarbone. In 1985 he announced his retirement.

To replace Bill Narduzzi, Youngstown State University hired a new football coach in December 1985, a thirty-two-year-old assistant coach from Ohio State University named Jim Tressel.

GIANTS HURLER: Another Boardman standout, Dave Dravecky, pitched for the San Francisco Giants. Before the Giants, Dravecky was on the mound for the San Diego Padres.

The Youngstown Pride, formed in 1988, quickly rose to prominence in the new World Basketball League, a summer enterprise for professional athletes six-foot-four and under. Hometown fans cheered the following year as the Pride won the WBL Championship by beating the Calgary '88s at YSU's Beeghly Center.

National League Appoints Warren Man Its President

In 1989 the City of Warren was justifiably proud when native son Bill White was named the new president of baseball's National League.

The whole valley suffered with Boardman native Dave Dravecky, a pitcher with the San Francisco Giants, when he broke his left arm during a game in August 1989, and two months later broke it again as his team celebrated its National League championship. The entire community would rally around him and his family in the early nineties as he fought cancer, retired, and ultimately lost his arm to amputation.

In 1983 motorists had cause to be joyful with the reopening of a new $12 million Market Street Bridge, smoothing travel from the city's South Side to its downtown, but in 1986 the South Avenue Bridge closed, not to open again until the next decade.

Tracks running through downtown Youngstown, a source of controversy in the early part of the century until they were finally sunk into the hillside, were abandoned and pulled up beginning in 1984 after Conrail received approval to do so from the Interstate Commerce Commission.

In 1986 two chemical-truck accidents sent emergency crews scrambling to protect Youngstown's water supply at Meander Reservoir. That same year scavengers at Lake Milton looked for souvenirs on the dried lake bed while area merchants grumbled about the long repairs to the dam and the adverse effects an empty lake exerts on a community's life and livelihood.

In a development belying the difficulties endured locally, LTV Corporation reported in 1980 that its profits rose to $146.6 million. Lost in the small print was the fact that 1980's earnings report was the first to include figures from the Lykes Corporation.

In another sign that the hands of time could not be turned back, the Edward J. DeBartolo Corporation bought the former Youngstown Sheet & Tube headquarters in Boardman in 1980.

McDonald Steel Starts Up; Hunt Retrofits Brier Hill Mill

One economic success story made headlines at its inception in November 1981: After sixteen months of preparation, McDonald Steel Corporation cranked up production at U.S. Steel Corporation's forsaken McDonald Works, putting seventy-five steelworkers back to work. In 1983 it added a new mill.

Although there was great satisfaction in 1983 when the Hunt Steel Company began making casing pipe at a refurbished plant that had once been Youngstown Sheet & Tube's Brier Hill Works, the company fell half a million dollars behind in its gas bill later

AN AIR OF FINALITY: A padlock and chain say it all at Gate 3 of U.S. Steel's Ohio Works, the community's oldest steel company. Established in the 1890s, it also grew into one of the largest producers. The city would later promote the land for industrial redevelopment.

that year, causing East Ohio Gas to disconnect service to the plant.

In 1984 continuing problems in the steel industry forced further retrenchment at the few remaining steel facilities.

Uneven Production, Lower Profits Hit Valley Industries

Many Mahoning Valley companies, including those involved in steelmaking and fabrication, traveled a bumpy road of off-and-on production, shrinking profits, and rising layoffs. Large steel companies cut executive salaries in 1982, and General Motors' Lordstown Assembly Division and Packard Electric Division developed into a crazy-quilt pattern of layoffs, callbacks, and more layoffs. As the decade progressed, old mills and blast furnaces were razed one by one.

In July 1986 LTV Corporation filed for reorganization under Chapter Eleven of the federal bankruptcy code, a move that threatened the financial future of thousands, not only steelworkers still on the job, but also pensioners whose benefits were on the line. Fortunately, LTV agreed in April 1987 to a one-time payment to steelmakers who had lost their benefits when the government took over their pension plans.

Warren Consolidated Sale Arises from LTV Bankruptcy

After grueling negotiations in bankruptcy court, LTV received the go-ahead in June 1988 to sell its Warren steel plant and Republic Drainage Products for some $147 million, including $112 million in cash. The buyer, a company called the Renco Group, was about to be accepted when BMAC Corporation of California tossed in a surprise $157 million all-cash bid on the plant. The Renco Group, however, upped its cash offer by $5 million and promised a faster sale.

By September, Renco had com-

VANISHING AMERICANA: Workers left their jobs at Youngstown's LTV for the last time July 18, 1986. The steel company had filed for reorganization under Chapter Eleven of the federal bankruptcy code. Warren Consolidated Industries was one outcome of the bankruptcy case. As the years passed, old mills and blast furnaces were dismantled.

pleted the transactions and worked out a contract with the United Steel Workers of America. After all was said and done, the plant, Warren Consolidated Industries, began producing flat-rolled steel, and LTV had completed part of the reorganization required by its declaration of bankruptcy two years earlier.

Times were tough in the Shenango Valley as well. In 1987 Sharon Steel, the nation's twelfth-largest steelmaker, filed a petition in federal bankruptcy court to reorganize its operation and, hopefully, preserve its position as Mercer County's largest employer. The next year Victor Posner, Sharon Steel's chairman of the board, president, and chief executive of-

JANUARY 1983: The five-year-old son of a laid-off autoworker holds up his end at one of the rallies common to the early 1980s.

IN COURT: What began as the Sharon Steel Hoop in 1900 under the watchful eyes of Sharon industrialists ended up in 1987 under the watchful eyes of a bankruptcy trustee. From making barrel hoops, Sharon had evolved into the the twelfth-largest steelmaker.

ficer, found himself powerless when a judge appointed a trustee to run the company after creditors said that recovery was too slow under Posner's leadership.

Posner resigned in April as president and CEO, but remained as chairman; although he still owned more than seventy percent of the company's stock, he no longer had any say in running it. In November, the trustee, James W. Toren, submitted his own resignation.

Youngstown Commerce Park; An Ill-Fated Brewery Project

Bright spots came in patches. Youngstown Commerce Park, for example, welcomed its first tenants in 1983. Plans to move a German brewery there moved closer to completion in 1984, but the project disintegrated in 1985 when city government missed crucial deadlines, causing the federal government to cancel a $9.3 million development grant.

More bright spots appeared in 1986. That year, North Star Steel went into production on the site of the former Hunt Steel Company, and General Motors' newest au-

tomotive arm, Saturn Corporation, announced it would be ordering components from the Packard Electric Division in Warren.

Monus Develops Phar-Mor As Deep-Discount Chain

The area also witnessed the genesis of a new business concern, Phar-Mor, a discount drug and retail store, brainchild of Youngstown's own Mickey Monus.

Phar-Mor acquired the former

Strouss-Hirshberg building in downtown Youngstown and began developing it for offices and shops. As the decade closed, Federal Plaza seemed to be coming back into its own as the Phar-Mor Centre became a commercial success.

In 1987 the valley welcomed the New Avanti Motor Corporation when it joined forces with the Cafaro Company and moved here in 1988 from South Bend, Indiana, to open a new car-production plant in the Ross Industrial Park. Thou-

ENTREPRENEUR: Mickey Monus pushed the concept of deep discounting to the limits when he created Phar-Mor. As it later turned out, he pushed the law to the limits, too.

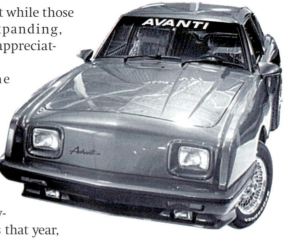

sands of residents lined up for days at the employment office on South Avenue in hopes of landing a job at the Albert Street plant.

In 1989 the Peter J. Schmitt Co. opened a warehouse in Jackson Township and announced plans to open a second; that warehouse and a second the company opened in Austintown would be closed before the company filed for Chapter Eleven bankruptcy protection in May 1992, putting more than five hundred employees out of work.

When Avanti sent its president, Michael E. Kelly, packing in January 1989, it foreshadowed the disillusionment the auto company, Peter J. Schmitt, and Phar-Mor would visit on the local economy

in the early 1990s, but while those companies were expanding, Greater Youngstown appreciated their presence.

Complicating the local economy, a drought of epic proportion struck in 1988. Northeastern Ohio farmers lost twenty to thirty percent of their corn, hay, soybeans, and oats crops that year, prompting many to sign up for emergency aid.

In August farmers in Maine sent more than ten thousand bales of hay to help Mahoning Valley farmers. The entire state was declared a natural-disaster area by the Department of Agriculture.

Interestingly, the valley bit off a piece of one of the country's fastest-growing industries in 1988 when plans for construction of a

AN OLDIE BUT GOODIE: The all-too-brief revival of Studebaker's Avanti sports car at Ross Industrial Park on Albert Street.

HOPEFUL: Thousands stood in line at the Ohio Bureau of Unemployment Services—some all night—to apply for jobs at the New Avanti Motor Corporation.

FEBRUARY 20, 1984: The Lincoln Park Bridge on Youngstown's East Side gives way under the weight of a truck, sending the truck, its driver, and a car carrying two women seventy feet into the gorge of Dry Run Creek. All recovered from their injuries.

new prison in northeast Ohio began making headlines.

Of the four locations under consideration for the state penitentiary, Youngstown was the leading contender until industrial waste was found on the proposed site.

Warren Becomes the First To Capitalize on Prison Boom

In the end, the announcement came that the valley would get the $35.4 million facility, but Youngstown was out of the running; the prison would go to Warren, where the local opposition with its concerns about safety and land devaluation had been vocal

and unyielding.

Bits of good news occasionally flashed across the horizon.

In 1989 CSC Industries of Warren, parent company of Copperweld, reported a profit for the first time since becoming independent two years earlier, and rumors circulated that Toys R Us was looking at the valley for a new regional distribution center. In October of that year, dodging a bullet, Commercial Intertech successfully fought off a buyout proposal from Haas & Partners.

As Decade Ends, Concern About GF, Standard, and GM

Yet as the eighties drew to a close and the local economy appeared to be recovering marginally with a bit of diversification, the Mahoning Valley experienced three more setbacks that further aggravated the uncertainty that had been part of people's lives since 1977.

First came the announcement that GF Corporation would probably close in 1990; then that Standard Slag, a Youngstown mainstay for seventy-five years, would be sold to Standard LaFarge; and finally that General Motors would close its Lordstown van plant in 1991, a loss of twenty-five hundred high-paying jobs (although Lordstown would be the exclusive producer of the Chevrolet Cavaliers beginning that same year).

OCTOBER 1988: A summer drought nearly dries up the south branch of Meander Creek near Kirk Road in Austintown. The creek, a tributary of the Meander watershed, feeds into Meander Reservoir, the source of domestic water for Youngstown, Niles, and suburban customers of the Mahoning Valley Sanitary District.

News from the Mahoning and Shenango Valleys

1990

JAN. 10: Flames from a natural-gas explosion damage East Ohio Gas equipment at Wick and Lincoln avenues; state investigators later say the gas line was unmarked.

APRIL 5: A bomb damages the Cafaro Company office building on Belmont Avenue and shatters windows in homes and other buildings.

AUG. 8: A crew from CBS-TV's top-rated "60 Minutes" visits Youngstown to gather data for a profile of U.S. Rep. James A. Traficant, Jr.

DEC. 3: The space shuttle Columbia lifts off; aboard is payload specialist Ron Parise, a Warren native.

1991

FEB. 27: In the Persian Gulf war, an Iraqi missile destroys a barracks near Farrell's 475th Quartermaster Unit, killing a New Castle man. A Liberty couple learns their son-in-law died when his helicopter went down in enemy territory.

APRIL 21: The Youngstown Metropolitan Housing Authority plans a night basketball league to keep teen-agers off the streets.

AUG. 7: Metal flies into a crowd watching explosive demolition of six Boardman radio towers once used by WFMJ; two are injured.

OCT. 15: Six prisoners use a makeshift rope to escape from the Mahoning County Jail.

OCT. 31: St. Elizabeth Hospital Medical Center will close its eighty-year-old nursing school and provide clinical training for Gannon University nursing students.

1992

JAN. 20: THE COLUMBUS DISPATCH names Jim Tressel of Youngstown State University Ohio football coach of the year for the third time.

FEB. 5: School officials curtail the use of book bags after two Campbell Memorial High School students are found to be carrying knives.

JUNE 26: Cuts in state aid cause Youngstown State to lay off thirty-two nonteaching employees.

AUG. 2: Krista Blake, Columbiana, a national figure in AIDS education, is on the cover of NEWSWEEK magazine. She will die in April 1994.

SEPT. 4: The women's professional golf tournament will be renamed Youngstown-Warren LPGA Classic and will move to Avalon Lakes.

NOV. 21: The final leg of Pennsylvania's Beaver Valley Expressway opens to traffic with a ribbon-cutting ceremony near New Castle.

DEC. 8: Federal Aviation Administration OKs transferring Youngstown-Warren Regional Airport to Western Reserve Port Authority.

1993

JAN. 27: John Antonucci's departure as chairman and CEO cuts local ties to Denver's Colorado Rockies baseball team; he and Mickey Monus had acquired the franchise.

MARCH 23: A $3 million state loan will enable Exal Corporation, maker of aerosol cans, to build on reclaimed LTV land in Youngstown.

APRIL 17: At University Hospital, Pittsburgh, surgeons transplant a liver, pancreas, stomach, and intestines into Vincent Ryan of Canfield.

JUNE 11: South High confers one hundred-nine diplomas at its final commencement, ending more than eighty years of education.

1994

MARCH 23: Mahoning County's 911 emergency calling system debuts quietly; on June 22, Trumbull County goes on line, the last major population center in Ohio to do so.

APRIL 1: Smoking banned in all Mahoning County buildings.

JULY 4: At Niles' Great East Plaza, a stray bullet hits Kim Williams, a player in the Youngstown-Warren LPGA Classic. A target shooter practicing a mile away turns himself in.

OCT. 7: Singer Tony Bennett achieves the first museum exhibit of his paintings at Butler Institute of American Art, which is celebrating its seventy-fifth anniversary.

NOV. 6: Fulfilling a wish broadcast over TV, Alex Trebek, host of "Jeopardy!," conducts the Greenville Symphony at Thiel College in the overture to Rossini's "Cinderella."

1995

FEB. 9: Isaiah Jackson, who directs the Dayton Philharmonic, will replace David Effron as conductor of the Youngstown Symphony; Jackson will be only the sixth conductor in sixty-nine years.

MAY 22: Rodney King, whose videotaped beating by police caused the Los Angeles riots three years ago, is charged near New Castle with drunken driving.

JUNE 22: The Senate Judiciary

Committee approves Common Pleas Judge Peter C. Economus of Mahoning County for the federal bench. The full Senate confirms the nomination July 1; he is sworn in July fourth and assigned to Youngstown.

JULY 13: St. Elizabeth Hospital Medical Center will close its thirty-year-old poison-control center August 1, leaving residents of four counties without a hotline for emergency information.

SEPT. 10: Amtrak's New York-Chicago Broadway Limited rolls through the valley for the last time, once more leaving Youngstown without passenger service.

SEPT. 14: Mahoning, Columbiana, and most of Trumbull County will become part of the 330 area code in March 1996, ending years in 216.

OCT. 13: Seven women sue Tippecanoe Country Club for sex discrimination, saying they can't golf on weekend mornings, can't use a dining room, and must reapply for membership if their husbands die.

1996

JAN. 13: Rocker Bruce Springsteen entertains a sell-out crowd at Stambaugh Auditorium. His composition "Youngstown" refers to the "Jenny," a steel-industry landmark, the Jeannette Blast Furnace.

MARCH 28: Western Reserve Care System closes its Southside Hospital emergency room and consolidates services elsewhere. Northside to get inpatient surgery; Southside, an urgent-care center; and Beeghly Medical Park, expanded hours.

APRIL 29: Melanie Valerio, twenty-seven, a Campbell native, makes the U.S. Olympic swimming team.

AUG. 3: Rod White of Hermitage, Pennsylvania, helps the U.S. archery team beat South Korea for the gold medal in the Atlanta Olympics.

AUG. 29: Campbell's is the only public school system in Ohio mandating uniforms for all grades.

SEPT. 22: Archbishop Spyridon, born George Papageorgiou in Warren, is the first native-born head of the U.S. Greek Orthodox Church.

DEC. 22: Christmas sensation: Thirty VINDICATOR classifieds offer Tickle Me Elmo, a Sesame Street doll that laughs, talks, and shakes. "Best offer" to $600.00 asked.

1997

MARCH 21: Thomas Bopp, forty-

seven, a Chaney High graduate and amateur astronomer in Arizona, was one of two who discovered the Hale-Bopp Comet on July 23, 1995.

APRIL 12: State health officials consider air drops of rabies vaccine after twelve cases of rabid raccoons turn up in Mahoning County, including one in Youngstown.

NOV. 14: Five hundred honor Pat Ungaro, Youngstown's departing and longest-serving mayor. It's like "a wedding and a funeral all in one," he says at Mr. Anthony's.

DEC. 3: The Vocal Group Hall of Fame and Museum opens as a tourist attraction in Sharon; it will enshrine musical groups yearly.

1998

APRIL 2: INDUSTRY WEEK magazine ranks Youngstown-Warren twelfth-best U.S. manufacturing area, calling it a "bounce-back community."

JUNE 2: Inspectors investigate a paint-department explosion at General Motors that killed an Atwater man, Dennis Schaefer, fifty-two.

JUNE 11: MONEY magazine lists Youngstown nineteenth of the twenty-four best places to live among medium-size Midwest communities; it was 291st and 224th the previous two years. Sharon is fourteenth of twenty-one small areas in the eastern U.S.

JULY 2: The Fox television network will begin broadcasting by September 1 on channels 40 and 62.

SEPT. 26: Pennsylvania's strongest earthquake–5.2 on the Richter scale –is centered near Greenville but causes minimal damage.

NOV. 20: The Wick-Pollock Inn, Youngstown's last full-service hotel, closes its doors.

1999

MARCH 17: Plans for an $11.2 million federal building and courthouse at Commerce and Wick avenues receive final approval.

MARCH 27: The Golden Eagle boys' basketball team of Kennedy Christian High School, Hermitage, Pennsylvania, earns its fourth Pennsylvania state crown in five years.

MAY 18: Minor league basketball may come to South Field House next winter as a franchise of the International Basketball Association.

JUNE 16: The National Packard Museum in Warren will open July 4.

Chapter

RISING FROM THE ASHES

STATE OFFICE BUILDING: Site preparation begins for the George V. Voinovich Government Center, a project of the Youngstown Central Area Community Improvement Corporation. The CIC, a body of civic-minded business people and public officials, devotes itself to the revitalization of downtown Youngstown. The Voinovich center, named for the Ohio governor who backed the project, opened in 1999 and houses state offices that serve eastern Ohio.

At last, the requiem was over, and the clouds parted a bit to admit the sunlight of the future. Some good things happened, and for once they had nothing to do with iron or steel.

What ever happened to vinyl records? For that matter, where did the milkman go? Has anyone bought a girdle recently, or made multiple copies with carbon paper, or ordered a malted at a soda fountain?.... Many objects and concepts that we once took for granted as part of everyday life either have vanished or seem destined to disappear. Shoe-fitting fluoroscopes, blue laws, and men's garters are distant memories. Landfills and hotel keys are just beginning to pass into history....

SUSAN JONAS AND MARILYN NISSENSON
"GOING, GOING, GONE: VANISHING AMERICANA"

NEW LIFE: The Voinovich Government Center gets the once-over from Bill Cushwa, Community Improvement Corporation executive director (with hard hat), and James Conrad, administrator-CEO of the Ohio Bureau of Workers Compensation.

MANY OF THE PROBLEMS that troubled the Mahoning Valley as the eighties drew to a close continued right into the 1990s, mindless of the change in calendar. People struggled to come to terms with a mixed economic picture and a declining and aging population, along with headline-grabbing murder trials, antiabortion protests, bombings, and labor strikes.

Yet for an eight-month period beginning in the summer of 1990, the focus of the region and the country turned half a world away to the Middle East when Iraq's Saddam Hussein engineered a surprise invasion of Kuwait. In the months that followed, as the United States and its allies banded together, first in Operation Desert Shield and afterward in Operation Desert Storm in January 1991, residents of the Mahoning and Shenango valleys prayed for the safety of area service personnel who had been sent to the war zone.

What has since come to be known as the Gulf War proceeded to a relatively quick conclusion, but eight years later new worries troubled area residents, particularly those of eastern European descent, as the United States and the North Atlantic Treaty Organization determined to bring down President Slobodan Milosevic of Yugoslavia and thereby stop the massacre of ethnic minorities numbering in the hundreds of thousands.

On the home front, a political cause that made repeated headlines through the summer and fall of 1990 was that of antiabortion demonstrations at the Mahoning Women's Center on Market Street. In July a man drove his van into a

MARCH 7, 1991: A U.S. Marine patrol performing perimeter security walks across the charred landscape near a burning oil well near Kuwait City during the Persian Gulf War.

doctors in Philadelphia performed corrective heart surgery on infant Jared Ausnehmer of Austintown.

But the politics of local medicine made news as well when the Mahoning County coroner's office endured a shake-up in April 1993 with the indictment of Dr. Nathan D. Belinky for illegally providing prescription medicines to drug dealers and his lover, a woman who had died of a drug overdose in 1991.

Belinky, seventy-nine, who became a deputy coroner in 1946 and was appointed county coroner in 1974 to succeed his deceased brother, was also accused of writing prescriptions for several women in exchange for Saturday morning sex in his office. Belinky was one of the

NATHAN D. BELINKY, M.D.

most successful politicians in the county, winning his first election

crowd of abortion protesters across the street from the clinic, then two demonstrators blocking the clinic driveway were run over in November when the driver of a sport-utility vehicle apparently did not see them lying on the sidewalk.

Despite judicial orders restricting demonstrations and forbidding threats and intimidation of workers or patients, tactical and mounted police had to head off a confrontation November 12 between hundreds of demonstrators and counter-demonstrators.

Twenty Protesters from Clinic Withhold Names, Sit in Jail

Five days later, twenty abortion protesters who identified themselves only as "sacrificial lambs" were arrested at the clinic. Fourteen of them blocked doors for five hours by locking themselves to each other and cars with chains, pipes, locks, and seatbelts. For twelve days they sat in jail, refusing to reveal their identities to police.

Before it was over, the Peace Council of Youngstown offered to mediate the dispute between the demonstrators and counter-demonstrators, Ohio's first lady, Dagmar Celeste, visited the clinic to plead for peace and to support the right to abortion, and the Most Reverend James W. Malone, bishop of Youngstown, came forward to say that however much the Catholic Church opposed abortion, the Youngstown Catholic Diocese also opposed violent confrontations at the abortion clinic.

Medical miracles also made news that spring when three-week-old Justin Sopkovich of Youngstown got a new heart in a three-hour transplant operation in Pittsburgh, and a few days later

1990: Youngstown police converge on a truck that struck antiabortion protesters during one of the many demonstrations at the Mahoning Women's Center on Market Street.

in 1976 and holding the post until his resignation in May 1993.

Belinky pleaded guilty to nineteen charges of drug trafficking and illegal possession of drug documents. The court sentenced him to thirty days in minimum-security prison, followed by a year of house arrest and five years of probation. He also surrendered his medical license and received a fine of $76,500.

Internet Case Raises Issue Of Limits on Free Speech

As society learned to negotiate the new information highway of the Internet, THE VINDICATOR carried a story in 1995 of a Boardman man attending the University of Michigan at Ann Arbor.

Arrested for using the name of a classmate as the victim in a gruesome fantasy, he was charged with interstate transmission of a threat by the United State's attorney's office in Detroit, a move that drew national headlines and provoked debate across the country about the free-speech ramifications of the government's actions.

SEPTEMBER 1990: Bombers target the home of County Prosecutor James A. Philomena. He would figure prominently in the news as the decade advanced.

Shades of Youngstown's reputation as "Little Chicago" three decades earlier, bombs were detonated near the Cafaro Company on Belmont Avenue in April 1990 and at the home of the Mahoning County prosecutor, James Philomena, in September. Another bomb injured a sixty-three-year-old South Side woman in December of that year when it exploded in her hand on her front porch.

The newspaper also highlighted lighter notes, however, as in 1990, when fairgoers bade farewell to the sometimes silly messages over the sound tower at the Canfield Fair, and the Ohio Lottery made millionaires of several valley residents.

When matters of religious import touched the Mahoning Valley, THE VINDICATOR memorialized those as well, as occurred when Pope John Paul II selected the fourth bishop of the Youngstown Diocese, the Most Reverend Thomas J. Tobin, in December of 1995. Bishop Tobin was installed in a special ceremony in Saint Columba Cathedral two months later.

The unpleasant side of human nature revealed itself time and time again.

TAMI ENGSTROM

In February 1991 a young woman named Tami Engstrom disappeared from a tavern in the community of Masury,

KENNETH BIROS

only to have the last person seen with her, Kenneth Biros, direct police a couple of days later to her headless torso along a wooded road in Irwin Township, Pennsylvania, and a day after that to her head and other body parts along another wooded road in Butler County, Pennsylvania.

Biros was subsequently convicted and sentenced to death, but Mrs. Engstrom's relatives declared the electric chair too good for him and announced they would burn him in effigy at a Halloween party.

Twice in the decade homicide rates in Youngstown hit highs. In 1991, fifty-nine were killed; in 1995,

APRIL 1990: An agent of the Treasury Department's Alcohol, Tobacco & Firearms division walks through broken glass from a bomb blast at the Cafaro Building on Belmont Avenue.

that number rose to sixty-six, the majority of whom were under twenty-five years of age. In a report November 6, 1995, the paper noted that killings were averaging 1.3 a week for the year. With eight weeks left in the year, Youngstown already had thirteen more killings than Pittsburgh, a city four times its size. It would finish the year fourteen ahead of its neighbor to the southeast.

In a society that became remarkably mobile during the twentieth century, numerous valley residents mourned the loss of loved ones in airline crashes during the decade. Several airline accidents made national and international news, but the one that

MAY 22, 1991: Capt. Robert George, right, and firefighter Ed Holcomb retrieve the body of a slain woman from Crab Creek below the Oak Street Bridge. Youngstown had fifty-nine killings in 1991 and sixty-six in 1995—more than Pittsburgh.

touched the Youngstown locality most deeply was that of USAir Flight 427, which literally seemed to fall out of the sky on September 8, 1994, ten miles northwest of Pittsburgh International Airport.

All 132 people on board were killed when the flight, en route from Chicago's O'Hare to Pittsburgh and West Palm Beach, Florida, crashed into a ravine near Aliquippa, Pennsylvania. Among the dead were Todd Johnston of Alliance, Robert E. Leonhardt of Neshannock Township, Randall J. Dellefield, a former Canfield resident, Leonard Grasso, formerly of the Greenville, Pennsylvania, area, and Paula and Anthony Rich, former Poland residents, and their unborn child.

Back on terra firma, a convoy of about one hundred slow-moving semitrailers made news in September 1990 when it tied up traffic on Interstate 80 to protest rising gasoline prices and a federal proposal to outlaw truck radios.

Gov. Tom Ridge of Pennsylvania shortened the time necessary to drive across his state in June 1995 when he signed into law a bill raising the speed limit for cars and trucks to sixty-five mph from fifty-five on rural interstates. Maximum speed limits in the state had been fifty-five since the Arab oil embargo two decades earlier.

Rabies Epidemic in '97 Hits Raccoon Population Hardest

The animal kingdom also showed evidence of its mobility, or at least that of its diseases, during the nineties when an epidemic that had been slowly spreading west from the east coast over the previous two decades reached Ohio.

In 1997 local cases of rabies were discovered for the first time in decades, and more than half the 1,309 raccoons tested for rabies statewide were from Mahoning, Trumbull, and Columbiana counties, according to figures from the Ohio Department of Health. The state launched a full-scale emergency operation that

SEPTEMBER 8, 1994: The wreckage of US-Air Flight 427 litters a gorge near Aliquippa, Pennsylvania.

AUGUST 6, 1997: The placard reads "Official Raccoon Rabies Baiting Vehicle." The state deposited vaccine-laced bait for wildlife in areas with the highest incidence of rabies.

April. By public health order, the owners of all dogs and cats in Mahoning, Trumbull, Columbiana, and Ashtabula counties were required to keep their pets under restraint and have them vaccinated against rabies. As a means of preventing the epidemic's spread, the state dropped vaccine-laced bait for wild animals over heavily infested areas.

Traficant Makes the Circuit Of Television News Shows

Looking back on 1990, THE VINDICATOR observed, "This was the year the Youngstown area shared its good-old-boy congressman with the rest of the nation and world."

The newspaper was referring, of course, to two appearances by James A. Traficant, Jr. on the "Donahue" talk show, frequent guest spots on the Cable News Network's political-commentary program "Crossfire," a profile on the CBS News program "60 Minutes," and an interview with a Japanese television network for a documentary on U.S.-Japanese trade.

What was viewed as an unflattering portrayal of Youngstown in the "60 Minutes" segment inspired

a local public-relations consultant and twelve YSU students to mount a letter-writing campaign denouncing the "Youngstown bashing."

At one point that year, the congressman made headlines when, speaking on the floor of the U.S. House of Representatives, he likened his colleagues there to prostitutes. He later apologized for the remark.

On the education front, a political turn was taken in Youngstown State University's search for a new president when five of the nine members of its board of trustees voted privately in 1991 to appoint a Youngstown lawyer, Paul M. Dutton, to succeed the outgoing president, Neil Humphrey. Dutton had withdrawn his name from consideration a month earlier, but when none of the three finalists received a majority vote, Trustee Mickey Monus nominated Dutton, a business associate.

Ultimately, Dutton's appointment was withdrawn. That took place, however, only after an uprising by the university community, a public outcry, and legal steps by THE VINDICATOR protesting obvious violations of Ohio's open-meetings law made Dutton's selection untenable.

Several other educational institutions and the public libraries struggled with labor conflicts and financing challenges.

School employees at Beaver Local, New Castle, Bristol, Neshannock Township, and Girard

AFTERTHOUGHTS: Federal Plaza, the 1974 revamp of Central Square, was not a unanimous favorite: some thought it turned people and commerce away. By the nineties, the city was looking into reconnecting east and west to again allow free access to Federal Street.

staged walkouts in 1990. Another strike closed the Mahoning County library system for the month of February that year.

Union Strikes Bring Backlash From Voters on School Taxes

Other school strikes included those at Springfield Local in 1992, and Youngstown, Niles, Champion, Newton Falls, Laurel, Mathews, and Wilmington in Pennsylvania in 1997.

Tax issues to fund education were defeated repeatedly as frustrated taxpayers used the voting booths as a means of protesting the state's structure for financing education. And just as changing tastes and shifts in population had doomed Pennsylvania's Villa Maria High School in 1989, War-

IN 1999, the magazine CONGRESSIONAL QUARTERLY termed U.S. Rep. James A. Traficant, Jr. a "party of one," highly popular at home.

GOING, GOING, GONE

REQUIESCAT IN PACE: Implosion obliterates one of the last reminders of the Steel Valley, Republic Steel headquarters at the foot of the the Market Street Bridge, on February 15, 1995.

ren students bade farewell in the fall of 1990 to Warren Western Reserve High School. The closing of the West Side school consolidated high-school classes once again at the older Warren Harding on the East Side.

The difficulties faced by the Youngstown City School District were singular, however, when it found itself at the center of a power struggle.

New Superintendent Causes A Stir in Youngstown Schools

From the moment Dr. Alfred Tutela arrived from Cleveland to become superintendent in August 1992, school board members, teachers, and he agreed on nothing. By September 1993, with the district facing a multimillion-dollar budget deficit, the teachers went on strike, the principal of a junior high school accused a board member of assaulting him in school, and another board member called for Tutela's resignation.

With no progress at the bargaining table, the board tried opening a school for seniors only, but the teachers spiked that plan. After nearly three weeks, marathon negotiations were called in the Common Pleas courtroom of Judge R. Scott Krichbaum, but after four days without progress, the judge accepted Congressman Traficant's offer to mediate.

At that point, the bargaining units went into round-the-clock talks at the Ramada Inn in Liberty. Ninety hours later, a settlement was announced, but only after the impatient congressman threatened to throw the negotiators in jail.

Eighteen months later, in June 1994, Tutela announced that he was leaving Youngstown to take a superintendency in Massachusetts.

On the national political scene, the Mahoning Valley's

PENTAGON PROJECT: Until Secretary of Defense Les Aspin and President Clinton changed the rules, the valley was in the running for a Defense Finance & Accounting Services center—and four thousand jobs.

emotions turned on hope, frustration, and, finally, dejection as it tried to have President Clinton make good in 1993 on a promise he had made as a presidential candidate a year earlier.

Political Expediency Dashes Hopes for Accounting Center

At stake was a Pentagon facility that would be assigned under the previous administration's plan to consolidate Defense Finance & Accounting Services centers. Overjoyed by the possibility of four thousand new jobs, the valley assembled a $525-million application, an alluring plan in which it offered to build the government a huge complex in Liberty Township.

Pentagon records showed that the valley's plan, much of it coordinated by the Cafaro Company, scored second-highest

THREE PENITENTIARIES, THREE STORIES

AS IT HAD in the late eighties, the national growth industry of correctional institutions continued to exert an impact on the valley. Columbiana County officials and residents endured a series of delays during 1992 after the U.S. Bureau of Prisons announced plans in January to build a 2,750-bed prison in Elkton Township (as had first been reported by THE VINDICATOR in May 1991). As Columbiana County debated the federal plan, Youngstown's mayor, Patrick Ungaro, announced that Youngstown was waiting for a shot at landing the prison.

EXPONENTS and detractors met repeatedly in turbulent gatherings, and twenty-five property owners learned that the federal government planned to appropriate their land for the project, a total of 336 acres.

When the federal bureau released an environmental-impact study claiming there were no serious environmental problems at the chosen site, the prison's opposition and five YSU professors disputed the claim. A deluge of letters delayed settlement of the impact statement until early 1993, and construction didn't begin until 1995.

The following year the Ohio Department of Rehabilitation & Correction announced a $60 million prison for Youngstown to house five hundred of the state's most dangerous inmates.

The so-called super-maximum lockup, planned for the south-

YOUNGSTOWN: The Ohio State Penitentiary is on the East Side. The idea of a super-secure prison for the most dangerous inmates grew out of the 1993 Lucasville riot.

west corner of McGuffey and Coitsville Center roads, would hold one prisoner per cell, and each would be allowed out of his cell for only one hour a day. The "super-max" concept developed in Ohio after a riot at the Southern Ohio Correctional Facility in Lucasville killed nine inmates and a guard in April 1993. A camp to quarter 250 minimum-security inmates was also planned.

YOUNGSTOWN: The privately owned Northeast Ohio Correctional Center found the going rough after it opened.

IN SUMMER 1998, national news stories were generated about the valley's newest prison, the Northeast Ohio Correctional Center, which had opened on Hubbard Road in 1997. NOCC, operated by Corrections Corporation of America, was the first private prison in Ohio and had a contract to

house prisoners from the District of Columbia.

STABBINGS AND the slayings of two inmates in winter 1998 brought court orders to transfer the most dangerous inmates elsewhere, but then, in July, six prisoners escaped. Five were caught within days, but the sixth wasn't found till nearly five weeks later in Buffalo.

After a study, the Justice Department recommended improvements. In November 1998, after months of hard work under Warden Jimmy Turner, the American Correctional Association recommended NOCC for accreditation.

ELKTON: Years passed and the debate intensified before the the Elkton Federal Correctional Institution got under way.

in the country, outshining those of more than one hundred other communities. A study said that the DFAS and spinoff jobs could pump as much as $128 million into the local economy each year.

Yet despite the high ranking, President Clinton and his defense secretary, Les Aspin, rejected the overall competition in July 1993. For the record, the administration said it didn't like the idea of communities paying for government services, but the local application team laid the rejection to arm-twisting and jawboning by powerful politicians whose areas would have lost the competition.

Though the original competition was rejected, the twenty finalists were promised first consideration under a new plan comprising a center with seven hundred fifty to one thousand jobs.

Amended Rules Put Pentagon Center Beyond Area's Reach

The new site-selection process, however, had a catch: It specified using closed military bases and expanding existing accounting centers, of which the Mahoning Valley had neither. The government extended consideration to the valley only under the option of renting available office space. Government officials went through the motions of looking at some properties, but no one was really surprised when nothing happened. In the end, the accounting centers went elsewhere, and the Mahoning Valley added another disappointment to what was becoming an endless list.

As 1991 ended THE VINDICATOR reported that Congressman Traficant and Youngstown Mayor Patrick J. Ungaro were riding out the year on a crest, having successfully flexed their political muscles on behalf of the airport.

Ungaro had threatened to close the airport at year's end unless a solution were found to the city's fiscal problems. The Youngstown

JULY 4, 1996: President Clinton finds time for a little political glad-handing after presenting an $11.5 million grant for expansion of Youngstown-Warren Regional Airport.

and Warren chambers of commerce took the threat seriously and pushed the idea of a regional airport owned by Mahoning and Trumbull counties. But someone had to persuade the commissioners of both counties to take over the airport and cover any losses.

As described by Bertram de Souza, VINDICATOR columnist:

> Enter Traficant.... The congressman denies strong-arming anyone, but the fact remains that four of the six commissioners are running for reelection next year. Traficant is the region's most powerful politician. Today a port authority is in place appointed by the commissioners, and Mahoning and Trumbull counties have each pledged up to $100,000 to cover any operating shortage in 1992.

Come 1996, President Clinton, running for reelection, aware that people held him accountable for breaking his campaign promise of four years earlier, came through with $11.5 million in federal money to help enlarge Youngstown-Warren Regional Airport. It was obviously a political peace offering, Clinton's way of acknowl-

MICHAEL MORLEY

edging that the Mahoning Valley's support would be critical to his carrying Ohio in November.

The complexion of Mahoning County politics changed abruptly in 1994 when Michael Morley, a Boardman lawyer, and his Mahoning County Democrats for Change dethroned longtime party chairman Don L. Hanni, Jr.

In a bitter campaign, Hanni's detractors derided him as a disciple of the spoils system, who, to the detriment of the Mahoning Valley, ran the party for personal and political gain. Morley and his cadre of party reformers put up nearly four hundred candidates for precinct-committee posts across the county, pledging a platform of political cooperation and professionalism.

A Commissioner and Party Chief Resign Unexpectedly

Although he ultimately lost his party position to Morley, Hanni still managed to gain a four-year term on the county board of elections.

In a political development of consequence in the final year of the decade, Michael Morley, Mahoning County Democratic Party chairman, and County Commissioner David L. Engler resigned their positions in June, stating in a press conference that they had accomplished most of what they had hoped to in their respective offices and were looking forward to pursuing other opportunities.

As the twentieth century drew to a close, the Mahoning Valley's political structure came increasingly under the microscope of criminal investigators, prosecutors, and judges. Even criminal-defense lawyers who had thought they'd seen it all marveled as federal and state prosecutors peeled back layer after layer of corruption and criminality, deceit, and deception.

Investigations Target Mafia Infiltration of Government

In 1994, accused of excessive spending and violating state bidding regulations, James Fiorenzo, the Democrat Trumbull County engineer, was convicted of theft in office, imprisoned, and removed from his post.

That same year an investment scandal in its treasurer's office rocked Columbiana County. Ardel Strabala, the county's treasurer of twenty-five years, had invested millions of the county's money through his son Stephen, who didn't even have a license to handle securities. More than $6 million of the $9.9 million thus invested then disappeared, most of it simply lost in high-risk stock options.

In March 1996, after decades of allegations and suspicion, a Mahoning County grand jury began an investigation of political fraud in the area, and the FBI alleged that the mob had ties to the county's sheriff's department, judges and other public officials.

Although nine people were indicted the next year, many of the headlines focused on the dismissal of Special Prosecutor Jonathan E. Rosenbaum for flouting local rules of evidence. In the weeks that followed, Harry A. Hanna, the visiting common pleas judge, stepped aside himself at the re-

Special Prosecutor Robert A. Ruggeri was one of six special prosecutors who handled phases of a local investigation into political corruption and public fraud.

quest of the chief justice of the Ohio Supreme Court amid allegations that his discharge of Rosenbaum had been inappropriate. So

the investigation could continue, Robert A. Ruggeri, a criminal-defense lawyer from Cleveland, became the new special prosecutor, and Tommy L. Thompson of Columbus was appointed the new visiting judge.

YSU's Penguins Make Their Mark on the Football Field

Youngstown State University's football program generated national headlines throughout the nineties.

In 1991, the Penguins, coached by Jim Tressel, were selected to appear in their third straight national playoff, and four games later defeated West Virginia's Marshall twenty-five to seventeen to win the national title. YSU lost to Marshall the following year but came roaring back to beat Marshall for the national title once again in 1993.

In December 1994 the Penguins defeated Boise State twenty-eight to fourteen to win the Division 1-AA national championship for the third time in four years. The Penguins won the title once again by beating McNeese State in December 1997.

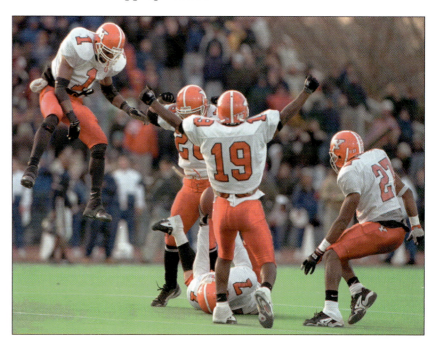

DECEMBER 6, 1997: Youngstown State University's Penguins beat McNeese State to capture their fourth national title in the decade.

For Cleveland Browns stalwarts in the Mahoning Valley, 1993 began a tough stretch as coach Bill Belichick cut quarterback Bernie Kosar.

Kosar Joins the Cowboys; The Browns Leave Cleveland

Kosar fans, however, were rewarded to find their man hired by the Dallas Cowboys, who then went on to win the 1994 Super Bowl a couple of months later. In 1997 Kosar announced his retirement after twelve years in professional football.

As for the original Browns, owner Art Modell announced in November 1995 that he would move the team from Cleveland's Municipal Stadium to Maryland, claiming that the relocation was necessary to keep the team afloat financially.

Fans, advertisers, and the press speculated that, in fact, Modell was irritated that the Browns had been left out of Cleveland's Gateway project, which produced Gund Arena for the Cleveland Cavaliers of the National Basketball Association and Jacobs Field for the American League's Cleveland Indians baseball team.

SEPTEMBER 1998: From left: Bernie Kosar, former Cleveland Browns quarterback, Carmen A. Policy, and Alfred Lerner at a news conference after the National Football League unanimously accepted Lerner's $530 million offer for the Browns expansion franchise.

Municipal Stadium, home of the Browns from 1946 until they became the Baltimore Ravens, was razed in 1996. A new stadium for the expansion Browns opened in 1999.

PENALTY FLAG: Edward DeBartolo, Jr. lost control of the San Francisco 49ers after the National Football League banned him from managing the team. DeBartolo got caught up in a federal investigation.

Whatever the reason, the Browns became the Ravens in Baltimore. In September 1998, however, northeast Ohio was given cause to look forward to the 1999 National Football League season when Alfred Lerner bought a new

JULY 23, 1999: Se Ri Pak, 1998 winner of the Giant Eagle LPGA Tournament, is back in the Mahoning Valley for another shot at the title, but it isn't in the cards. The nineteen ninety-nine championship belongs to someone else: Jackie Gallagher-Smith.

THE MOB, THE MVSD, AND THE PUBLIC OFFICIALS IN THE CROSSHAIRS

THE KILLING of Ernest A. Biondillo, Jr. in June 1996 placed the Mafia squarely in the headlines. Though the murder remained mysterious for nearly a year, when the pieces began coming together, the focus fell on the underworld of Pittsburgh's La Cosa Nostra. When Lenine ("Lenny") Strollo of Canfield and Bernard Altshuler of Liberty were arrested by the FBI in December 1997 in an ongoing investigation of gambling and public corruption, the two also faced charges in the Biondillo case.

ON THE STAND: Lenny Strollo testifies in Federal District Court about the mob he commanded, the rivals he fought, and the politicians he corrupted.

ERNEST A. BIONDILLO, JR.

The Mahoning Valley Sanitary District entered the headlines in summer 1997 when the Ohio auditor's office called for recovery of some $2.7 million in improper expenditures. The auditor also issued citations and recommendations concerning questionable practices within the MVSD. Edward A. Flask, an MVSD director, was fired after the audit revealed he had benefited personally and politically, receiving nearly $1.9 million in consulting fees from MVSD vendors and subcontractors. Moreover, THE VINDICATOR revealed that he had received $1.5 million more from Medical Mutual of Ohio in so-called consulting fees.

CORRUPTION INVESTIGATIONS now flooded the headlines. In 1998 a Mahoning County grand jury found probable cause to believe that an illicit organization was being run through the sheriff's department Major Crimes Unit, directed by the brother of Sheriff Phil Chance. Allegations also surfaced that mob money was passed to Sheriff Chance for his 1996 campaign, aided by Charles O'Nesti, an aide to Congressman Traficant. O'Nesti pleaded guilty to bribery and other charges in a plea agreement be-

EDWARD A. FLASK

fore retiring from Traficant's employ in March 1998.

IN FEBRUARY 1999 Lenny Strollo turned state's evidence, and that same winter Sheriff Chance was placed under house arrest to await trial on federal corruption charges. At the county level, a jury convicted Commissioner Frank Lordi of theft in office and violating state ethics statutes. He received eighteen months in prison. The FBI's war on the Mafia, conducted by a beefed-up Youngstown branch, peeled away layer after layer of bribery, payoffs, and other crimes by public officials, lawyers, judges, and mobsters.

The mob's previously impregnable fortress of illegal enterprise collapsed under the pressure of an investigation led by Special Agent Robert G. Kroner, Jr., a veteran of the Youngstown FBI office. In March 1999 Strollo's testimony led to the conviction in federal court of Bernie Altshuler, and Youngstowners Jeff Riddle and LaVance Turnage for killing Biondillo and conspiring to kill Paul J. Gains, Mahoning County prosecutor-elect. In December 1998, before taking office, Gains had been wounded in a failed gangland hit. In May, the same three were

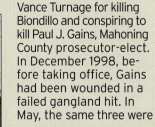

EX-SHERIFF: A jury convicted Phil Chance on all charges.

CHARLES O'NESTI

convicted in Mahoning County—again on Strollo's testimony—of using hired guns to further organized crime.

IN JULY a federal jury convicted Sheriff Chance of public corruption. THE VINDICATOR felt so strongly that his conviction provided an opportunity to clean house that it ran a rare front-page editorial July 14 urging the appointment of a former Youngstown police chief, Randall Wellington, to succeed Chance. Wellington, who had run unsuccessfully against Chance in 1996, possessed a record of public service that remained unblemished throughout the long FBI investigation. In a vote, Democratic precinct committeemen later voted Wellington the appointment.

OTHERS WHOSE CRIMES put them on the front page included William Fergus, a former Mahoning County engineer who pleaded guilty in 1998 to accepting kickbacks on county paving contracts; Richard D. Goldberg, a lawyer who pleaded guilty in August 1999 to federal charges of defrauding twenty-three clients of almost $4.5 million; James A. Philomena, who pleaded guilty in September 1999 to accepting bribes to fix cases during his eight years as Mahoning County prosecutor; and Fred Bailey, who pocketed bribes over an eight-year period as a Mahoning County Court judge.

Cleveland Browns franchise for $530 million, with Carmen Policy, a former Youngstown lawyer and 49ers executive, as a ten percent owner.

Two of the decade's biggest sports stories were closely intertwined with local business stories.

The first was the Phar-Mor Million Dollar Ladies Professional Golf Association Championship, the first of which saw Beth Daniel pocket a sudden-death victory in July 1990.

When a financial scandal brought the fall of Phar-Mor head Mickey Monus in the summer of 1992, the company discontinued the tournament. Fortunately for the valley, the LPGA and local business leaders had an agreement by September 1992 to continue the annual event, renaming it the Giant Eagle LPGA Classic.

DeBartolo, Jr. and a Former Governor Figure in Probe

The second sports-business story emerged in 1997 when Youngstown native Edward J. DeBartolo, Jr. resigned the presidency of the San Francisco 49ers, along with all his corporate responsibilities at the Edward J. DeBartolo Corporation.

Underlying his resignation was a federal investigation of gambling fraud in Louisiana, including reports that DeBartolo had given Edwin Edwards, governor of Louisiana, about four hundred thousand dollars before receiving

that state's last riverboat casino license.

In October of 1998 DeBartolo pleaded guilty to knowing about but not reporting an extortion scheme. He was fined $1 million and was placed on probation for two years; additionally, the NFL banned his involvement in the management of the 49ers.

By the annual meeting of the Edward J. DeBartolo Corporation in March 1999, however, Eddie, Jr. was planning his return to power and negotiating a larger board of directors for the corporation. Meanwhile, his sister, Denise DeBartolo York, had taken over management of the corporation and the 49ers when her brother stepped down, and the corporation had filed suit against Eddie, Jr. seeking to recover funds advanced to him. He in turn filed a $100 million countersuit for "damages." Local 49ers fans could only wonder how the NFL would view such developments.

Despite a strike in professional

baseball, the Cleveland Indians delighted their fans in 1995 by breaking a forty-one-year pennant drought.

Although winning the American League title, they lost the World Series in six games to the Atlanta Braves. Two years later fans cheered when the Indians found themselves in the World Series again, only to see their hopes dashed when the team lost the title, this time to the Florida Marlins expansion team. The Indians would make the playoffs again in 1998 and 1999, but they did not make it to the World Series.

At Long Last, the Valley Gets A Baseball Team of Its Own

In 1998 the valley prepared to welcome a Class A baseball team to a new stadium in Niles after the Erie Sea Wolves, a New York-Pennsylvania League farm team for the Indians, found that they needed a new home when their stadium was given over to a Class AA team.

After several plans to build a stadium fell through, the Cafaro Company stepped up to the plate with the private financial participation needed to make the deal. As a way to honor the valley's steel-making heritage, the principals named the new team the Mahoning Valley Scrappers, and baseball fans throughout the region looked forward to the team's inaugural season in 1999.

The economic picture as the decade began was mixed. GF Office Furniture filed for bankruptcy in 1990, and Avanti Automotive Corporation laid off most of its work force, but on the positive side, union officials at General Motor Corporation's Lordstown plant disclosed that December that GM would build its 1994 J-car at the plant. And the area watched with more than passing interest the accelerating growth of Youngstown-based Phar-Mor.

1991: An incinerator for hazardous waste built by Waste Technologies, Inc. generates protests, demonstrations, civil disobedience, and arrests in East Liverpool. Entertainers and politicians made cameo appearances on the side of those who viewed it as a potential health hazard.

GM Gets Future Production Of Cavalier and Sunbird

In July 1991, despite a wretched year corporate-wide, GM ended several years of suspense, during which the valley wondered if production at the Lordstown plant would extend beyond 1993. The company announced that Lordstown would, in fact, build the next generations of the Chevrolet Cavalier and Pontiac Sunbird, and that a third crew would be added to drive up production of the popular cars, guaranteeing jobs for the van plant workers.

Four months later, Lordstown hired more than one hundred employees on layoff from

idled GM plants in Missouri and Georgia. The influx of seventeen-dollar-an-hour industrial workers led real estate agents to predict a sellers' market for the next spring, citing a windfall of potential homeowners and apartment renters.

By the start of 1998, the Mahoning Valley finally seemed to be on the rebound from the pernicious financial ailments that dogged it for two decades. The job pool totaled 271,000 in 1997, the first year the valley had more jobs

than it had in 1974. Some questioned the quality of the jobs produced in comparison to the jobs that had been available before, but there was also recognition of the investment in the valley's future that had been made with the expansion of existing industrial parks and construction of several new ones.

Before the decade's end, however, the long-term fate of GM's Lordstown plant became an issue once again as the corporation began to debate other ways to do business, like modular composition, outsourcing, and foreign production. In fall 1998 the Youngstown/Warren Regional Chamber of Commerce spearheaded the "Bring it Home" campaign, a local effort to show GM how much the valley valued and appreciated the Lordstown facility and the jobs it provided.

2000 Chevrolet Cavalier

Phar-Mor wasn't the only story of concern to the area's communities, businesses, and industries. Meander Reservoir had sustained only low-water levels through 1991, and after a dry spring in 1992, water restrictions entered the headlines.

Although it had been hoped that precipitation over the winter months would bring the reservoir back to normal capacity, by January 1992 voluntary conservation measures were adopted. In February, however, Meander's level dropped to 35.6 percent of capacity, a record low for that date, and the U.S. Army Corps of Engineers, after refusing the use of Berlin Reservoir as a backup supply, instructed the Mahoning Valley Sanitary District to seek mandatory restrictions.

Hazardous-Waste Project Provokes Public Opposition

Water restrictions and fines were imposed, then eased to allow residents to wash cars and water lawns once a week. In June the restrictions were extended a month while a drought task force compiled a new plan, but then the rains fell through July and into August. On July 28 the reservoir's level had reached 79.3 percent; by August 2, it was over 100 percent.

Down on the Ohio River, meanwhile, the presence of Waste Technologies Industries made headlines in 1992 with arrests and delays as officials and opposition fought over the company's plans to fire up a hazardous-waste incinerator in East Liverpool.

A permit for the incinerator had been issued by the Ohio Hazardous Waste Facility Approval Board eight years earlier, but construction took until 1992. The lapse was due in part to a halt necessitated when the U.S. Environmental Protection Agency filed a complaint that certain parts were being installed without authori-

THE FALL OF MICKEY MONUS AND PHAR-MOR

THE FALL of retail king Phar-Mor and Mickey Monus, the most disturbing business story since Youngstown Sheet & Tube announced its closing in 1977, unfolded in summer 1992. Phar-Mor had begun ten years earlier in Niles with a deep-discount drugstore, Monus's brainchild. By July 1992, with stores in thirty-three states, Phar-Mor and Monus, its president, celebrated the opening in Ashtabula of the chain's three hundredth outlet.

A WEEK LATER, David S. Shapira, Phar-Mor chief executive, fired Monus, saying he and others had defrauded the company of $350 million by cooking the books, inflating inventories, devaluing losses, and duping potential investors into believing the company was on a fast track when it had actually been losing money since 1989.

The story drew national attention, and news reports eventually placed the loss even higher, $499 million. Phar-Mor filed for Chapter 11 bankruptcy protection from creditors, closed dozens of stores, and laid off employees at its local stores and subsidiaries. Local financial institutions had to absorb losses on loans made to the company, Monus, and his associates. Many local Phar-Mor suppliers shut down temporarily, or closed for good, and the City of Youngstown worried that the company's headquarters would be moved from the city. Charities lost Phar-Mor donations and corporate sponsorships.

While other businessmen stepped in to preserve the yearly LPGA event, Monus's World Basketball League, founded in 1988, folded the day before the allegations against him came to light. Among the accusations was one to the effect that Monus had transferred as much as $15 million to prop up the money-losing league. As federal investigators evaluated the company's claims against Monus, he occupied himself with preserving his partnerships in the Colorado Rockies baseball expansion team and other businesses, as well as his personal bankruptcy and divorce proceedings.

In 1993 a federal grand jury indicted Monus, accusing him of perpetrating one of the largest fraud and embezzlement schemes in the state's history, even as Monus was claiming that he himself was about to uncover irregularities in the company's financial records when he was fired.

PHAR-MOR'S former chief financial officer, Patrick B. Finn, who had secretly taped conversations with Monus and other officials, bargained a plea with the government and was sentenced to thirty-three months in prison in November 1993. Monus went through two trials, the first of which began in February 1994 and ended with a hung jury. In May 1995 a second jury convicted him of 109 felonies. Authorities believed the case to be the largest corporate fraud and embezzlement in United States history, totaling $1.1 billion or more. That December Monus was handed nearly twenty years in prison and fined $1 million.

JANUARY 1998: Sheet & Tube's old administration building comes down at Poland Avenue and Walton Street. In back is the former office building.

zation. Protesters professing concern about possible health hazards that might be carried downwind of the plant were banned from demonstrating on WTI's property in November 1991. They insisted, however, on violating the court order, and arrests were made for everything from disorderly conduct and trespassing to criminal mischief and criminal trespassing.

Among the celebrities and public figures involved were the actor Martin Sheen, the singer Richard Marx, and Jerry Brown, a former California governor who was then a Democratic presidential candidate. Vice-president-elect Al Gore announced in 1992 that the Clinton administration would try to halt operations until Congress could investigate the plant's safety.

The merger in 1996 of the longtime Youngstown business DeBartolo Realty Corporation with Indianapolis-based Simon Property Group came as a blow to many. Some workers at the Boardman headquarters were laid off quickly by the newly minted Simon-DeBartolo Group, but the company wouldn't say how many employees would remain on the job there.

The $1.41 billion merger of what analysts termed the top mall developer and best mall manager may have created the country's largest real estate development company, but unfortunately for Youngstown, the new entity was headquartered in Indianapolis. Fortunately for the valley, another long-time Youngstown concern, Commercial Intertech, in 1996 once again succeeded in fighting off a takeover attempt, this time by United Dominion Industries of Charlotte, North Carolina. Commercial beat the takeover with a master plan that reorganized its core business and spun off the company's most profitable unit.

Elsewhere, strikes kept labor-management relations on the front page. In May 1997 workers at Delphi Packard Electric struck for the first time in more than twenty years, protesting the company's sending work to Mexico to capitalize on the business opportunities offered by the North American Free Trade Agreement, which had been negotiated by the United States, Mexico and Canada. Because the company made wiring for all General Motors assembly plants, the brief strike threatened to shut down all North American operations.

In Niles, five hundred workers struck RMI Titanium over wages, pensions, and profit-sharing in the fall of 1998. The strike, marred by violent skirmishes, dragged on more than five months.

The steel industry continued to make headlines, although the news was good only on occasion.

Sharon Steel endured cash-flow problems from the day it emerged from Chapter 11 bankruptcy reorganization at the end of 1990. In November 1992, the company returned to Chapter 11, and it was

FEBRUARY 12, 1999: Police subdue a striker at RMI Titanium in Niles. The violent strike resulted in damage to company property, harrassment, and picket-line confrontations.

OCTOBER 27, 1994: The gates at Sharon Steel were reopened in 1995 after a St. Louis-based company bought the steelmaker at a bankruptcy auction in Erie.

harder the second time around.

During the first round of bankruptcy, which lasted just over three and one-half years, the organization never missed a payday and workers lost no health-care benefits. In 1992, however, all but about one hundred of the twenty-seven hundred people at its steel plant in Farrell were laid off, together with a couple of hundred workers at most of its other divisions. Plant workers also lost health-care insurance because the company couldn't cover its self-funded insurance program.

Competition and Falling Prices Figure in Bankruptcy

The company's treasurer disclosed that the company had had negative cash flow since January 1991 and actually began to run out of operating money in October 1991. Despite a modest profit reported for 1991, in reality the company lost $32.4 million that year and $41.2 million more during the first nine months of 1992.

In its bankruptcy filing, Sharon Steel blamed the nationwide recession, declining steel prices, and increased competition in an al-

ready tight steel market for its inability to meet its post-bankruptcy projects. Average prices in October and November 1990 stood at four hundred-fifty dollars a ton, but the price had dropped to four hundred dollars by 1992.

Through 1993, Sharon Steel devoted its energies to paying off its $80 million in debts. It sold off its Damascus Tubular Products division in Transfer, Pennsylvania, for $10 million and a continuous caster at its Monessen plant for $6.3 million, and turned over its inventory to lenders. In November 1994 Caparo, Inc. of St. Louis, Missouri, bought the bulk of the former Sharon Steel Corporation plant in Federal Bankruptcy Court and closed the $26 million deal in early December. Caparo began hiring hourly production employees in January 1995.

In September 1995 seventeen hundred workers walked out at WCI Steel in Warren when two locals of the United Steel Workers of America called a strike at the expiration of the contract. WCI tried to operate with replacement employees, but the plant had to be closed by the end of the month because of escalating violence. The strike idled WCI for nearly two months, and a full recovery took several months beyond that.

UNDERCUTTING: In winter 1998-1999, U.S. steelmakers rebelled against the dumping of foreign steel on the American market by former members of the Soviet Union and Pacific rim countries. Many of those countries sold their product well below cost.

The Life, Times, and People of The Youngstown Vindicator

EVENTS FROM THE HISTORY OF THE VINDICATOR

FEB. 28, 1850: William F. Maag born to Johannes and Catherine Maag, Ebingen, Germany. At fourteen, he begins a four-year printing apprenticeship, coming to the U.S. in 1867.

JUNE 25, 1869: First issue of the weekly MAHONING VINDICATOR hopes for "speedy triumph" of Democratic party principles. Page one pleads the cause of women's rights, a provocative concept then.

OCT. 22, 1869: Publisher J.H. Odell forms a partnership with Mark Sharkey, another Democrat. By September 1870, only Odell remains.

SEPT. 26, 1873: O.P. Wharton buys THE VINDICATOR; Odell is editor.

FEB. 26, 1875: S.L. Everett buys the paper, only to sell it five months later to one of its writers, W. L. Brown. Odell fades from view.

APRIL 7, 1876: MAHONING VINDICATOR renamed YOUNGSTOWN VINDICATOR as Youngstown becomes county seat.

APRIL 14, 1876: William F. Maag buys German-language RUNDSCHAU (Review) from Henry Gentz. He has worked at Wisconsin and Indiana papers.

APRIL 16, 1880: W.L. Brown sells VINDICATOR to Charles A. Vallandigham and John H. Clarke, Lisbon lawyer and future U.S. Supreme Court justice. Brown later buys NEW YORK DAILY NEWS.

APRIL 22, 1881: VINDICATOR sells two thousand copies weekly. A year later, Vallandigham sells his share to Judge Leroy D. Thoman, later the first U.S. civil service commissioner.

AUG. 24, 1882: THE VINDICATOR changes hands again: Dr. Thomas Patton editor and publisher. Son Will H. takes over when he dies in 1884.

MAY 22, 1885: John M. Webb's name appears with Patton's as co-publisher and editor. Webb, an influential Democrat with a sharp pen, will play a major role in the paper's future.

SEPT. 28, 1886: Still another ownership change: J.A. Caldwell and Charles Underwood take the helm.

JULY 25, 1887: Fire destroys North Phelps Street print shop (where Erie Terminal Building now stands.)

DEC. 22, 1887: At sheriff's sale, William F. Maag enters the only bid for VINDICATOR nameplate and remnants of the print shop. He persuades Webb, a past editor, to be his partner.

JUNE 8, 1888: Weekly VINDICATOR

resumes publication; Webb and Maag "publishers and proprietors."

SEPT. 3, 1889: Investors organize Vindicator Printing Company with $20 thousand capital. Officers are Maag, Webb, John H. Clarke, and Judge D.M. Wilson. Capital stock increased to $40 thousand three years later.

SEPT. 23, 1889: The paper shifts to daily publication as the EVENING VINDICATOR. Volume I, Number I is four pages.

JAN. 2, 1890: Webb is president and managing editor, Maag, business manager and treasurer.

AUG. 9, 1892: THE VINDICATOR will vacate 12-13 S. Phelps when a new building is finished on the southwest corner of Boardman and Phelps.

FEB. 22, 1893: John M. Webb, VINDICATOR president and guiding light of its editorial department, dies.

MARCH 25, 1893: THE VINDICATOR moves into its new building. An open house a month later is followed in four days by a special industrial issue with a press run of forty thousand copies.

MARCH 7, 1896: First printing using Mergenthaler typesetters. The Linotype ends laborious hand-composition and speeds production.

SPRING 1896: THE VINDICATOR exposes the bigoted American Protective Association. Courageous Republicans break ranks, help the paper elect a Democratic mayor, Edmund H. Moore, and stop the APA's takeover of the city. Moore later becomes Democratic national chairman.

JUNE 7, 1896: VINDICATOR publishes first Sunday issue, competing with the Republican TELEGRAM, which was founded in 1885 by merging THE YOUNGSTOWN NEWS REGISTER, YOUNGSTOWN DAILY NEWS, and SUNDAY MORNING.

1900: THE VINDICATOR becomes a charter member of the reorganized Associated Press, preserving a relationship that began in the early eighteen-nineties when the first United Press failed. Today, the relationship is in its second century.

JAN. 16, 1900: Youngstown Arc Engraving chartered with $25 thousand capital. Principals include Maag and Clarke. Arc will make the paper's engravings for most of the century.

APRIL 7, 1901: First printing of color photographs.

MAY 19, 1907: Color comics appear

for the first time.

SEPT. 19, 1913: New Goss Sexduble press is the largest press in Ohio.

1919: Maag retires his German weekly, THE RUNDSCHAU.

1923: THE VINDICATOR wages war on Ku Klux Klan and its political toadies. Unlike the APA of 1896, the Klan is stronger, and the paper's mayoral candidate loses to the Klan puppet. To steal VINDICATOR subscribers, THE TELEGRAM sides with the Klan, a blunder that will hasten its end.

APRIL 10, 1924: William F. Maag, the German immigrant who molded THE VINDICATOR from the clay of good citizenship, dies at seventy-four. Son William F., Jr., managing editor, becomes general manager and, later, editor, and publisher.

APRIL 4, 1925: First bulldog edition of the Sunday VINDICATOR printed for Saturday afternoon distribution. It remains in the lineup till the sixties, long after radio and TV have the competitive edge on breaking news and play-by-play sports.

JULY 2, 1936: William F. Maag, Jr. buys THE TELEGRAM from Scripps-Howard. Public disapproval of its Ku Klux Klan leanings and the trial of top executives for padding circulation and defrauding advertisers had irreparably harmed THE TELEGRAM.

JULY 25, 1937: First issue published in the TELEGRAM building Scripps-Howard built in 1931 at Boardman and Chestnut streets. THE VINDICATOR added a third story, part of a fourth, and made other improvements. WFMJ later moves into a new building at Boardman and Phelps.

MARCH 27, 1938: "The People's Paper" motto appears on page one for the first time, forty-five years after its first publication in the paper's statement of philosophy.

MARCH 22, 1945: Justice John H. Clarke, a VINDICATOR investor from the beginning, dies at eighty-seven. He had moved to Cleveland in 1897 and served on the U.S. Supreme Court from 1916 to 1922, resigning to head the failed campaign for America's entry into the League of Nations.

APRIL 22, 1966: THE VINDICATOR places sixth among seven hundred papers in the Ayer Cup competition for excellence in makeup, typography, and printing.

FEB. 29, 1968: William F. Maag,

Jr., editor and publisher, dies at eighty-four. His association with THE VINDICATOR spanned four foreign wars, the worst depression, the discovery of atomic energy, and the dawn of the space age. His nephew, William J. Brown, general manager, becomes publisher and president of the Vindicator Printing Company.

NOV. 3, 1969: Work begins on a new production facility across Boardman Street from the present building. An eighteen-unit Goss Mark II press rolls for the first time in December 1972.

MAY 1974: The One-Star, a morning edition originally hawked downtown and sold on newsstands, is discontinued, leaving the paper with four daily editions.

AUG. 14, 1981: Publisher William J. Brown dies at 68. His widow, Betty H., becomes editor and publisher, and president of the Vindicator Printing Company. Their son, Mark A. Brown, is general manager and treasurer. Brown's sister, Elizabeth M., continues as vice president and secretary.

JULY 6, 1986: Dogged by prohibitive printing costs, the Sunday pictorial section, the "Roto," makes its final appearance. The brown-toned section, last of its kind in the U.S., first appeared November 7, 1926.

APRIL 1988: The news staff and library move to the production building. A $4 million newsroom includes a replacement for the paper's eleven-year-old computer system. Computers would be upgraded again in 1993, when pagination begins, and in 1998.

JAN. 27, 1989: The end of the Stocks-Sports Edition. Printed in late afternoon, it had been in the repertoire well over a half-century.

OCT. 28, 1990: THE VINDICATOR unveils its first top-to-bottom redesign since 1937; layout and typography tailored for faster, easier reading.

JULY 7, 1997: First run of the Blue Streak. Earliest edition of the day, it prints in midmorning for coin box and newsstand sales. Named for an edition published in the thirties.

SEPT. 4, 1999: First issue of the Saturday morning VINDICATOR. It reaches out to sports fans, shoppers, parents, and others who prefer a morning paper on weekends.

1869 **11** 1999

THE VINDICATOR

The People's Paper

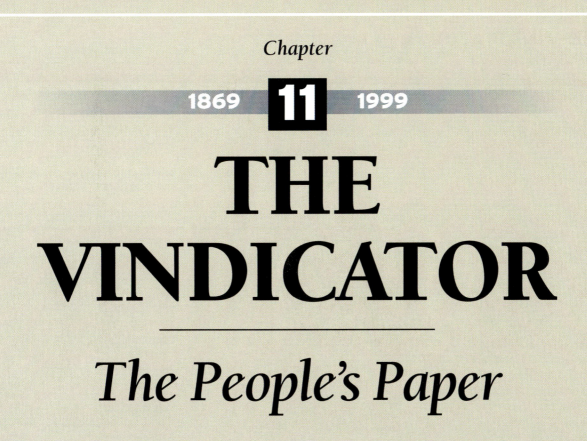

PAST AND PRESENT: THE VINDICATOR's multi-million-dollar printing plant, which opened in 1972 on Vindicator Square, represents a commitment to downtown Youngstown by a past publisher, William J. Brown. The newsroom is located there, along with all production facilities. Directly north, across Boardman Street, is the building THE VINDICATOR acquired in 1936 with its purchase of THE YOUNGSTOWN TELEGRAM. The business office is located there, along with the advertising and circulation departments.

*In the end, a day's newspaper becomes one small piece in
the larger mosaic that reflects a place, its people, and
the time in which they find themselves.*

"Thus passed one who by industry, integrity, high standards of living, and the gift of vision to see and trust in the future of this valley, became one of its most honored citizens and the founder of an institution destined long to survive him."

JOHN H. CLARKE, FORMER U.S. SUPREME COURT JUSTICE,
UPON THE DEATH OF WILLIAM F. MAAG, SR. APRIL 10, 1924

THE ONE WHO STARTED IT ALL

STRANGERS most often remark about the name: Why THE VINDICATOR? We wonder about that, too. Legend has it the paper's founder in 1869, James H. Odell, called it the MAHONING VINDICATOR because he found vindication of his Democratic political beliefs in Youngstown. Why he thought that is a source of wonder itself, because Youngstown was solidly Republican, as was most of the postbellum North.

WHATEVER THE CASE, nothing official exists to confirm that bit of miscellany, just as there is no way to prove or disprove that Odell had been run out of Beaver County, Pennsylvania, for offending that Republican stronghold with his Democratic thunderbolts. While there, he briefly owned the WESTERN STAR paper, and in those days, the publisher's political passions most often set the paper's tone.

Odell was a better politician than moneymaker. Before long, he lost THE VINDICATOR, leading to a succession of would-be publishers hanging on by their fingernails. In time, he moved to Columbus, and thereafter to Minnesota after the deaths of his wife and two boys. He died in the late 1870s in Minneapolis.

THE VINDICATOR still carries the banner of fiercely independent journalism that began with Odell. Of the 1,477 daily U.S. newspapers, only 271 independents remain. The others belong to chains and publishing conglomerates. Of the 271 independents, the family-owned VINDICATOR ranks seventeenth in size and twenty-fourth in length of ownership. Among all 1,477 papers, it has had the same ownership longer than all but thirty-seven.

LATE 1880s: The reborn VINDICATOR sets up shop at 12-13 South Phelps Street. William F. Maag, Sr., who bought the paper at sheriff's sale, is at the right edge of the brickwork.

THE MAHONING VINDICATOR's inaugural issue hit the streets June 25, 1869. The new periodical, a weekly under the guidance of publisher J. H. Odell, received immediate recognition from the other paper in town, THE REGISTER, which noted: "Received the first number of THE MAHONING VINDICATOR today...and we are inclined to the belief THE VINDICATOR will make things lively after a while in Mahoning County."

As the voice for the principles of the Democratic party in what at the time was a strongly Republican city and county, however, the fledgling newspaper struggled desperately to survive.

Unable to gain and maintain the steady support it needed to endure, the newspaper's ownership changed hands several times over the next two decades. By 1887 THE

WILLIAM F. MAAG SR.

VINDICATOR was owned by J.A. Caldwell and Charles Underwood, and its North Phelps Street plant was located on land that would later accommodate the Erie Railroad baggage room.

On July 25 of that year a fire struck, causing one thousand dollars in damage, and, consequently, the newspaper, its presses, and the remains of the plant were offered for public bid at a sheriff's sale. William F. Maag, Sr., a spectator who had had no intention of taking part in the auction, made the first offer. As fortune would have it, Maag's was the only offer, and thereby he became the owner of the forerunner of today's VINDICATOR.

Maag had come to the United States in 1867 at the age of seventeen, and at the time of the fateful auction edited the weekly German paper RUNDSCHAU, which he

Mahoning Vindicator.

VOL. 1—NO. 1.   YOUNGSTOWN, OHIO, FRIDAY, JUNE 25, 1869. $2 A YEAR.

continued to publish until 1919.

Of his new acquisition, a retrospective in THE VINDICATOR of March 27, 1938, observed:

Although he had little money to complete the purchase, he had courage, enterprise, and industry. He persuaded John M. Webb, a newspaperman of more than ordinary ability, to join with him.... They made a good team, Webb's trenchant pen giving new life to the editorial columns, and Mr. Maag's experience as a publisher bringing the paper the capable management it had always lacked.

Determined to succeed, but faced with competition from THE TELEGRAM, which had been organized by local business interests in 1885 and was published every evening, Mr. Maag formed a small stock company so THE VINDICATOR, too, could become a daily newspaper, which it did in September 1889.

Democratic in Philosophy But Expansive in Scope

Explaining its principles in that first daily edition, THE VINDICATOR stated:

The paper will be politically Democratic, but free from the rancor and violence of personal politics, and all the business and material interests of the city and county will be represented in its columns, which will be sustained upon the principle of the common good and welfare of the whole people.

As treasurer and general man-

ager, positions he held the rest of his life, Maag worked side by side with Webb as president, Judge D. M. Wilson as vice president, and John H. Clarke as secretary.

Within a few years the new daily had been established to such a degree that construction began in 1892 on an up-to-date printing facility on the southwest corner of Boardman and Phelps streets, even as observers wondered about the wisdom of such a move in an era when the success rate among newspapers was very low and buildings in which to print them were expensive. Yet Maag was determined and the risk proved worthwhile.

Renewing its philosophy once again upon moving into its new, three-story building in 1893, THE VINDICATOR declared:

This newspaper is ever faithful to public interests. It is bound by no entangling ties, circumscribed by no rules but equal and exact justice, hedged by no lobbies, haltered by no hindrance of corporate influence. It is free to publish all the news, to show the facts as they are without coloring or fear of offending corporate interests. It is dis-

THE VINDICATOR STAFF, 1891: Reading from left: Carl DuCasse, Samuel M. Muter, C.E. Fifield, John M. Webb, Carl Maag, Ellis Johnston, Herman Gasser, Charles Smith, Martin Gerlach, John S. Stigleman, L.W. Miller, Ray M. Owen, James Lightbody, Charges G. Muter, Charles T. Gaither, A.V. Huth, William H. Stigleman, Frank S. Brenner, J.D. Hurford, Byron Williams, Clate A. Smith, Emil Braun, William F. Maag, Sr., Charles Christy, Fred Oertly, John M. Boyle, William Uber, J.B. Wallace, W.S. Stigleman.

tinctively the people's paper, the organ of the many.

On June 7, 1896, shortly before the Niles-born William McKinley would be nominated the Republican candidate for the U.S. presidency, the first Sunday VINDICATOR appeared, twenty-four pages, with information about the upcoming Republican convention in St. Louis. It also noted in a brief that a Niles man, Charles Harris, made the gavel to be used there, some of the wood having been taken from the house in which McKinley was born.

The paper said that its Sunday issue would not contain the "fierce asperities" often found in the daily issue: "THE VINDICATOR believes in the cessation of such warfare on the Sabbath except when extraordinary cases arise." Finally, an editorial declared that the paper "will take the part of the oppressed against the oppressor, the weak against the strong, right against wrong, as it understands it, always."

Technologically, THE VINDICATOR kept pace with larger papers in larger cities, and outstripped them in many areas. The Youngstown paper was the first in America to use a halftone printed on a

INVENTIVE: Pressroom foreman Charles T. Gaither designed, built, and sold his Fredonia auto in Youngstown.

high-speed rotary press to reproduce a photographic image.

Pioneering Work in the Use Of Pictures to Tell the Story

With financial backing from Maag, Charles T. Gaither, VINDICATOR pressroom foreman, and Frank Hubler used their ingenuity to bend a copper etching of the Mahoning Valley industrialist Chauncey Andrews to fit the curved printing plate. The picture ran in the December 26, 1893, issue. Before that halftone ran, and for years afterward until the method could be perfected, the paper relied on hand-drawn illustrations, as did newspapers generally around the world.

Gaither presently directed his mechanical skill to the fledgling auto industry and, in 1895, became the first person to make a car in Ohio. For a time, he built an auto called the Fredonia in Youngstown.

In many other respects, THE VINDICATOR, an early member of the Associated Press, was a tech-

nological leader. It had increased to an eight-page format in 1893 and on April 29 of that year issued a special forty-page industrial edition. The newspaper printed the first issue assembled with ma-

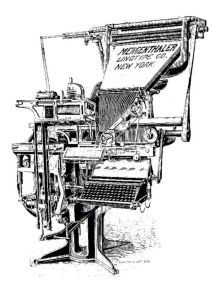

PROGRESS: By 1901, the paper was using Merganthaler typesetting machines, greatly reducing the amount of type set by hand.

1924: Frederick A. Douglas was editor from 1901 to 1936. He succeeded "Uncle Billy" Dawson, a jovial Santa Claus look-alike.

chine-set type on March 7, 1896. On February 20, 1899, Maag gave a tour of the VINDICATOR building to the high-tech mastermind of that day, inventor Thomas Edison.

In March 1901 the paper upgraded to a Merganthaler Linotype machine for typesetting and later that year published a special sixty-six page issue for Thanksgiving and a sixty-four page issue for Christmas; each issue included a four-page color section.

In 1902 the paper installed a new Goss press that enabled it to produce a piece that was slightly smaller (and thereby more easily handled) but with more pages for reading matter and advertising. At the time the press was the largest, most-improved, and most-expensive between Cleveland and Pittsburgh. It could print and fold twenty-five thousand twelve-page sections an hour, count them out in bundles of fifty, and print two colors in addition to black. THE VINDICATOR also installed an electric-light plant in 1902.

In a special industrial issue published November 9, 1902, THE VINDICATOR remarked that its new building of nine years, which had so much room to start that the upper hall and a half were rented to societies and church groups, was already being taxed to its limits to accommodate the many depart-

SECOND HOME: The VINDICATOR published from this building at West Boardman and South Phelps streets from 1893 until it moved to the former TELEGRAM building in 1937.

ments and enterprises operated in conjunction with the newspaper.

The Arc Engraving Company and the Beil Bindery occupied the top floors; the composing and editorial rooms were on the second; the business and business manager's offices, the job rooms, and Maag's RUNDSCHAU were on the first; and the pressroom was in the basement. On May 19, 1907, THE VINDICATOR published its first Sunday color comic, "Willie Cute," a panel about the exploits of a mischievous tomboy.

On page three of the issue of Sunday, April 26, 1908, the paper told how it had snapped and developed a photograph in only nine minutes. Another Goss press, one that printed twenty-eight pages at a clip, went into operation September 23, 1910, and the paper printed a special industrial issue June 27, 1911, "marking the

arrival of Youngstown in the class of the big cities of the country [that] must be reckoned with in the financial and monetary history of the Nation for the future...."

Its distribution, the paper stated proudly, was "not only to the regular readers of Youngstown's great Daily but to tens of thousands of financiers, boards of trade, chambers of commerce, bankers, steel men, and real-estate men scattered all over Ohio and the United States."

For a Time, The Vindicator Has the Largest Press in Ohio

By September 1913 THE VINDICATOR was being published on the largest press in Ohio, a new, high-speed Goss Sexduble. The first Rotogravure section appeared November 7, 1926, and the Sunday novel and magazine section were being printed in color in January 1934.

In his bicentennial history of the Mahoning Valley, Howard Aley tells of "Telephone 25," a revered piece of news-gathering equipment, a "battered old instrument of fifteen years' service in THE VIN-

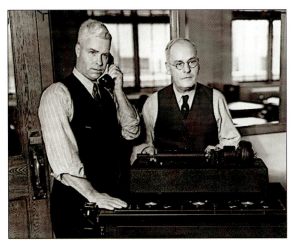

SEPTEMBER 1938: The paper adds the Associated Press wirephoto service whereby pictures can be transmitted from anywhere in the world by telephone line and cable.

DICATOR editorial room, cited as being responsible for funneling as much as fifty percent of the news into the ears of on-duty reporters, the source of thousands of reports, stories, and tips each year." Aley concluded by pointing out that a "sister phone" was placed on the same desk in 1932.

Information also came in by telegraph, but whereas one Morse telegraph wire had been enough to meet the paper's needs in 1893, eleven high-speed Teletype wires were in place by 1937 to receive the news of the nation and the world from the Associated Press, United Press, and International News Service. In 1938 the paper added the Associated Press electronic photo service, making it one of the most up-to-the-minute publications in the country.

Through the years, THE VINDICATOR has championed myriad causes and contributed to many crusades for the common good.

In its early years, it campaigned vigorously against the bigotry and nativism of the American Protective Association in the eighteen-

1932: The business office as it appeared when the VINDICATOR was still at Boardman and Phelps. The electric-powered adding machine looks primitive, but it was a marvel of its day.

nineties and the Ku Klux Klan in the nineteen-twenties; each of those stands cost the paper subscribers. It stood by Gov. James M. Cox as he struggled to establish a workers' compensation act, supported creation of the Federal Reserve System, spoke against Prohibition, pushed for the election of United States senators by pop-

ular vote, and editorialized vigorously for women's suffrage and the League of Nations. The newspaper lent its voice to the efforts to establish Mill Creek Park and a public library system, repeatedly demanded the elimination of railroad grades throughout Youngstown, and campaigned for clean water and construction of a Lake Erie-to-Ohio River waterway.

WKBN and Vindicator Team Up to Report Election Results

In November 1926, THE VINDICATOR sponsored the broadcast of election returns over WKBN Radio from the porch of Warren P. Williamson's house on Auburndale Avenue. In the years leading up to World War II, it supported the Roosevelt administration's Lend Lease plan and prepared its readers for the United States' inevitable entry into the conflict.

In 1874 THE VINDICATOR supported construction of the Opera House and the cultural opportunities it would bring to the area. Later, it supported (or "boomed," in the jargon of the day) creation of the Arms Museum and development of Joseph Butler's museum of American art.

OCTOBER 1921: People stand elbow-to-elbow to follow World Series play between the Yankees and New York Giants on the VINDICATOR scoreboard. Before radio, the paper regularly used bulletin boards to update news between editions. The Giants won the series.

When an economic depression struck in 1896, the paper organized a relief movement to help the poor and provided Christmas dinners for newsboys and distressed families. In the Great Panic of 1907, the paper sponsored relief efforts again and organized a fresh-air camp for city children that continued for many summers. In those same decades it actively contributed to the welfare of the community, supporting cause after cause for the common good.

Youngstown's first Christmas dinner baskets were distributed in 1913 through the paper's creation of a Christmas drive that raised $1,370 to buy food for the poor. Before radio took hold, the paper maintained a scoreboard downtown during the World Series so the crowds could keep up with developments inning by inning. In 1924, twenty thousand children were THE VINDICATOR'S guests at Idora Park during its first annual Before School Day, which soon developed into the annual VINDICATOR Kiddies Day and continued for years.

In 1928 THE VINDICATOR spoke up for Herbert Hoover, the first time the paper had supported a Republican presidential candidate. The VINDICATOR Spelling Bee, a tradition that continues today, was first held in 1934. In recent times the newspa-

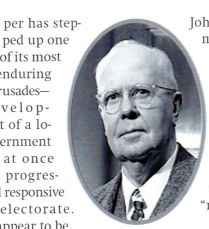

THE TELEGRAM: Scripps-Howard erected this building in 1931 for its TELEGRAM, which had been formed in 1885 by merging the YOUNGSTOWN NEWS REGISTER, YOUNGSTOWN DAILY NEWS, and SUNDAY MORNING.

WILLIAM F. MAAG SR.
In later years

WILLIAM O. BROWN
Succeeded Justice Clark

JOHN H. CLARKE
Vindicator president

per has stepped up one of its most enduring crusades—development of a local government that is at once honest, progressive, and responsive to the electorate. While that may appear to be a goal easily attained, the people's best opportunity for achieving it in the twentieth century took shape only in the 1990s as the FBI dismantled the Youngstown underworld with a stunning series of convictions, and as local government itself nibbled at the edges of public corruption by impaneling special grand juries. VINDICATOR reports that at times cast a harsh spotlight on government inspired some of the investigations.

William F. Maag, Sr. died on April 10, 1924.

John H. Clarke, former justice of the Supreme Court of the United States and Maag's business associate of thirty-seven years, eulogized him as the newspaper's "managing director and inspiring spirit since the daily was first issued in 1889." His obituary noted that he had been elected to the state legislature, serving on its committee on railroads and public printing; had been a presidential elector in 1912; had risen to become a thirty-second degree

Mason; and had served as a member of the Draft Board during World War I. "He loved to be among the newsboys," the obituary said, "and in the course of years he became acquainted with thousands of them who took their places in the life of the city feeling that he was their personal friend."

Owner Entrusts Supervision Of Newsroom to Elder Son

The elder Maag's son William F., Jr., born in 1883, had spent a great deal of time in THE VINDICATOR's offices and plant while he was growing up. After graduating magna cum laude from Harvard University, he became a VINDICATOR reporter. His father, essentially a businessman, looked to him to take on more and more respon-

sibility in the newsroom. Shortly after World War I, he became managing editor and retained that title until his father's death in 1924, at which time he became general manager.

On July 2, 1936, THE VINDICATOR acquired THE YOUNGSTOWN TELEGRAM, which had been sold to the Scripps-Howard chain in 1922. "Editor" was added to the younger Maag's list of titles as he managed both papers, and John H. Clarke became president of the company.

After the death of Justice Clark in 1945, Maag, Jr. became editor and publisher, and his brother-in-law, William O. Brown, became president. After Brown's death in 1956, Maag also became president of The Vindicator Printing Company.

For twenty-two years after the merger, the notice "and THE YOUNGSTOWN TELEGRAM" ran right under the VINDICATOR flag on the front page. An editorial on July 27, 1937, in the new, larger publication reaffirmed its enduring commitment to the community it served, saying: "Those directing THE VINDICATOR's policy realize that although Youngstown has only one paper, it can't rest on its past achievements or rely on its monopoly, either as a matter of ethics or of practical success."

After the merger, THE TELEGRAM plant on Telegram Square, built in 1931, was remodeled and enlarged to accommodate the combined operation. New telephones and a battery of automatic

JANUARY 1948: THE VINDICATOR adds radio Teletype service to its growing technology base.

teletypewriter machines were installed; the libraries (or "morgues") of the two papers were cleaned out and combined; and the business office and advertising and circulation departments were packed up and moved.

Last-Minute Move Ensures Continuity of Publication

At the last possible moment, the mechanical department—the equipment that could not be spared lest even one edition go unprinted—was transferred as quickly as possible. That included twenty-seven Linotype machines, each weighing nearly a ton, and about 350 tons of type metal, an alloy of lead, zinc, and other metals. The paper's newest Goss press could turn out sixty thousand papers an hour.

To mark the paper's seventieth anniversary and relocation to its building on the renamed Vindicator Square, the newspaper published a special 224-page issue, weighing three pounds, on March 27, 1938. The new premises were described as including "60,095 square feet of floor space." The description continued:

The building and the huge Goss press rest on two separate foundations so that the vibrations of the 400-ton press are not com-

BROADCASTING: After the move, the former offices of THE VINDICATOR underwent a top-to-bottom renovation in 1938 and became the home of WFMJ Radio and, later, WFMJ-TV.

municated to the structure.... To dull the clatter of typewriters and hum of wire machines, acoustically treated ceilings have been installed in the editorial and press wire rooms and the business office....

A telephone system of the very latest type has been installed. An intricate system connecting one hundred telephones through a double switchboard insures prompt service for The Vindicator's countless incoming, outgoing, and intra-office calls....

All the steel furniture was made in Youngstown.... Pneumatic tubes carry copy from the classified advertising department on the third floor, the business office, and editorial room, to the composing room. From the tubes the copy is distributed to men operating the typesetting machines.

The article also described the "miniature railroad with two hundred feet of narrow-gauge track" that transported paper from the storage rooms to feed the press:

As efficiently as on a regular railway line, small trucks are loaded with seventeen-hundred-pound rolls of paper and pass along the little track with its switches and turntables to the point where they enter the press.

In those days, a roll of newsprint contained about two and one-half miles of paper.

The first Sunday issue of the paper in 1896 contained twenty-four pages. By 1936 the Sunday VINDICATOR contained eight sections: First News, Second News, Society, Sports, Magazine, Rotogravure, a complete novel, and twenty-four pages of comics. As the century draws to a close, a typical Sunday issue of THE VINDICATOR numbers more than one hundred pages and contains twelve sections, including inserted grocery coupons and advertising circulars for local goods and services. A daily Peach Edition, containing the latest sports and stock-market news printed on peach-colored stock, began in the mid-nineteen twenties and continued until the middle of 1937. "Because the red-lined sports and blue-lined stock editions are now so well recognized by the five stars in the upper right-hand corner of the stock edition and the six stars on the sports edition," the Peach was being retired, the paper explained. Starting in September

HOT OFF THE PRESS: Mailer Lou Fratino gathering copies of the Stocks-Sports Edition from a mailroom conveyor in the early 1950s. The mailroom is the last stop before the loading dock and delivery trucks.

ESTHER HAMILTON: Though better known as a columnist, Esther was an enterprising reporter in the twenties and thirties when the big papers staffed "sob sisters" to cover the most sensational crimes and hottest human-interest stories. Esther was at THE TELEGRAM then, always striving to scoop her VINDICATOR rival, Ella Kerber Resch.

1939, just in time for Hitler's advance across Europe, THE VINDICATOR broadcast a fifteen-minute news program from its editorial room over WFMJ Radio at 7:15 a.m. each day.

That same year, the paper cosponsored with the Ohio State Archeological Society a project by the Works Projects Administration to file and index local papers, including microfilming the complete files of THE VINDICATOR. As part of the yearly newspaper carriers' convention, the paper held a Mummers Parade with huge, inflated character floats.

On January 29, 1950, the paper issued a special supplement looking back at the first half of the twentieth century and the remarkable progress that had been made over a broad spectrum, including, among others, steel, transportation, medicine, and warfare. In June 1953 photos of Queen Elizabeth II's coronation were ready for developing at THE VINDICATOR within seven to ten minutes of their transmission from London.

The Alias Santa Claus shows of reporter-columnist Esther Hamilton, which annually brought in

HOT TYPE: Before computerized typesetting arrived in the 1970s, machines cast type one line at a time in a melted lead alloy. The lines of type, or "slugs," were locked in a form to make a page. The page was then pressed into a fiber matrix, which was used to make a curved plate to fit the press cylinder.

top-name talent and raised money for relief agencies, received the paper's full support when Miss Hamilton came to The Vindicator from The Telegram in the papers' merger.

For her efforts there and elsewhere, the Junior Chamber of Commerce honored her in November 1955 with the Frank Purnell Memorial Award for outstanding community service. In October 1966 she was named Woman of the Year by the Youngstown Business & Professional Women's Club.

Meanwhile, The Vindicator's politics editor, Clingan Jackson, who had served as a state representative and senator, was named to the Ohio Pardon & Parole Commission by Gov. William O'Neill

in 1957, and also was approached by the Mahoning County Democratic Party to consider running for governor. The paper had evolved from the partisan views of its early days and now preferred to support causes and candidates whose goals seemed best to fit the needs of the people. During the Little-Steel strike of 1937, The Vindicator worked so hard to present the facts impartially that it made enemies on both sides of the bargaining table.

In the Youngstown mayoral campaign of 1947, the paper endorsed Charles P. Henderson, the Republican candidate; in 1948, it spoke up for Thomas Dewey over Harry Truman in the national election; in 1952 and 1956, it took Dwight Eisenhower's side over Adlai Stevenson; and in 1960 it chose Richard Nixon rather than the young John F. Kennedy. No longer was The Vindicator wed to the Democratic Party and its doctrines. It had matured politically, embracing an editorial philosophy that judged issues and candidates on merit, not along party lines.

The first application ever made to the Federal Communications Commission for a license to build and operate a television station in Youngstown came from The Vindicator in April 1952, and that July both The Vindicator and WKBN Broadcasting Corporation were granted licenses.

In the late nineteen-fifties, Vindicator stories about wide-open gambling at various joints led to Internal Revenue Service raids and crackdowns on the illegal activities.

By the nineteen-sixties, mob warfare busied reporters with the bombings, shootings, and other mayhem associated with underworld factionalism and power-grabbing; and where the gangsters went, one inevitably found its compliant groupie—government corruption. For weeks, Vindicator readers followed Lynn B. Griffith, Jr.'s riveting prosecution of Warren councilmen, an underworld figure, and the chairman of the Trumbull County Democratic Party in a scandal involving contractor shakedowns on a federally funded sewerage project.

Civic Honors for the Paper, Then a Protracted Strike

The Vindicator's achievements and contributions inspired the Mahoning Valley Historical Society to honor Maag on his eightieth birthday in July 1963, and the Chamber of Commerce a few months later to honor him for civic leadership and service.

Although Local 11 of the American Newspaper Guild called a strike on August 18, 1964, management continued to put out an abbreviated version of the paper, carrying reports from the Associated Press, United Press International, Chicago Daily News Service, New York Herald-Tribune Service, London Observer Service, and Vindicator State Wire.

When the strike ended April 15, 1965, the paper stated simply, under the headline BACK TOWARD NORMAL that "THE VINDICATOR is resuming home delivery after an interruption since August 18."

William F. Maag, Jr., the lanky, bespectacled editor his employees called "The Boss" in almost reverential tones, died February 29, 1968, having played a large role as a leader of the community and the newspaper industry.

A classicist schooled in economics and passionately interested in foreign affairs, Maag was the right man to steer the editorial ship through the murky waters of World War II.

As the storm clouds gathered, the lifelong bachelor accepted appointment to the committee that nominated members of various draft boards and later sat as a trustee of the Ohio division of the National War Fund. At one point, in utmost secrecy, he flew to England at the behest of the British

WILLIAM F. MAAG, JR.
Student of World Affairs

Embassy. Upon his return, he declared that "more Flying Fortresses" would be the best contribution to a speedy ending of the war.

In 1949 he served on the jury that selected the Pulitzer Prize winners for that year. He served as a trustee of the Red Cross and as a board member and treasurer of the Fresh Air Camp.

He was also a trustee and early supporter of the Youngstown Civil

Liberties Union. During the nineteen-thirties, he bought the land needed for the city's new municipal airport and continued to pay options on the property until the city was prepared to begin the airport's construction.

A New Leader Blazes a Trail In the High-Tech Wilderness

But in addition to the impact he made on the Mahoning Valley through his charitable work and with THE VINDICATOR, Maag spearheaded development of two other notable contributions to the Mahoning Valley news media—WFMJ Radio and WFMJ-TV. The television station, an NBC affiliate, broadcasts over Channel 21; WFMJ Radio was sold to other interests in 1990.

William J. Brown was a grandson of the newspaper's founder and the son of William O. Brown. The elder Brown, known as "W.O" to friends and associates, was married to William F. Maag, Sr.'s daughter, Alma, and was the paper's business manager for many years. Until his death in 1956, he

APRIL 1971: A new production building goes up on Vindicator Square. It will surround a Goss Mark II press numbering eighteen units.

was also president of The Vindicator Printing Company.

After the death of his father, the younger Brown, an alumnus of the University of Virginia, took command of the paper's business department. Upon the death of Maag Jr., he succeeded his uncle as publisher of the leading newspaper between Cleveland and Pittsburgh.

During Brown's years at the helm, THE VINDICATOR continued to expand until, by the late nineteen-sixties, the need for a new plant became inescapable.

Bill Brown Honors a Family Commitment to Downtown

The suburbs had grown remarkably in the years after World War II, and many businesses were moving out of Youngstown's central business district to be closer to the consumers; however, Bill Brown, determined to honor his family's tradition, vowed that Youngstown's only daily paper would maintain its commitment to the downtown area and remain there. In 1967 the company acquired property on Front Street, across Boardman Street from the VINDICATOR building, for construction of a new printing plant. Five years later, in December 1972, the paper was printed in the new plant.

Satellite Transmissions Bring A Bigger Selection of News

By the mid-seventies the days of the telegraph key were long gone, and the Teletype machine would soon clatter its last syllable. News from beyond the Mahoning and Shenango valleys now arrived by computer, and transmissions had increased to include news, features, and columns from such alternative sources as North American Newspaper Alliance, Chicago Daily News Service, New York Times News Service, Los Angeles Times/Washington Post News Ser-

vice, and many of the country's top syndicates.

Besides the national wire, Associated Press news came in over an Ohio wire, a sports wire, and a Pennsylvania wire. Additionally, a special Associated Press service was in place to receive high-speed photos covering prime domestic and foreign news, and another service was in place to receive high-speed transmissions of stock quotations and financial news. By February 1977 the paper's reporters and editors were using video-display terminals to write the daily and Sunday issues. In March 1981 the paper installed a new Associated Press earth satellite to receive wire-service dispatches.

By that point THE VINDICATOR was being printed on two new Goss presses, each of which could print 144 black-and-white pages at a time and fold seventy thousand copies an hour at top end. The paper's daily circulation had topped 100 thousand, and its subscribers were living in Mahoning, Trumbull, Columbiana, Ashtabula, and Portage counties in Ohio, and in Mercer and Lawrence counties in Pennsylvania. Sunday distribution stretched even farther, to the New York line and the West Virginia panhandle.

During Brown's tenure, the newsrooms, composing rooms,

OUR NAME IN LIGHTS: Richard Cook of the Peskin Sign Company makes repairs to the neon tubes on the downtown landmark.

pressrooms, mailrooms, and business offices of newspapers across the country entered the

DECEMBER 1972: The paper prints its first issue in the production building. By then, photocomposition has replaced hot type. In 1988, the editorial staff will relocate to a high-tech newsroom developed by Mark A. Brown, Bill Brown's son and the paper's general manager.

computer age.

During the middle years of the twentieth century, columns of type were still being set in a molten lead alloy by Linotype machines, the invention of a German-born machinist named Ottmar Mergenthaler in the latter part of the nineteenth century. When the metal cooled, the letterforms appeared in relief on thin strips, or "slugs." Many such slugs made up a column of type. The so-called hot-type process was cumbersome, slow, and labor-intensive—inappreciably improved from Mergenthaler's day.

Computers, Film, and Digital Typesetting Replace Hot Type

By 1976 the printing process had fully converted to "cold type," a form of computerized typesetting using photosensitive paper. Columns of type were cut from the paper and, along with pictures and other graphics, pasted into place on page-size grid sheets. Negatives were then made from the grid sheets and press plates from the page negatives. Since that day, improvements in technology have come at geometric pace because of the increasingly rapid development of computers. Entering the new millennium, whole pages are composed and designed, with artwork, text, and photographs in place, directly on computer screens. With the press of a keyboard command, digital pages flow into digital typesetters that make negatives for the plate-making process. The middle step of pasting up grid sheets has been eliminated, and newspapers are now experimenting with eliminating negatives by transmitting the digitized pages directly to plate-making machines.

As it had done since its founding, THE VINDICATOR continued under Bill Brown's leadership to champion causes it felt were in the best interests of the Mahoning and Shenango valleys. In May 1970 the Associated Press Society

WILLIAM J. BROWN
Exponent of latest technology

of Ohio recognized THE VINDICATOR with an award in the community-service category for its campaign marshaling public support for a crucial Youngstown school levy. During the Iranian hostage crisis in the late nineteen seventies, as a sense of frustration and futility weighed heavily on Americans at home, THE VINDICATOR showed its support, as did many other news organizations, by keeping a daily count of the duration of the affair. A boxed notice appeared on the front page stating "Lest We Forget" and listing the number of days since those fifty-six Americans had tasted the sweetness of freedom.

An Untimely Death Brings New Leaders, More Progress

On August 14, 1981, THE VINDICATOR family suffered the death of publisher Bill Brown, a painful loss. Like his grandfather and uncle before him, he had been highly active in community affairs.

He had been appointed by Gov. James A. Rhodes as one of the nine original trustees for Youngstown State University, and he served as trustee on dozens of other boards as well, among them the Reuben McMillan Free Library Association, the Youngstown Hospital Association, and the Youngstown YMCA. He was also one of the biggest supporters of the Buckeye Elks, and Lodge 73 made him an honorary member in 1976 in recognition of his services for human relations.

From college on, Brown's service to THE VINDICATOR was inter-

1970s: Cold type replaces hot type. Laser-driven typesetters reproduce text, pictures, and graphics on photosensitive paper. The elements are then pasted onto a page grid. A negative is made of each finished page and from that an aluminum plate for the press.

rupted only by four years in the Army Air Forces during World War II. Upon his death, Donald J. McKay, president of Home Savings & Loan, where Brown had served on the board of directors, summed up the loss to the Mahoning and Shenango valleys by calling Brown the kind of person "a community can't afford to lose." "There is no replacement," McKay said.

Brown's death ushered in a new era of journalism but did not materially change the newspaper's founding principles or family ownership. Brown's widow, Betty, and the couple's son, Mark, assumed leadership of the paper, she as president and publisher, he as general manager. As the century ends, THE VINDICATOR remains a home-grown newspaper, one of the few remaining independents in a sea of cookie-cutter newspapers owned by large chains and absentee corporations.

Reaffirming the Commitment To Excellence in Coverage

With the changing of the guard in 1981 came new approaches to news-gathering, new ways of presenting and displaying the news, and a new aggressiveness in monitoring government and politics. Wasteful spending, questionable contracts, dubious practices, and bureaucratic sophistry made headlines more frequently. In 1992, for example, THE VINDICATOR acquired confidential files showing that the Ohio governor's office knew all along about the Peter J. Schmitt Company's shaky finances and doubtful future, and in 1996 reporters dug up questionable gas-card purchases in the Mahoning County Sheriff's Department.

Later in the decade, FBI investigations led to the conviction of, or guilty pleas from, among others, a municipal judge, a county judge, a Campbell police chief, a former county engineer, a former county prosecutor, an incumbent

BETTY H. BROWN JAGNOW
Vindicator President and Publisher

county sheriff, crooked lawyers, mob associates, and hired guns recruited to kill a county prosecutor and rivals of the entrenched Mafia leadership.

Testimony from Lenny Strollo, Mafia boss turned informer, was instrumental in convicting a sitting Mahoning County sheriff, Phil Chance who received a prison sentence of seventy-one months for taking bribes from the mob. Among the others pleading guilty to federal charges were William Fergus, a former county engineer; James Philomena, a former county prosecutor; Patrick Kerrigan, a Youngstown municipal judge; and Charles Xenakis, police chief of Campbell.

THE VINDICATOR aggressively covered the federal investigations, a county investigation of public corruption, and an investigation of the Mahoning Valley Sanitary District, printing more than one thousand articles over four years.

For THE VINDICATOR, the 1980s occasioned some of the biggest changes in the second half of the century. One of them was the relocation of the newsroom and morgue across Boardman Street to the second floor of the production building in 1988.

A vigorous modernization plan developed by the general manager, Mark Brown, created a state-of-the-art newsroom equipped with a computerized text-creation, editing and typesetting system much faster and more powerful than the first, which had been in use since the mid-seventies. The newsroom layout and amenities were so innovative that THE VINDICATOR found itself written up in national architectural journals.

Arriving at a Design to Meet The Needs of Today's Reader

About the same time, it became apparent that the newspaper's look had not kept pace with the times, so planning commenced on a major overhaul of the newspaper's design. A modest redesign in 1984, conducted in house, had reduced the number of columns to six from eight, ended the practice of capitalizing most words in headlines, and introduced a sense of order to page layouts. Wider columns improved readability and conformed to an industry-wide change to standard widths for advertisements.

For the new design, however, THE VINDICATOR went outside, hiring Robert Lockwood, an artist

MARK A. BROWN
Vindicator General Manager

whose pioneering work in the seventies at THE ALLENTOWN MORNING CALL in Pennsylvania rewrote the book on contemporary newspaper design. Lockwood, a visionary who views newspaper design from the reader's perspective, roughed out the new VINDICATOR on a Macintosh computer in one intense week of collaboration with key newsroom personnel. In October 1990, the newspaper launched an entirely fresh appearance that capitalized on shorter stories, informational graphics, stronger pictures, modular layouts, and, most important, better-organized news sections.

Changes in the Newsroom: Defining a Regional Outlook

Another imperative took shape in 1989 with reorganization of the separate news-gathering departments into a regional desk comprising regional editors and assistants supervised by a senior editor.

The objective was a gradual remolding of the news columns to better address the regional cause and effect of the news. Community-specific coverage continued, as always, but news events were more often examined from a perspective consistent with, and pertinent to, the multicounty area THE VINDICATOR served.

As part of its increasingly vigorous coverage of politics, the newspaper renewed its involvement in pre-election polling, using scientific methods. In 1984, it teamed with Youngstown State University for the first time to poll the races between James A. Traficant, Jr. and incumbent Lyle Williams for U.S. Congress, and Vincent E. Gilmartin and Gary L. Van Brocklin for Mahoning County prosecutor. Since then, polling has become a frequent element of election coverage.

In 1994, the paper lent its editorial support to the Democrats for Change, an ad hoc organization that challenged the Democ-

PAGINATION: The computer revolutionized newspaper publishing. Pages are now composed entirely on Macintosh computers and digitally typeset to negative film from which the printing plates are made.

ratic machine, displaced the party leadership, and declared a new order. In summer 1999, the paper invoked the seldom-used power of the front-page editorial to rally behind Randall Wellington for the vacancy created by the resignation of the county's convicted sheriff, Phil Chance, and to urge voter approval of a crucial half-percent sales tax for county government. Democratic committeemen voted Wellington in, and voters passed the tax in November.

Safeguarding the People's Right to Public Information

The curious (and illegal) propensity of government officials to conduct business in secret, foreclose public access to meetings, and withhold official records to which the public and press are entitled formed a disturbing trend of the eighties and nineties.

In one notable case, the newspaper sued Youngstown State University in the Supreme Court of Ohio in 1991 for not providing meeting minutes, as required by law, in respect to the selection of a new university president. Over the years, the newspaper has spent thousands upon thousands in legal fees to preserve and pro-

tect the people's right to acquire public records in a timely fashion and take their rightful place in meetings of governmental bodies.

Ten decades ago THE VINDICATOR published a five-cent Sunday paper and a two-cent daily that could be twenty-four pages, with headlines and copy of both published in the same dense typeface over eight ruled columns. It has grown steadily, and its history intertwines tightly with the progress of development in the Mahoning and Shenango valleys. As the twentieth century draws to a close, the paper costs thirty-five cents on weekdays and Saturdays and a dollar on Sundays. It has a circulation of eighty-five thousand daily and 120 thousand Sunday.

Our Second Century Serving 'The Privileged of the Earth'

As the world, its peoples, and times change, THE VINDICATOR and other newspapers change and adapt, readers' needs evolve, and the paper's pages take shape to meet those needs. In the end, a day's newspaper becomes one small piece in the larger mosaic that reflects a place, its people, and the time in which they find themselves.

In his work "Rebel Angels," novelist Robertson Davies writes, "Everything that can be recovered from the past throws light on our time, and guides us toward the future." May the struggles and lessons endured by the peoples of the Mahoning Valley and its neighbors over the past one hundred years, and reported in the pages of THE VINDICATOR, *The People's Paper,* be taken to heart and lead to a better century ahead.

As THE VINDICATOR of November 11, 1946, editorialized:

Americans are the privileged of the earth. This did not simply happen. It came because generations worked and planned and fought and died to make it so. We, too, have an obligation to build well for those who come after us.

INDEX

INDEX

INDEX

INDEX

PICTURE CREDITS

WHILE MOST PHOTOGRAPHS in this publication are from the archives of The Vindicator or its holdings, some are of unknown origin. Although efforts have been made to trace present copyright holders, apologies are made for any unintentional omissions. Appropriate acknowledgement to companies or individuals will gladly be inserted in any subsequent printings of the book.

Photographs from other sources:

Chapter 1: 1900-1909

2 Wright Brothers first flight: Associated Press; Albert Einstein theory of relativity, $E=mc^2$: Associated Press.

Chapter 2: 1910-1919

13 Floodwaters and Baltimore & Ohio Railroad station, U.F. Webb.

14 WWI poster, Argonne Forest: Acme Newspictures, Acme Photo.

15 Women's suffrage: Associated Press.

18 Clarence Darrow: Associated Press.

21 Opera House: Mahoning Valley Historical Society.

Chapter 3: 1920-1929

24 Mein Kampf: Associated Press; Robert Goddard and rocket: Associated Press.

28 KKK: Cleveland State University, Cleveland Press collection.

30 Oil derrick: Associated Press.

Chapter 4: 1930-1939

34 Hindenburg: Associated Press.

35 Breadline: Associated Press.

36 Bringing Up Father: King Features Syndicate; Radio: Associated Press.

38 Central Square 1936: Nick Petrella, Boulevard Tavern.

40 Pierce Arrow: Associated Press.

Chapter 5: 1940-1949

46 Adolf Hitler: Newspaper PM; Wartime poster: International News Photos.

47 World War II: Associated Press.

53 Cleveland Indians: Associated Press.

Chapter 6: 1950-1959

60 Hydrogen Bomb: Associated Press/U.S. Air Force; Korean War: Associated Press.

62 Television: Associated Press.

64 Jonas Salk: Associated Press.

Chapter 7: 1960-1969

70 Moon landing: Associated Press; Vietnam War: Associated Press.

74 Youngstown State University: Youngstown Area Chamber of Commerce.

75 Youngstown business district: Youngstown Area Chamber of Commerce.

Chapter 8: 1970-1979

80 Mars: Associated Press; Kent State: Associated Press.

81 Nixon resignation: Associated Press; Rose Mary Woods: Associated Press.

87 Steelworkers Rally: Associated Press.

Chapter 9: 1980-1989

90 Challenger explosion: Associated Press.

91 Unemployment: Associated Press.

92 Traficant hugging jury foreman: United Press International.

93 Iran hostage release: Associated Press.

96 Clyde Lee Conrad: Associated Press.

99 Ohio Works Gate 3: United Press International.

Chapter 10: 1990-1999

106 Oklahoma City Bombing: Associated Press.

107 Persian Gulf War: Associated Press.

109 USAir Flight 427: Associated Press/Pittsburgh Tribune-Review, Tod Gombar.

111 Aspin and Clinton: Associated Press.

115 New Cleveland Browns: Associated Press; Browns stadium: Associated Press; Edward DeBartolo, Jr.: Associated Press.

118 WTI Incinerator: Associated Press; Incinerator opponents: Associated Press; Cavalier: General Motors.

119 Mickey Monus: Associated Press.